Chinese Nation
Global Era

Chinese Nationalism in the Global Era presents an analysis of the tension between nationalism and globalisation in China since the beginning of the 'reform and opening' period in the late 1970s to the present day. It makes a unique contribution to the on-going debate on the nature of Chinese nationalism by showing how nationalism is used to link together key areas of policy-making including economic policy, national unification and foreign policy. The book looks in detail at the areas of policy-making where the preservation of Chinese identity and the impact of external influences, such as education and information technology, converge.

Hughes provides historical context to the debate by examining how nationalism became incorporated into the ideology of the Chinese Communist Party in the 1980s and the ways in which this strengthened and combined with globalisation discourse through the domestic crisis of the Tiananmen Massacre and the external shock of the Cold War's conclusion. The different perspectives towards this resulting orthodoxy are discussed including those of the state and dissent in mainland China and the alternative views from Taiwan and Hong Kong.

Chinese Nationalism in the Global Era offers a systematic treatment of Chinese nationalism during the period of 'reform and opening', providing conceptual insights that will allow the reader to grasp the complex weave of Chinese nationalist sentiment today and its implications for the future. It is essential reading for China specialists, and scholars interested in nationalism and the nature of Chinese foreign policy and domestic politics.

Christopher R. Hughes is Senior Lecturer in International Relations at the London School of Economics, where he was Director of the Asia Research Centre, 2002–2005. He has published extensively on Chinese nationalism, including *Taiwan and Chinese Nationalism* (Routledge, 1997) and *China and the Internet: Politics of the Digital Leap Forward* (ed. with Gudrun Wacker) (Routledge, 2003).

Politics in Asia series
Formerly edited by Michael Leifer
London School of Economics

ASEAN and the Security of South-East Asia
Michael Leifer

China's Policy towards Territorial Disputes
The case of the South China Sea Islands
Chi-kin Lo

India and Southeast Asia
Indian perceptions and policies
Mohammed Ayoob

Gorbachev and Southeast Asia
Leszek Buszynski

Indonesian Politics under Suharto
Order, development and pressure for change
Michael R.J. Vatikiotis

The State and Ethnic Politics in Southeast Asia
David Brown

The Politics of Nation Building and Citizenship in Singapore
Michael Hill and Lian Kwen Fee

Politics in Indonesia
Democracy, Islam and the ideology of tolerance
Douglas E. Ramage

Communitarian Ideology and Democracy in Singapore
Beng-Huat Chua

The Challenge of Democracy in Nepal
Louise Brown

Japan's Asia Policy
Wolf Mendl

The International Politics of the Asia-Pacific, 1945–1995
Michael Yahuda

Political Change in Southeast Asia
Trimming the Banyan Tree
Michael R.J. Vatikiotis

Hong Kong
China's challenge
Michael Yahuda

Korea versus Korea
A case of contested legitimacy
B. K. Gills

Managing Political Change in Singapore
The elected presidency
Kevin Y.L. Tan and Lam Peng Er

Islam in Malaysian Foreign Policy
Shanti Nair

Political Change in Thailand
Democracy and participation
Kevin Hewison

The Politics of NGOs in Southeast Asia
Participation and protest in the Philippines
Gerard Clarke

Malaysian Politics Under Mahathir
R. S. Milne and Diane K. Mauzy

Indonesia and China
The politics of a troubled relationship
Rizal Sukma

Arming the Two Koreas
State, capital and military power
Taik-young Hamm

Engaging China
The management of an emerging
power
*Edited by Alastair Iain Johnston and
Robert S. Ross*

Singapore's Foreign Policy
Coping with vulnerability
Michael Leifer

**Philippine Politics and Society in the
Twentieth Century**
Colonial legacies, post-colonial
trajectories
*Eva-Lotta E. Hedman and
John T. Sidel*

**Constructing a Security Community
in Southeast Asia**
ASEAN and the problem of regional
order
Amitav Acharya

Monarchy in South East Asia
The faces of tradition in transition
Roger Kershaw

Korea After the Crash
The politics of economic recovery
Brian Bridges

The Future of North Korea
Edited by Tsuneo Akaha

**The International Relations of Japan
and South East Asia**
Forging a new regionalism
Sueo Sudo

Power and Change in Central Asia
Edited by Sally N. Cummings

**The Politics of Human Rights in
Southeast Asia**
Philip Eldridge

Political Business in East Asia
Edited by Edmund Terence Gomez

**Singapore Politics under the People's
Action Party**
Diane K. Mauzy and R. S. Milne

Media and Politics in Pacific Asia
Duncan McCargo

Japanese Governance
Beyond Japan Inc
*Edited by Jennifer Amyx and
Peter Drysdale*

China and the Internet
Politics of the digital leap forward
*Edited by Christopher R. Hughes and
Gudrun Wacker*

**Challenging Authoritarianism in
Southeast Asia**
Comparing Indonesia and Malaysia
*Edited by Ariel Heryanto and
Sumit K. Mandal*

**Cooperative Security and the Balance
of Power in ASEAN and the ARF**
Ralf Emmers

Islam in Indonesian Foreign Policy
Rizal Sukma

Media, War and Terrorism
Responses from the Middle East and
Asia
*Edited by Peter Van der Veer and
Shoma Munshi*

**China, Arms Control and
Nonproliferation**
Wendy Frieman

Communitarian Politics in Asia
Edited by Chua Beng Huat

**East Timor, Australia and Regional
Order**
Intervention and its Aftermath in
Southeast Asia
James Cotton

Domestic Politics, International
Bargaining and China's Territorial
Disputes
Chien-peng Chung

Democratic Development in East Asia
Becky Shelley

International Politics of the
Asia-Pacific since 1945
Michael Yahuda

Asian States
Beyond the developmental
perspective
*Edited by Richard Boyd and
Tak-Wing Ngo*

Civil Life, Globalization, and
Political Change in Asia
Organizing between family and state
Edited by Robert P. Weller

Realism and Interdependence in
Singapore's Foreign Policy
Narayanan Ganesan

Party Politics in Taiwan
Party change and the democratic
evolution of Taiwan, 1991–2004
Dafydd Fell

State Terrorism and Political Identity
in Indonesia
Fatally belonging
Ariel Heryanto

China's Rise, Taiwan's Dilemmas
and International Peace
Edited by Edward Friedman

Japan and China in the World
Political Economy
*Edited by Saadia M. Pekkanen and
Kellee S. Tsai*

Order and Security in Southeast Asia
Essays in memory of Michael Leifer
*Edited by Joseph Chinyong Liow and
Ralf Emmers*

State Making in Asia
*Edited by Richard Boyd and
Tak-Wing Ngo*

US-China Relations in the
21st Century
Power transition and peace
Zhiqun Zhu

Empire and Neoliberalism in Asia
Edited by Vedi R. Hadiz

Chinese Nationalism in the Global
Era
Christopher R. Hughes

Indonesia's War over Aceh
Last stand on Mecca's Porch
Matthew N. Davis

Chinese Nationalism in the Global Era

Christopher R. Hughes

Routledge
Taylor & Francis Group

LONDON AND NEW YORK

First published 2006
by Routledge
2 Park Square, Milton Park, Abingdon, Oxon OX14 4RN

Simultaneously published in the USA and Canada
by Routledge
270 Madison Ave, New York, NY 10016

*Routledge is an imprint of the Taylor & Francis Group, an
informa business*

© 2006 Christopher R. Hughes

Typeset in Sabon by
RefineCatch Limited, Bungay, Suffolk
Printed and bound in Great Britain by
TJ International Ltd, Padstow, Cornwall

British Library Cataloguing in Publication Data
A catalogue record for this book is available from the British Library

Library of Congress Cataloging in Publication Data
Hughes, Christopher R., 1960–
Chinese nationalism in the global era / by Christopher R. Hughes.
p. cm. – (Politics in Asia series)
Includes bibliographical references and index.
1. Nationalism–China. I. Title. II. Series.
DS779.215.H86 2006
320.54′0951–dc22
2005023709

ISBN10: 0–415–18265–4 (hbk)
ISBN10: 0–415–18266–2 (pbk)

ISBN13: 978–0–415–18265–2 (hbk)
ISBN13: 978–0–415–18266–9 (pbk)

To my father

Contents

Note on romanisation   xi
List of abbreviations   xii

Introduction: Chinese nationalism in the global era   1
Nationalism and globalisation as discursive
   concepts 2
Nationalism and policy-making 7

1 The globalisation of nationalism under 'reform and opening'   11
Patriotism and policy-making 14
Patriotism between foreign policy and unification 16
The nation as discursive subject 19
The compromise of 'socialist spiritual civilisation' 22
'Spiritual pollution': nationalism and
   factionalism 26
The world scientific and technological revolution 30
The genesis of techno-nationalism 34
Fighting 'bourgeois liberalisation' 39
Consolidating techno-nationalism at the Thirteenth
   Congress 43
The road to Tiananmen 49
Conclusion 53

2 After 1989: nationalism and the new global elite   55
Jiang Zemin's patriotic turn 56
Forging the new technocratic consensus 58
Towards 'Deng Xiaoping Theory' 62

Teaching the nation 69
Personnel power: from 'Deng Xiaoping Theory' to
   the 'Three Represents' 76
Unification and foreign policy interrupt 80
The powerlessness of the powerful 85
Facing the past: facing the future 89

3   **Globalisation and its discontents**   92

Nationalism and political strategy 93
Globalisation and political change 98
China Can Say No *104*
The liberal dilemma 106
The WTO: contradictions among the people 115

4   **What kind of a status quo power?**   122

The value of unification 122
Multipolarity, multilateralism and shaping
   norms 130
Rethinking security under globalisation 135
Taiwan: the limits of China's 'peaceful rise' 139
Japan: popular nationalism and the limits of elite
   discourse 146
Chinese nationalism in the global era 151

Notes   157
Bibliography   159
Index   177

Note on romanisation

The standard Pinyin system of romanisation has been used throughout this text. The exception is when individuals in Taiwan and Hong Kong have chosen to use a certain spelling for their own names. For place names in Taiwan, the conventions used on the island, such as 'Taipei' rather than 'Taibei' for the capital city, have been followed here. The convention of using 'Peking University' rather than 'Beijing University' and 'Tsinghua University' rather than 'Qinghua University' has also been followed.

List of abbreviations

ARF	ASEAN Regional Forum
ASEAN	Association of Southeast Asian Nations
CAS	Chinese Academy of Sciences
CASS	Chinese Academy of Social Sciences
CCP	Chinese Communist Party
CPSU	Communist Party of the Soviet Union
DPP	Democratic Progressive Party
GATT	General Agreement on Tariffs and Trade
HKSAR	Hong Kong Special Administrative Region
KMT	Kuomintang (Guomindang)
ODA	Official development assistance
SCO	Shanghai Cooperation Organisation
SOE	State Owned Enterprise
SEZ	Special Economic Zone
UN	United Nations
WHA	World Health Assembly
WHO	World Health Organization
WTO	World Trade Organization

Introduction
Chinese nationalism in the global era

Taken together, the events of the opening years of the twenty-first century symbolise how China has risen to become a major force in the international economic and security system just over ten years after being cast as a pariah after the 1989 Tiananmen Massacre. The reaching of the long-awaited agreement on China's accession to the World Trade Organization (WTO) in September 2001 symbolised its membership of the world trade system. Following the terrorist attacks on the United States that took place that same month, President Jiang Zemin met his American counterpart at the Asia Pacific Economic Cooperation (APEC) summit in Shanghai in October, and China became a partner in the war on terrorism with a global reach. With Beijing scheduled to hold the summer Olympic Games in 2008, it seems that a growing degree of 'soft power' has secured China's place in the global cultural system, too.

This rise to respectability has been accompanied by an increasing visibility of Chinese nationalism. At times, this has spilled over into foreign relations in ways that have threatened regional stability, as with the military stand-off with the United States Navy over Taiwan in 1995–6. Nationalistic passions have also appeared to threaten the domestic legitimacy of China's leaders, as when Premier Zhu Rongji returned empty-handed from his negotiations with President Clinton over China's WTO accession in April 1999. The following month, angry crowds took to the streets in Chinese cities after the destruction of the Chinese Embassy in Belgrade by American missiles. As the new century began, relations with the United States were further aggravated by the Bush administration's original hawkish stance towards China and the heightening of popular passions that occurred when an American reconnaissance plane collided with a Chinese interceptor off Hainan Island on 1 April 2001. Despite Jiang Zemin's telegraph of support to the American people after the terrorist attacks on

New York and Washington, reports in the Western media claimed that many Chinese citizens reacted with delight over the tragedy inflicted on their perceived adversary. Whether the improvement in relations that followed is of a lasting character, or whether the structure of the international system is such that a rising power will inevitably challenge the status quo, are questions of critical importance for world order in the new millennium.

Nationalism and globalisation as discursive concepts

Given such phenomena, the discussion of nationalism and globalisation has come to permeate all levels of political debate in China. When Jiang Zemin addressed the Chinese Sixteenth Congress of the Chinese Communist Party (CCP) in his capacity as General Secretary in November 2002, he thus described a world characterised by 'political multipolarity and economic globalisation', in which the Chinese people are bent on 'bringing about a great rejuvenation of the Chinese nation on its road to socialism with Chinese characteristics' (Jiang 2002). Younger writers address a growing commercial market by speaking ominously about 'China under the shadow of globalization' (Fang, N. *et al.* 1999), or boost the sales of popular books by combining a defiance of American power with despair over the lack of national self-confidence that is revealed by the proliferation in Chinese streets of signs advertising 'China's Long Island', and 'The Manhattan of the East' (Tang 1996).

As for academics, some idea of the extent of the discussion of nationalism and globalisation can be gained from a full-text search for these terms on the China National Knowledge Infrastructure (CNKI) database[1] (Table 1).

Understanding the relationship between nationalism and globalisation in Chinese political discussions is complicated by the fact that neither of these concepts is susceptible to clear definition. Ultimately, any definition of 'nationalism' has its limitations due to the fact that it is a 'fuzzy concept' that changes as it is used for different purposes over time. A survey of some of the most recent works covering the nationalist revival in China in the 1990s reveals the following array of subthemes: anti-traditionalism, anti-Westernisation, new authoritarianism, Confucianism, culturalism, statism, (neo)-conservatism, neo-leftism, developmentalism, anti-Americanism, academic nativism, post-modernism, civilisationism, populism, elitism, concerns over social justice.[2]

The meaning of 'globalisation' is equally fuzzy. The best working

Table 1 Number of articles with the terms 'globalisation' (*quanqiuhua*) and 'nationalism' (*minzu zhuyi*) on China National Knowledge Infrastructure database, 1994 to 2004

	Globalisation	Nationalism	Events
1994	34	35	
1995	73	35	Taiwan crisis
1996	63	69	
1997	132	142	15th CCP Congress
1998	415	50	
1999	927	83	Belgrade Incident
2000	2329	98	
2001	2868	99	WTO accession 9/11 Incident EP3 Incident
2002	5131	101	
2003	5021	148	
2004	3896	140	

definition is provided by David Held and his co-authors, who describe it as:

> [. . .] a process (or set of processes) which embodies a transformation in the spatial organization of social relations and transactions – assessed in terms of their extensity, intensity, velocity and impact – generating transcontinental or interregional flows and networks of activity, interaction and the exercise of power.
>
> (Held *et al.* 1999: 16)

Yet even such a carefully worded formula fails to stipulate whether globalisation involves one or many processes, or to address the issue of periodicity. Held's analysis thus incorporates much of world history and a vast range of political, military, cultural and economic processes, rendering the concept so general that it becomes unwieldy for use in academic analysis.

There is little agreement in political science over the relationship between nationalism and globalisation, either. While hyper-globalists foresee the end of the nation-state, sceptics see national governments maintaining their grip on power in a world characterised by growing regionalism and North–South inequality (Held *et al.* 1999: 1–10). Moreover, the continuing scourge of war in the former Yugoslavia and Rwanda indicates that globalisation can actually lead to the resurgence

4 *Introduction*

and strengthening of local identities (Giddens 1990: 50). New concepts, such as the 'global state', try to capture the paradox of states that might do some things less well than they used to, but have taken on new responsibilities in exchange (Clark 2001: 645–6).

That so much discussion of these concepts and their relationship takes place in China means that they can at least be treated as essentially contested concepts. This has the advantage of circumventing the problem of definitions, because the task of research is to look at the divergent uses to which the concepts can be put. The question of whether nationalism is 'top-down' or 'bottom-up' also becomes less important when the task is to reveal how a range of actors try to appeal to both rulers and ruled by articulating the discussion of nationalism and globalisation. By treating nationalism and globalisation as discursive concepts, it is also possible to resolve the problem of periodicity by limiting the focus to a systematic account to the post-Mao years, which the Chinese call the period of 'reform and opening'. This is because under 'reform and opening' it is possible to trace how the discussion of nationalism has been conditioned by themes associated with globalisation, such as the world technological revolution and the transformation of the international trade and financial systems. Finally, by looking at the relationship between the two concepts, it is possible to narrow down the focus of research. The result is thus narrower than the broader surveys of the revival of popular nationalism in the 1990s that have already been provided by Zhao (1997), Zheng (1999) and Gries (2004), although the historical scope is somewhat longer, starting with the genesis of 'reform and opening' in the late 1970s. This longer focus is essential, given that the most important sources of the present ideology of 'Deng Xiaoping Theory' span the period from the late 1970s up to Deng's landmark 1992 'Southern Tour'.

This work does not attempt an extensive historical account of the origins of Chinese nationalism and the debates that surround this topic, something that has already been masterfully accomplished by Zhao (2004). From the longer historical perspective, however, it is important to note that discussion of the relationship between nationalism and what have recently become identified as the processes of globalisation has a long pedigree in China. Those who believe that it is the information revolution of the late twentieth century that has broken down 'Chinese walls' would do well to remember that in 1820 China accounted for 30 per cent of global GDP (World Bank 1998: 2). By the 1870s, the Jiangnan arsenal had become one of the largest in the world, the China Merchants' Steam Navigation Company had been established, and telegraph cables were being laid that linked Hong

Kong, Guangzhou and Shanghai with London and San Francisco. The constitutional reformer Kang Youwei wrote a memorial to the emperor in 1897; his language is remarkably similar to today's talk about globalisation when he states:

> China is one country in a world of 800,000 *li*; China is one country among more than fifty. The globe (*diqiu*) has been connected since the end of the Ming dynasty, transportation has boomed since the reigns of Jiaqing and Daoguang [1796–1851]. The new events of the past hundred years represent change that is unprecedented in the preceding 4,000 years.
>
> (Kang 1897: 191)

By the end of the nineteenth century, dichotomies were already proliferating to explain how Chinese orthodoxy could be maintained while importing knowledge from abroad, such as 'Self sufficiency as essence, promote sincerity as function', 'defence as essence, war as function', 'rely on industry for essence, rely on commerce for function', and 'metaphysics (*li xue*) for essence, economics for function' (Li, Kuo-chih 1984: 34). The best-known example of this is found in Zhang Zhidong (1837–1909), the late Qing dynasty 'self-strengthening' governor general of Hubei and Hunan, who advocated achieving state power through the construction of railroads, heavy industry and a foreign policy based on the balancing principle of 'use barbarians to control barbarians'. His *Exhortation to Study*, written in 1898, is commonly identified with the '*ti-yong*' call to appropriate Western functional knowledge (*yong*) to preserve Chinese essence (*ti*). As such language demonstrates, the discussion by the 'self-strengtheners' of the Qing dynasty of local military, political and economic issues in terms of 'world order' was already typical of what sociologists would call a 'globalistic mentality' (Waters 1995: 42).

It is this mentality that made it possible for Kang Youwei's fellow reformer, Liang Qichao, to import the Chinese term for nationalism (*minzu zhuyi*) from Japan, in articles he wrote between 1899 and 1901 (Jiang, Yongjing 1985: 177–8). After the fall of the Qing, the claim to be able to use Western functional knowledge to preserve Chinese essence remained at the centre of the claim to legitimacy made by nationalist and communist elites. When president Yuan Shikai tried to make himself emperor during the early years of the Chinese Republic, he did so by reviving Confucianism as the state ideology. Sun Yatsen, the 'National Father', maintained a strong aversion to cosmopolitanism and a belief in the revival of Chinese tradition throughout his life.

Chiang Kaishek continued this when he combined propagation of Sun's nationalist orthodoxy of the 'Three Principles of the People' with the Confucian morality of the New Life movement after the 1927 Northern Expedition left much of the former empire under Nationalist control. This ideological strategy even survived under the KMT in Taiwan, until the island's democratisation in the 1980s made it unsustainable.

The Communists, too, had to reconcile their Chinese identity with the promise of modernity offered by socialist internationalism. Mao Zedong is said to have achieved the 'sinification of Marxism'. When he claimed leadership of the United Front in the conflict with Japan, he presented the CCP as the true inheritor of what he considered to be the essence of 'a splendid old culture' that was created during the long period of Chinese history and which could be used selectively to develop the 'new national culture' (Mao 1967: 381). Not only did Mao advocate learning from socialist cultures, but also from capitalist countries in the Age of Enlightenment. Yet, at the same time, he warned, 'We should not gulp any of this foreign material down uncritically, but must treat it as we do our food – first chewing it, then submitting it to the working of the stomach and intestines with their juices and secretions, and separating it into nutriment to be absorbed and waste matter to be discarded – before it can nourish us' (Mao 1967a: 380). The dilemma of balancing the preservation of political orthodoxy with learning from abroad is even clearer under 'reform and opening'. China's leaders since Mao have always been careful to balance the importation of investment and know-how from abroad with a call to build 'socialism with Chinese characteristics' and 'socialist spiritual civilization', and to insist that the nation combats the tendency of 'worshipping things foreign, or fawning on foreigners' (Deng, X. 1984a: 320).

To search for logical consistency in this discourse, however, is to overlook how such actors are not concerned with talking to philosophical circles. The issues they address are essentially political, in the sense that there is no possibility of a logical solution, only the hope of achieving some kind of social compromise. As Zhang Zhidong realised at the end of the Qing dynasty, it is humiliation at the hands of foreigners that provides the conditions under which the apparently incommensurable positions of dogmatic conservatives and radical reformers can be reconciled. Zhang did this by reducing Confucianism to a symbol of loyalty rather than a practical guide for living. In the same way, China's leaders under 'reform and opening' have reduced socialism to a symbol of patriotic loyalty, while the technological and market orthodoxies of globalisation have been introduced as the guide for policy. The condition for achieving this, however, is to portray the nation as threatened and humiliated by a coalition of enemies within and abroad, from which only the CCP can promise deliverance. It is thus that the legacy of the impact of colonialism and civil war has made possible the discourse on nationalism and globalisation that is so central to Chinese politics at the start of the new millennium.

Nationalism and policy-making

The focus of this work is also narrower than existing surveys of the rise of China's 'new nationalism' in the 1990s, because it explores how certain themes have been used by the post-Mao CCP elite to articulate, influence and test the limits of orthodox political discourse that they inherited, by taking a relatively narrow view of 'politics' as an activity related to policy-making. While this entails looking at areas of policy-making that are at the interface between the preservation of the national essence (*ti*) and reception of foreign 'function' (*yong*), such as education and information technology, the research is mainly structured around foreign policy, unification policy and economic policy. These are the areas in which the 'three main historical tasks' were established by Deng Xiaoping as the litmus test for the legitimacy of the post-Mao CCP leadership, namely opposing hegemonism and striving to preserve world peace, returning Taiwan to the motherland for China's reunification, and stepping up economic construction. That Deng established these tasks in January 1980, at the same time that he was articulating patriotism as the main value system to delimit the legitimate boundaries of dissent, created the dynamics of nationalist and globalist discourse that have remained in place and been developed by Deng's successors, as can be seen in Jiang Zemin's speech to the Sixteenth Party Congress, when he handed over power to the new leadership team under Hu Jintao.

It was originally intended to divide the analysis into chapters devoted to these three specific areas of policy-making. However, as the research developed it became apparent that an exploration of the linkages that patriotism creates between policies is required in order to illuminate the dynamics of the discourse on nationalism and globalisation. Rather than try to repeat a detailed account of the economic transition that has occurred under 'reform and opening', which has already been provided by other authors (Zweig: 2002), the first chapter thus tries to unravel how patriotism was deployed in the late 1970s and throughout the 1980s up to the Tiananmen Massacre by a CCP leadership that was introducing market mechanisms into the command economy. During this time, the attempt to build an elite consensus around concepts such as the building of 'socialist spiritual civilisation' merely raised the discussion of the nation to a new level of significance. In the process of the factional disputes and popular discontent that arose over the nature of stepping up economic construction at this time, the other 'major tasks' of national unification and opposing international hegemony were imbued with a new kind of ideological significance that set the context for the increasing salience of nationalism in the decade that followed.

The second chapter takes this analysis further by looking at how the orthodox version of patriotism was 'globalised' as elements of the CCP deployed themes such as the 'world scientific and technological revolution' to legitimate the introduction of market mechanisms. The impact that this had on the education system and the class relations in Chinese society meant that ideology had to be further transformed. This was to make the development of an elitist techno-nationalism compatible with meeting the challenges of globalisation, making possible the later development of the current ideological orthodoxy of Jiang Zemin's theory of the 'Three Represents' as an alternative to the increasingly sterile debates between 'Left' and 'Right' that had come to dominate discussion.

Having established the basic dynamics of CCP ideological orthodoxy under 'reform and opening', the chapter goes on to examine the way in which this political dispensation was articulated in new ways to respond to the crisis of socialism posed by the 1989 Tiananmen Massacre and the end of the Cold War. By locating developments such as the 'patriotic education campaign' of the 1990s within the strategies deployed by various actors in the intense factional discussions over the nature of socialism, it becomes possible to show the variety of ways in which nationalistic rhetoric can be articulated to accommodate the pressures of policy-making, and ultimately to appropriate the discourse on globalisation within the new orthodoxy of 'Deng Xiaoping Theory'. Without such an analysis, the variety of uses to which nationalist themes are put in political discussion tends to be either overlooked, or addressed in terms of the old debate between ill-defined categories of 'Right' and 'Left'. While these terms are certainly still used in political arguments in China, it is a mistake to see nationalism as belonging to one or the other. Those who advocate liberal economic reforms are in fact just as prone to using nationalist arguments to bolster their legitimacy as are guardians of the old socialist system.

In order to understand the full range of these strategies, though, it is also necessary to look at how the ideology of 'reform and opening' has been articulated to accommodate the changing structure of Chinese society. New social groups that do not fit the old categories of Left and Right have been empowered by the introduction of market mechanisms and the belief that science and education can 'rejuvenate the nation'. This is reflected in the way that the new ideology of the 'Three Represents' recognises entrepreneurs, technical personnel, and managers of non-public and foreign enterprises as 'builders of socialism with Chinese characteristics'. The political implications of the rise of what might be called a 'new global class' are analysed in some depth, by looking at the relationship between the development of a scientific and technical knowledge base and the transformation of nationalist rhetoric.

While there have certainly been winners under 'reform and opening', there have also been losers as the security provided by the state sector has been eroded. Key constituencies upon whom the Party has traditionally relied to safeguard and disseminate its orthodoxy, such as 'intellectuals' and educators, have come under new pressures that threaten their social status. The third chapter will look at how the discontent of such groups has fed into a broader public discussion of nationalism and globalisation through new outlets for expression, such as the Internet and a more commercialised publishing industry. This has magnified the political impact of the external crises that beset the CCP from the Taiwan Strait crisis of 1995–6 onwards, allowing the 'new nationalism' of the 1990s to become a force that shapes and articulates the limits of a Party orthodoxy that still determines what may be spoken about.

The final chapter looks more closely at the political implications of the ways in which the evolving discourse on nationalism and globalisation ties together domestic politics with issues of national unification and foreign policy. The resulting dynamics have important implications for a wide range of people, from populations in Tibet and Xinjiang who reject the imposition of Chinese identity, through those in Hong Kong and Taiwan who use democracy to challenge the reduction of patriotism to loyalty to the CCP, to neighbouring states who are concerned about the impact of domestic nationalism on the foreign policy of a rising power. Equally significant, though, is the way in which such problems rebound back on a Chinese leadership that continues to legitimate its rule by deploying the ideological formula of what has become known as 'Deng Xiaoping Theory' that has its origins in the legitimacy crisis of a Communist party overseeing the introduction of market-based reforms.

1 The globalisation of nationalism under 'reform and opening'

By the time Mao Zedong died on 9 September 1976, China's population had suffered the Great Leap Forward and the Cultural Revolution. Sixty per cent of the people had to survive on less than the internationally accepted poverty line of one US dollar per day. Productivity in agriculture and industry was either standing still or in decline. There were serious economic imbalances across the country, with underdevelopment of the western regions creating a huge drain on the eastern economy. The non-Han populations who populated the border regions suffered deeper feelings of alienation than most after being subjected to nation-building through 'class struggle'. In foreign affairs, the People's Republic of China (PRC) not only had tense relations with both superpowers, it had even alienated the non-aligned states, thanks largely to attempts to export Maoism. Meanwhile, the military was more of a bloated and inefficient welfare system engaged in maintaining domestic political stability than a professional fighting force.

Before these deep-seated problems could be addressed, the CCP had to resolve the issue of the leadership succession. After the fall of the 'Gang of Four', this was the subject of intense factional conflict between acting chairman Hua Guofeng and the supporters of Deng Xiaoping. Deng's supporters could portray Hua Guofeng as a dogmatist slavishly bound to Mao's policies and ideology. This strategy was complicated, however, by the fact that Hua was also a moderniser, insofar as he had previously worked with Deng and Zhou Enlai on formulating the 'Four Modernisations' of agriculture, industry, defence, and science and technology. Under Hua's leadership, this had been announced as the new policy orientation when the first Session of the Fifth National People's Congress convened in February and March 1978. Moreover, as Acting Chairman, Hua actively promoted foreign investment and the expansion of links with the non-socialist states, trying to achieve industrial modernisation through the wholescale importation of foreign plant and capital in a way that allowed his critics to christen his policies the 'Foreign Leap Forward' (*yang maojin*).

In this situation, the 'thought emancipation' campaign launched by Deng Xiaoping's supporters to discredit acting chairman Hua Guofeng's reliance on Mao's authority could never be a mere call for 'pragmatism'. The claim that 'practice is the sole criterion for testing truth' was, Deng asserted, 'a debate about ideological line, about politics, about the future and the destiny of our party and nation' (1984b: 154). Deng placed 'thought emancipation' in the CCP's narrative of national salvation when he pointed out that the slogan 'seek truth from facts' had been presented to the Central Party School in Yan'an during the war against Japan (1984c: 58). Deng's political programme, moreover, could be presented as the restoration of continuity with the 'period before and after Liberation', when the collectivisation of agriculture and the nationalisation of industry had brought to a peak the Party's triumphs in the civil war and the conflict with Japan. The struggle against the bourgeois class had been rendered obsolete. As Deng told a national conference on education in April 1978, that had been a time when the young 'were filled with love for their motherland, for the people and for labour, science and public property, and they struggled heroically and resourcefully against bad elements and enemies, setting the tone for the new era' (1984d: 121).

Calling for selfless devotion to the nation was a way to justify key elements of Deng's reform programme, such as the introduction of greater agricultural incentives, dismantling the commune system, introducing 'responsibility systems' and developing an elitist education system. As well as deploying an atavistic patriotism, though, Deng also had to articulate an ideological dispensation for the future that could win the loyalty of those sections of the population upon whose expertise modernisation would depend. He thus reassured the education conference that schools would no longer be the field of class struggle, but were to be used to build an army of working-class intellectuals combining the virtues of being both 'red and expert', capable of mastering and advancing modern science, culture and the new technologies in order to 'transform China into a modern and powerful socialist country and ultimately defeat bourgeois influences in the superstructure' (1984d: 120). When he spoke at a national science conference in December that year, he insisted that 'experts' would no longer be contrasted negatively with those who had *bona fide* 'red' political credentials, because 'If a person loves our socialist motherland and is serving socialism and the workers, peasants and soldiers of his own free will and accord, then it should be said that he has begun to acquire a proletarian world outlook' (1984e: 107–8).

After Deng had consolidated his leadership position in December 1978, he had to develop his appeal to patriotism in a way that could manage the growing dissatisfaction spreading among broader sections of the urban population. He began to do this in March 1979, when he marked the suppression of the Beijing Spring Democracy Wall movement by delivering a speech on the 'Four Cardinal Principles' within which political discussion would be permitted (1984f). These principles of 'keep to the socialist road', 'uphold Party leadership', 'uphold the dictatorship of the proletariat', and 'uphold Marxism-Leninism and Mao Zedong thought', were drawn from the Communist lexicon. Yet they make only a passing commitment to socialism, compared to the emphasis that is placed on patriotism. The commitment to public ownership expressed in the explanation of 'keeping to the socialist road' pales beside his portrayal of socialism as being important in the first place because, 'socialism and socialism alone can save China – this is the unshakeable historical conclusion that the Chinese people have drawn from their own experience in the 60 years since the May Fourth Movement' (1984f: 174–5), referring to the 1919 student demonstrations in Peking against the transfer of German concessions in China to Japan at Versailles.

Furthermore, 'Party leadership' and the 'dictatorship of the proletariat' are not explained in terms of a struggle between clearly defined social classes, but against an enemy conceived as a ragbag collection of 'counter-revolutionaries, enemy agents, criminals and other bad elements of all kinds who undermine socialist public order, as well as new exploiters who engage in corruption, embezzlement, speculation and profiteering'. Advocates of human rights are discredited as the stooges of foreign powers, contemptible for their supposed links with pernicious outside influences and inviting intervention in China's internal affairs. To make China turn towards capitalism, he warned, such people will seek political asylum overseas and make contact with KMT agents sent from Taiwan and abroad to plot sabotage (1984f: 181). Faced by such enemies, who are supposed to have developed inseparable links with the international forces of imperialism and hegemonism, it is inconceivable that the army, public security organs, courts and prisons can be allowed to 'wither away' (1984f: 176–7).

As for upholding 'Marxism-Leninism and Mao Zedong thought', this does not refer to the ideas of the man who had engineered the Great Leap Forward, the Cultural Revolution and internationalism. It meant remembering the leader who had allowed the Chinese people to 'stand up' in 1949, the statesman who had formulated the strategy of differentiating the 'three worlds' and personally ushered in a new stage in Sino-American and Sino-Japanese relations. These elements of Mao's heritage were further elaborated when the orthodox version of the past appeared in the form of the *Resolution on CCP History (1949–81)*, two years later. In this document, the essence of Mao Zedong thought was presented as the principles 'to seek truth from facts', the 'mass line', and 'independence'. The first of these had already become a safer formula than 'thought emancipation', because it could be presented to mean that the answers to China's problems have to be found in Chinese experience and not in foreign teaching. The 'mass line', which had traditionally meant that the Party should canvass the opinions of the general population when developing its policies, was now presented as proof that the Party 'exists and fights for the interests of the people'. 'Independence' was taken to represent Mao's belief that China must find its own path to modernity, rejecting any kind of interference in national sovereignty.

Patriotism and policy-making

Deng set out the 'three major tasks' for the future in his speech to the Central Committee in January 1980 on 'The Present Situation and the Tasks Before Us'. These were: 'oppose hegemonism and strive to preserve world peace', strive for 'the return of Taiwan to the motherland for China's unification', and 'step up economic construction' (1984g: 224–5). It is possible to interpret this formula as establishing the priority of economic development over politics, because it presents the argument that unification depends on whether China can catch up economically with the developed countries (Zheng 1999: 17). Deng certainly puts economic development first, when he states:

> . . . in the final analysis, the two tasks of opposing hegemonism and reunifying the country by achieving the return of Taiwan to the motherland both require that we do well in our economic development. Of course, we have to handle our other affairs well too, but economic development is primary.
>
> (1984g: 225)

Yet there is another way in which Deng's presentation of 'economic construction' as the condition for achieving unification and opposing international hegemony creates a link between patriotism and policy-making that has far-reaching implications for the ideology of 'reform and opening'. This is the implication that economic development is merely the condition for achieving the higher goals of foreign and unification policy. National unification and opposing international hegemony thus become criteria for measuring the success of the reforms. Questioning economic policy becomes forbidden not due to any departure from socialist principles, but because it will weaken China internationally and prevent unification. This makes it unpatriotic to question the movement towards a market-based economy.

The nationalist force of this speech is further illustrated by the way in which Deng goes to some lengths in deploying themes drawn from the Party's narrative of the nation's salvation, locating himself in the tradition of national fathers that runs through Mao to the 'National Father' Sun Yatsen. He does this by reminding his audience how China used to be described as a 'heap of loose sand' until 'the CCP came to power and rallied the whole country around it, bringing to an end the disunity resulting from the partitioning of the country by various forces' (1984g: 252), a metaphor that had been used by both Sun Yatsen and Mao Zedong. Looking to the future, he continues to emphasise patriotism, when he insists that the 'Four Modernisations' of agriculture, industry, defence, and science and technology cannot be achieved unless a political line is maintained according to the principle: 'Unite the people of all our nationalities and bring all positive forces into play so that we can work with one heart and one mind, go all out, aim high and achieve greater, faster, better and more economical results in building a modern, powerful socialist country.'

Again, little is said about the meaning of socialism in this formula, other than that it will express its superiority first and foremost though the rate of economic growth and the high degree of efficiency it delivers through development of the productive forces (1984g: 233–5). This theme was to be developed over the following years as patriotism was adapted to globalisation discourse. Welfarism is rejected in favour of public recognition and material rewards for those individuals and organisations that make outstanding contributions according to the principle of 'to each according to his work', with some parts of the population and certain localities becoming well-off before others. For Deng, socialist ideology has come to mean not much more than immunising an increasingly professionalised elite against the infiltration of bourgeois ideology as relations are developed with the capitalist world. In the process, the dissidents of Democracy Wall can be discredited by comparing their activities with the fanatics of the Cultural

Revolution. Such behaviour is condemned when what is needed is 'stability and unity' and the spirit to 'work hard with a pioneering spirit'.

Patriotism between foreign policy and unification

In January 1980 there were good reasons for Deng to establish this linkage between patriotism, reform and policy-making. Above all, Deng had gained a good deal of personal kudos from the normalisation of relations with Washington on 1 January 1979, having steered negotiations on the issue since the deterioration of Zhou Enlai's health in the early 1970s. His visit to Washington to mark the event had been used as a publicity coup, with images of Deng receiving the nine-gun salute on the White House lawn broadcast to the PRC by satellite (Hsu 1983: 72). Conceptually, moreover, Deng could identify with Mao's vision of international politics as power-balancing between the 'three worlds' of the superpowers, the developing countries of the Third World and an intermediate zone of developed countries (Mao 1998: 454). Deng had presented this theory to the United Nations General Assembly in 1974, and restated it in December 1977 when he argued that China could contribute to the struggle against international hegemonism because the United States was pre-occupied with Soviet expansionism and on the defensive after its defeat in Southeast Asia (1984i: 92–3). In his speech on upholding the Four Cardinal Principles, Deng had used the theory of the three worlds to justify the 'defensive counter-attack' against Vietnam, reminding his audience that Mao had called for China 'to side with the third world countries and strengthen its unity with them, try to win over the second-world countries for a concerted effort against hegemonism, and establish normal diplomatic relations with the United States and Japan' (1984f: 168).

Given that the theory of the three worlds is a product of the elements of statecraft in Mao Zedong's diplomacy, it was also useful for establishing a positive appraisal of Mao's foreign policy, even during the Cultural Revolution. It was made public that Deng himself had insisted that the definitive judgement of the past that was to appear in the form of the 1981 *Resolution on Party History*, should stress that these years had seen the improvement in China's status as a great nation, the visits of Henry Kissinger, the signing of the Shanghai Communiqué with the United States, return to the United Nations, restoration of diplomatic relations with Japan, and the warm reception that Deng had received when he addressed the UN General Assembly in 1974 (1984h: 291).

The drafters of the *Resolution* duly complied with Deng's wishes, stating that Mao's last years were a period 'when our country remained unified and exerted a significant influence on international affairs' and when Mao Zedong's 'correct foreign policy' correctly stood up to the 'pressure of the social-imperialists' and 'firmly supported the just struggles of all peoples, outlined the correct strategy of the three worlds and advanced the important principle that China would never seek hegemony' (41–2).

The state-centric nature of the fluid international situation described by the 'three worlds' was developed further by the revival of the formula of the 'Five Principles of Peaceful Coexistence', namely: respect for territorial integrity and sovereignty; mutual non-aggression; mutual non-interference in internal affairs; equality and mutual benefit; and peaceful coexistence. This has a certain resonance in domestic politics because the Five Priniciples formula is attributed to Zhou Enlai, reinforcing continuity with the popular face of the CCP's past and making a ready counterpart to Zhou's Four Modernisations. When Deng revived the slogan of 'seeking truth from facts' during the leadership struggle in September 1978 (1984j: 141–4), he presented Mao's theory of the three worlds as useful in domestic politics for distinguishing the correct attitude of maintaining the international conditions that enable the importation of foreign capital, technology and know-how, as opposed to the incorrect branding of economic relations with other countries as a kind of 'national betrayal' (1984j: 142). Over the years that followed, references to both proletarian internationalism and the three worlds were to be eclipsed by the Five Principles, which came to encapsulate the sovereignty-centred nature of PRC foreign policy.

The strong attachment to the principles of state sovereignty and non-intervention also meant that the Five Principles could be tied in with the pursuit of national unification. Zhou Enlai is said to have first presented the Five Principles in negotiations with India between December 1953 and April 1954, after which they were written into the 'Agreement between the PRC and the Republic of India on Trade and Intercourse between the Tibet Region of China and India'. Under Deng, even the origins of the 'one country, two systems' formula for unification with Taiwan, Hong Kong and Macao could be found in the foreign policy framework of the Five Principles of Peaceful Coexistence (Deng, X. 1993b: 96–7).

These linkages between patrioitsm, foreign policy and national unification were further cemented by the revival of the United Front strategy. With its origins traced back as far as the CCP's Second

Congress in Shanghai in July 1922, the strategy had been adopted as the theoretical justification for working with the Nationalists to unify much of China in the Northern Expedition under Chiang Kaishek and to defeat Japan in World War II. Again, it is also associated with the figure of Zhou Enlai, who applied it in July 1956 to the Taiwan problem when he appealed for a Third United Front with the KMT. There were thus good grounds both within Party history and the Marxist canon for presenting the United Front as an alternative to Maoist class struggle. When the United Front was resurrected in July 1977, it was directed mainly towards the non-Han populations living in the border regions of Tibet, Xinjiang and Inner Mongolia. The ethnically Mongolian cadre Ulanfu was appointed as its director, and measures were taken by the Central Committee to rehabilitate those who had been made to 'wear the hat' of 'local nationalism' since the anti-Rightist campaign of 1957.

When the United Front was extended to Taiwan, Hong Kong and Macao, however, the orthodox CCP definition of 'patriotism' (*aiguo zhuyi*), as loyalty to the state expressed by a variety of ethnic groups, was hard to sustain. Instead, an underlying *volkisch* conception of the nation was deployed when, on 1 January 1979, the National People's Congress issued a 'Message to Compatriots on Taiwan', stating:

> Every Chinese, in Taiwan or on the mainland, has a compelling responsibility for the survival, growth and prosperity of the Chinese nation (minzu) [. . .] If we do not quickly set about ending this disunity so that our motherland is reunified at an early date, how can we answer our ancestors and explain to our descendants? This sentiment is shared by all. Who among the descendants of the Yellow Emperor wishes to go down in history as a traitor?
>
> (NPC 1979)

With patriotism being equated with loyalty to the CCP and a belief in socialism in the CCP's domestic discourse, however, even this message for Chinese people living beyond Beijing's sovereignty became confused at times, as when Deng asked audiences in Hong Kong, Macao and Taiwan:

> Is loving the motherland something abstract? If you don't love new China led by the Communist Party, what motherland do you love? We do not ask all our patriotic compatriots in Xianggang (Hong Kong) and Aomen (Macao) and in Taiwan and abroad to

support socialism, but at the least, they should not oppose socialist New China. Otherwise, how can they be called patriotic?

(1984m)

Such inconsistencies were inevitable, given the way in which patriotism was being used to link together key areas of policy-making. While Deng had established important dynamics for political discourse under reform and opening, the deployment of nationalistic themes in this formula amounts to what Chinese writers often call a 'double-edged sword'. Within the domestic politics of 'reform and opening', nationalism could be appropriated by all sides. Those who supported more radical and faster economic reforms could present their opponents as unpatriotic because they endangered the ability of the nation to oppose hegemony and achieve unification; conversely, more cautious members of the elite could portray advocates of economic reform as unpatriotic whenever they failed to deliver the promised goals. This is why it makes no sense to talk of nationalism as the exclusive province of the 'Left' or the 'Right', or 'liberals' or 'hardliners'. Within the politics of 'reform and opening', all contenders for power and influence have to appropriate nationalism to achieve legitimacy for their respective programmes.

The nation as discursive subject

It is certainly difficult to categorise Deng Xiaoping as either 'Right' or 'Left'. On the one hand, he could advocate political reforms that would strengthen centrifugal social forces, such as separating party organs from state organs, enhancing the supervision of cadres by the public and enabling the different 'nationalities' to exercise regional autonomy (1984a: 302–25). He also raised hopes for Western-style political reform when he pointed out that Mao had criticised Stalin for making errors that would not have been possible in countries like Britain, France and the United States (1984a: 316). Yet, at the same time, Deng was cultivating his appeal to patriotism and stressing the need to combat the tendency of 'worshipping things foreign, or fawning on foreigners' (1984g: 320–1).

Given Deng's ambiguity, relatively cautious figures in the leadership could turn his patriotic rhetoric against the acceleration and broadening of the reform process if they so wished. Party elder Chen Yun, the cautious advocate of managed and limited economic liberalisation, expressed his concerns over the way in which some people had been convinced by seeing foreign skyscrapers and motorways that China was not as good as other countries and that socialism was not as good as capitalism (Wang 1997: 152–3). Deng is sympathetic to such fears when he insists that the values for the new era are to be culled not from Marxism-Leninism but from the heroic past of the 'new democratic revolution' when Party members were imbued with the spirit of slogans like 'Serve the people wholeheartedly', 'The individual is subordinate to the organisation', 'Be selfless', 'Utter devotion to others without any thought of self', and 'Fear neither hardship nor death' (1984k: 335–55).

As Party elders like Chen Yun and Deng Xiaoping attempted to retreat from policy-making in the early 1980s, patriotic ethics also had to be developed and deployed by the new leadership team of Hu Yaobang and Zhao Ziyang. As the new general secretary of the CCP, Hu was the key figure for the re-engineering of ideology, having used his positions of deputy head of the Central Party School and head of the Party's Central Organisation Department to steer the 'thought emancipation' campaign. His position was weak, though, because he was engineered into position by Deng without the formal authority of the Central Committee. Moreover, he was viewed with a degree of hostility by more conservative Party elders. Personally, he is said to have preferred cosmopolitan values. Moreover, he had to win the loyalty of a rising generation of cadres who had been scarred by the Cultural Revolution and were looking for alternative ideological explanations of the suffering that had occurred under 'socialism'.

While senior figures in the leadership were advocating an atavistic form of patriotism, Hu had to appeal to a highly cynical younger generation that had come to maturity during the Cultural Revolution. Within the political strategies of this 'scarred generation', there arose a contest to appropriate nationalism. Many of the new artistic movements that appeared at the time were not only critical of the Cultural Revolution but were also careful to relate themselves in a positive way to Chinese identity, claiming that there was no incompatibility between opposing the older style of nationalism and remaining loyal to 'nation' (*minzu*) and 'country' (*guojia*) (Larson 1993: 183). The novelist and dramatist and future Nobel laureate Gao Xingjian could argue that using Western literary techniques need not deprive a work of its national character. In his view, Chineseness could still emerge in the form of social customs, psychological modes, language and aesthetic tastes. The new generation of writers and artists maintained that so long as the national language was used and the subject remained the national people, the national spirit would remain clear. What was important for modernist poetry was to discard the form of traditional classical and folk genres, while retaining the Chinese 'spirit' of straightforwardness, scorn for wealth and influence, regard for truth, justice and friendship, and a hope and tenacity specific to the Chinese people (Larson 1993: 176–8). This contestation of patriotism posed a challenge to Deng's attempt to recover selfless ethics from the past. The scepticism with which his version of patriotism was viewed by those whose formative years had been spent during the Cultural Revolution is encapsulated by the dialogue between an idealistic student and a young woman who are returning from having been sent down to the countryside in the groundbreaking novel *Waves* by the poet Bei Dao (real name Zhao Zhenkai), written in 1974 and finally published in 1979 after several changes:

'Tell me something please', she brushed back the stray hairs, speaking slowly and emphatically. 'In your life, what is there worth believing in?'

I thought for a moment. 'Our country, for example.'

'Ha, that's an out-dated tune.'

'No, I don't mean some hackneyed political cliché, I mean our common suffering, our common way of life, our common cultural heritage, our common yearning ... this indivisible fate that constitutes everything: we have a duty to our country ...'

'Duty?' she cut me off coldly. 'What duty are you talking about? The duty to be an offering after having been slaughtered, or what?'

'Yes, if necessary, that kind of duty.'

'Forget it. I can just see you sitting in a spacious drawing room discussing the subject like this. What right have you to say 'we', what right?' She was becoming more and more agitated, her face growing flushed, tears filling her eyes. 'No thanks, this country's not mine! I don't have a country, I don't have one ...' She turned away.

(Zhao, Z. 1985: 21)

The party leadership appeared to be increasingly uncertain over how to deal with this kind of cynicism. Just one month after Deng delivered his August 1980 speech advocating political reform, the literary journal *Jintian* (*Today*), edited by Bei Dao and fellow poet Mang Ke, was proscribed. The following May saw a campaign of criticism against the script for the film *Bitter Love*, the story of a man passing through the travails of modern Chinese history. The main problem with this work appears to have been the way in which it did not allow the Party to play any kind of positive role. The icons of the orthodox narrative of national salvation were missing, from the Long March to Yan'an. Not one Communist leader was presented in a position of constructive authority and there was no mention of the Party as the vanguard leading the peasants or the workers (Spence 1992: 285). On 23 May, however, the scriptwriter, Bai Hua, received a writer's award, and in June officials at the *People's Daily* apparently refused a request from *Liberation Army News* to run a criticism of *Bitter Love* it had published in April. On 17 July, Deng Xiaoping himself remarked that no campaigns on the issue were necessary. Then, at the end of August 1981, Hu Yaobang gave a speech in which he emphasised that *Bitter Love* was 'not good for the people and socialism and therefore should be criticized' and that it was 'not an isolated matter' and represented a 'wrong tendency' (SWB FE/6817/B11, 2–9–81: 1–2). There was obviously deep disagreement at the top over how to present an orthodox version of patriotism that could be acceptable to all upon whom the success of 'reform and opening' would depend.

The compromise of 'socialist spiritual civilisation'

The main strategy to build a consensus in the discussion of the nation amongst the party elite emerged in the proposal to build 'socialist spiritual civilisation'. This had first been raised by Marshall Ye Jianying in a speech of 29 September 1979, to mark the thirtieth anniversary of the PRC. It appeared again when Central Committee member Li Chang wrote a letter to his colleagues recommending that the slogan 'Build a socialist spiritual civilisation' should be used as a complement to the Four Modernisations (*PD* 10–2–81, in Schram 1984: 431). Deng first gave the idea its authoritative form in a speech of 25 December 1980 (1984k: 335–55), during which he called for cadres to balance their technical learning with 'communist thinking, ideals, beliefs, morality and discipline, as well as a revolutionary stand and revolutionary principles, comradely relations among people, and so on' (1984k: 348). Building socialist spiritual civilisation was then enshrined in law as a duty of the state in Article 4 of the revised PRC Constitution when it was implemented on 4 December 1982. Its central values were defined in Article 24 as 'the civic virtues of love of the motherland, of the people, of labour, of science and of socialism; it educates the people in patriotism, collectivism, internationalism and communism, in dialectical and historical materialism'.

Although 'communism' still figured in this formula, its meaning had become so diluted that it had come to signify not much more than a kind of patriotic selflessness characteristic of a past era. When Deng addressed the Central Military Commission in July 1982, for example, he listed the fundamental elements of the 'revolutionary spirit' as being 'ideals, morality, culture and discipline'. From then on, these qualities were to be known as the 'Four Haves' and became central in the formulation of ideological education. The one glaring omission from the list, however, was 'communist thinking'. Until then, this had always been made one of the core values listed as elements of the 'revolutionary spirit'. As Peng Zhen, vice-chairman of the committee for the revision of the Constitution, made clear in his commentary on the new Constitution, however, 'socialist' principles were certainly not to be confused with egalitarianism. That would be tantamount to 'skipping a stage of historical development and pushing an economic and social system that can be realized only at a higher stage of communism'. Instead of this, at the present stage, socialist principles should be understood in terms of imperatives such as 'to each according to his work' and 'economic responsibility' (Peng 1983: 91).

When Peng Zhen traced the origin of the central values of socialist spiritual civilisation, he went back to the definition of civic virtues in the Common Programme, a kind of provisional constitution adopted after the foundation of the PRC, when the Party was still appealing for a broad united front between all progressive forces in the country. Deng even looked back as far as the spirit of Yan'an, reducing Mao's idea of 'revolutionary spirit' to an ethic that inspires people to 'work tirelessly, observe strict discipline, make sacrifices, act selflessly and put the interests of others first, the spirit that gives people revolutionary optimism and the determination to overwhelm all enemies and surmount all difficulties in order to win victory'. Deng believed that if this spirit could be fostered, not only amongst cadres but also amongst young people, 'Our country will then be looked up to by all revolutionary and progressive minded people in the world and admired by all who feel frustrated and suffer from spiritual emptiness for lack of purpose in their lives' (1984k: 349).

If class struggle was absent from these descriptions of ideological orthodoxy, they centred very much on presenting the age-old tension between using foreign functional knowledge to preserve the essence of

Chinese identity. This is plain from the way in which Deng explained the need to oppose any tendency to worship capitalism and bourgeois liberalisation while continuing to promote exchanges with friendly Western countries in order to learn whatever was useful from them. The condition for achieving this without being corrupted by capitalist influences was to encourage patriotism and a sense of national dignity and self-confidence (1984k: 350). This deployment of the function-essence dichotomy can be seen even more clearly in Peng Zhen's comments on the two facets involved in the work of building socialist spiritual civilisation. The first of these is the expansion of education for the sake of modernising science and technology and achieving the Four Modernisations. The second is the need to 'imbue more and more citizens with high ideals, moral integrity, general education, and a sense of discipline so that a new standard of morality is fostered and our nation acquires a revolutionary and vigorous mental outlook'. The state is thus expected to raise the technological capabilities of the population, while the 'fighting task on the ideological front' is that the state 'combats capitalist, feudal and other decadent ideas' (Peng 1983: 88–91).

Hu Yaobang eventually came round to the view that the attempt to build a patriotic set of ethics could be made compatible with 'thought emancipation' if it could be confined to a Party rectification campaign. This would be aimed at eradicating corruption and factionalism amongst the cadres, rather than being allowed to degenerate into a Maoist-style mass movement amongst the broader population. He thus gave the concept his personal endorsement in a September 1982 article in the *People's Daily*, where he stated that socialist spiritual civilisation 'not only gives tremendous impetus to the building of material civilisation, it also guarantees that it will develop according to a correct orientation' (*PD* 8–9–82; *BR* 37:1982: 21; cited in Schram 1984: 433). When the Twelfth Party Congress duly launched a rectification campaign, Hu told the meeting that that the concept of 'socialist spiritual civilisation' should be used to enrich the cultural life of the nation through policies such as media and education reform. Rather than giving any hint of xenophobia, he pointed out that it was dangerous to just attack 'criminal activities', while ignoring the need to maintain openness to the outside world (Hu 1982).

When Deng Xiaoping addressed the Congress, a new emphasis on economic development was visible in the way that the task of speeding up socialist modernisation had moved to first place in the list of the three major tasks for the CCP. Foreign policy, on the other hand, had fallen to third place. Moreover, the emphasis on Taiwan had been watered down somewhat with the call for the '. . . return of Taiwan to the motherland, realising the unification of the motherland' (*shixian Taiwan huigui zuguo, shixian zuguo tongyi*) (1984g1: 204), now phrased as a desire to 'realise unification of the motherland, including Taiwan' (*zhengqu shixian baokuo Taiwan zai nei de zuguo tongyi*) (Deng 1993c: 3).

This new ordering and phrasing of the three tasks can be explained in part by the growing confidence of the leadership in the domestic reform programme following successes posted in agriculture. The souring of relations with Washington after the failure to secure a cut-off date for American arms sales to Taiwan in the PRC-US Communiqué of August 1982 was already making it more difficult to deploy foreign policy and unification with Taiwan in the politics of legitimation. This latter issue was of vital importance to Deng's domestic standing, PRC foreign minister Huang Hua had made it an issue at the UN on 29 October 1981, and the foreign ministry lodged a formal protest with the US government on 12 January 1982. After the failure of the talks with Washington, it had become prudent to play down the use of opposing hegemony and achieving unification to legitimate economic reform in domestic politics.

The need for a loosening of the constraints imposed by nationalist discourse can also be seen in the attempt to replace Deng's originally bellicose practice of international power-balancing with the establishment of a foreign policy based on the principles of 'independence and self-reliance' (*zili zizhu, zili gengsheng*). The orthodox version of Deng Xiaoping Theory presents this development as due to Deng's realisation that there should be at least seventy years of international peace in which China could reconstruct and become a prosperous nation (Deng 1993d). Such a view overlooks the cumulative effect not only of the stalemate in Taiwan policy but also the humiliation suffered by Chinese forces in Vietnam in the winter of 1978/9 and the failure to win international support for this venture, along with the domestic changes taking place inside the Soviet Union with the decline of Leonid Brezhnev, who died in November 1982.

The way in which Deng uses patriotic themes to explain this change in outlook can be seen quite clearly in his emphasis on the way in which the Chinese people value their long history of struggle and achievement of independent sovereignty, together with his warning that foreign countries should not expect China to become a subordinate or 'swallow any bitter fruit' that will damage the national interest. While he accepts that opening to the outside world and expanding foreign relations on the basis of equality and mutual benefit will continue, he also insists that vigilance will be maintained in the fight against corruption by decadent ideas from abroad and the spread of a bourgeois lifestyle (1993c: 3).

The new phrasing of the call for unification could also provide more space for diverting unification discourse away from Taiwan and towards Hong Kong, as negotiations with the relatively weak adversary of the United Kingdom over the future of the colony provided a better opportunity to deploy unification discourse. On 24 September 1982, just three weeks after Deng's speech to the Twelfth Party Congress, Deng took full advantage of this situation. Whereas Mao had once told Henry Kissinger that he was in no hurry over Hong Kong (Kissinger 1973: 187), Deng raised the status of the issue in domestic politics when he told Margaret Thatcher that any Chinese leader or government that did not ensure Hong Kong's return to China would be rejected by the people as an equivalent of the Qing statesman, Li Hongzhang, who had signed the 'unequal treaties' with the powers in the nineteenth century (1993z).

When the National People's Congress (NPC) promulgated the revised version of the PRC Constitution in December 1982, it thus struck a careful balance between nationalist legitimation on the one hand and 'reform and opening' on the other. It emphasised the decentralisation of power, regional autonomy, the protection of ethnic minorities, the rule of law and gave a constitutional foundation for agricultural reforms, the role of the private sector, property rights and the use of the market for regulating the economy. At the same time, the centrifugal forces that could be generated by such reforms were to be contained by the building of 'socialist spiritual civilisation'. The preamble, moreover, included the demand that accomplishing unification with Taiwan is 'the lofty duty of the Chinese people, including our compatriots in Taiwan', while international relations were to be handled by adherence to an 'independent foreign policy' and the Five Principles of Peaceful Coexistence (NPC 1983: 7–8). The new limits of political discourse under 'reform and opening' had thus been delineated.

'Spiritual pollution': nationalism and factionalism

The difficulties of maintaining the ideological compromise reached at the Twelfth Party Congress can be seen in the way in which the rectification campaign escalated out of control and became a widespread campaign against 'spiritual pollution'. Initially, recommendations for ideological education issued in August and September 1983, which even covered nursery education, called for a fairly bland form of selfless patriotism, recommending that love of the motherland, love of the Party and love of socialism should be integrated into one body of thought. Patriotic education was to be made appealing to students through the use of a rich variety of activities to teach it, and by relating the fate of every student to that of the motherland. In the process, their duty was to accept that the welfare of the motherland comes above all other concerns. There was, therefore, no conflict between patriotism and socialism because patriotic awareness and nation-building sentiments would lead the young to establish communist ideals and faith (Education Commission 1983).

Local Party organisations, however, began to take this ideological campaign a step further, issuing instructions for the return to a kind of revolutionary puritanism, involving neat and simple dressing, and stronger organisation and discipline. When the Central Committee met for its Second Plenum in October and made a decision to consolidate the Party, this broadened out to become a campaign against 'spiritual pollution' that involved an indiscriminate and widespread onslaught against anybody whose dress or behaviour showed signs of foreign influence, be they inside or outside the Party. For this kind of behaviour to spread so fast in Chinese cities, the messages of the elite had to resonate with a festering resentment against foreign influences within the population. This, after all, is a characteristic of modern Chinese culture that goes back much further than distinctions between 'Left' and 'Right'. It is a condition that was most brilliantly captured and lampooned in 1922 by the dramatist and essayist Lu Xun, creator of the tragicomic peasant vagabond Ah Q, whose uselessness is only outweighed by his scorn for everything foreign. This condition was always present in Mao, and spontaneously came to the surface amongst the urban population in July 1979, just three months after the crackdown on the Beijing Spring, when Shanghai witnessed two days of clashes between Chinese and foreign students, resulting in injuries to some forty people.

Such a cultural explanation is overly deterministic, however. The widespread xenophobia of 1983 can also be explained by the uncertainty generated by the economic reform process. Farmers had been subjected to three years of encouragement to get rich, with some getting rich before others (Deng 1984g: 243). In the summer of 1983, talk of the introduction of an 'economic responsibility system' for industry and the extension of the practice of 'contracting out' from commerce and the service sector to industry threatened the security of many workers. Economic winners became convenient targets for the release of anger and frustration as they tended to indulge in foreign consumer goods and fashions, many of them influenced by popular culture in Taiwan and Hong Kong. Many of those who had not gained from the reforms were only too happy to interpret the calls from the top as an excuse to vent their envy (Schram 1984: 439–40). Yet it is also unlikely that this outbreak of xenophobia could have occurred without a division at the top of the Party itself. This is the view of Wang Ruoshui, a journalist at the *People's Daily* who had been a leading advocate in the rising generation of Party theorists of the need to explore the possibility that alienation could occur under socialism. According to Wang, those who had control over the propaganda organisations, namely Mao Zedong's former political secretary Hu Qiaomu and Deng Liqun, secretary of the Central Committee and director of the Propaganda Department, used the campaign to undermine Hu Yaobang. They gained the crucial support of Party elder Chen Yun, who complained to the Second Plenum about the need to educate or remove from their positions those in the Party who were entranced by foreign skyscrapers and motorways (Wang Ruoshui 1997: 152–61).

For such views to prevail, they still had to gain Deng's support. That support was forthcoming when Deng told the Plenum (1993f) that he was concerned about the way in which young theoreticians in the Party who were experimenting with the theory of alienation had been poisoned by the influence of 'spiritual pollution'. Resolute measures had to be taken to stop this contagion from affecting the successor generation, he insisted. The ideological struggle had to be extended beyond culture and theoretical work into education, news work, publishing, broadcasting and mass culture. The orientation and scope of the rectification campaign thus changed significantly, as Deng stated that the Party had focused too much of its time on struggling against the 'leftism' of the Cultural Revolution and been overly lenient towards the trouble-makers on the Right.

Although Deng's change of position undid Hu's attempt to limit the construction of 'socialist spiritual civilisation' to a rectification campaign within the Party, the leadership soon became sufficiently concerned about the spread of the campaign against 'spiritual pollution' to call for moderation. For the longer-term nature of the development of nationalist orthodoxy, it is highly significant that the final nail was hammered into the coffin of the campaign when Deng Xiaoping returned to Beijing from a tour of the Special Economic Zones (SEZ) in February 1984. It was on that occasion that he gave a speech to the Central Committee (1993e) in which he lauded the zones as the most radical experiment in the opening up of China to foreign influences, heaping special praise on the industrial zone of Shekou in the Shenzhen SEZ, adjacent to Hong Kong, which had coined the motto 'time is money, efficiency is life'. In the same vein, he recommended that some areas of the country should be encouraged to get rich before others in order to boost domestic demand.

Deng thus effectively used the SEZs to portray an alternative patriotism to the puritanical and xenophobic conservatism that had been encouraged to surface during the campaign against 'spiritual pollution'. In May, the Central Committee and State Council opened up fourteen more coastal cities to the world. This marks the beginning of the articulation of a new kind of outwardly orientated patriotism in the Party line, which was partly necessitated by the need to draw in resources from abroad as attempts were made to extend the economic reform programme to urban areas, after the agricultural boom that had been generated by decollectivisation in the countryside began to peak. Central to this version of patriotism is the erosion of the CCP's commitment to central planning and public ownership, and the reduction of socialism to the task of raising national production. As Deng explained to a delegation from Japan in June 1984, the meaning of 'socialism' could now be understood in terms of the Marxist emphasis on the development of the forces of production and that 'poverty is not socialism, and even less is it communism' (1993g: 64).

By locating this version of socialism in the CCP's narrative of national salvation since the Opium War, the problem of social polarisation could be dismissed as something that would be solved by the principle of distribution according to work done. The improbability of being able to realise communist society in the immediate future meant that socialism's task was to develop productive power at a rate faster than capitalism could achieve. The central message after the vicissitudes of the campaign against spiritual pollution, then, was all that was necessary for socialist modernisation to be achieved was to avoid having a closed attitude either to the outside world, or between regions and organisations within China itself (Deng 1993g: 62–6). The tension that had come to exist between preserving Chinese identity and importing foreign know-how is nowhere better expressed than by the way in which Deng Xiaoping, at the height of the campaign against 'spiritual pollution' in October 1993, presented a calligraphic inscription that coined what was to be known as the slogan of the 'Three Faces' over the coming years: 'Face modernisation, face the world, face the future' (Deng 1993f).

The world scientific and technological revolution

It was the emphasis on raising production that allowed a discussion of science and technology as the key to national power to rise to the centre of Party othodoxy over the next two decades. Deng had laid the foundations for this discourse on science and technology at least as early as a key 1977 speech to the national conference on science (1984l). It can be seen quite clearly in his January 1980 speech on 'The Present Situation and the Tasks Before Us', where he emphasises the need to keep up with new developments in science and technology and in international exchanges of personnel and information if the primary tasks of opposing international hegemony and achieving unification are to be achieved (1984g: 255).

The discussion of the world scientific and technological revolution had become increasingly popular amongst the CCP elite, thanks partly to the influence of works such as Alvin Toffler's *The Third Wave* (Lieberthal 1995: 139). Even at the height of the campaign against 'spiritual pollution', in December 1983, the State Council felt moved to issue guidelines to emphasise the importance Deng Xiaoping attached to science and technology. These pointed out that scientists and technicians should not mistake the inventions of modern science for 'sugar coated bullets of capitalism' and that freedom of thought in some areas of their work should not be confused with 'bourgeois liberalisation' (*PD* 18–12–83: 1). When Chen Yun's *Selected Works (1926–1949)* was published in January 1984, a commentary in the *People's Daily* by the biographer of the young Mao and head of the Organisation Department of the Central Committee (Li Rui 1984) presented it in the context of a world that was just entering the era of a new technical revolution that would act as a stimulus and a challenge for China to stand on its own two feet and catch up with and overtake the other nations of the world. Consequently, the ranks of cadres would have to meet unprecedented demands for increasing the number of intellectuals and specialists among them.

That the world technological revolution could be used to portray opponents of extending and deepening the reforms as 'leftists' who were holding back national development is shown by the propaganda campaign that was launched by the *People's Daily* during the spring of 1984. This opened with a near full-page story about Zheng Zhemin, a gifted scientist who had fought to return to the PRC from the US with a PhD in 1955, yet whose appointment as director of the Insitute of Mechanics at the Chinese Academy of Science and application for Party membership had been blocked. The reason for this kind of phenomenon was traced to the failure of the Party to tackle the problem of 'leftism' head on (*PD* 30–03–84; Schram 1984: 451).

Closely linked to the global technological revolution was the reduction of socialism to the raising of national production. Deng had already suggested this principle in his January 1980 speech, and he repeated this at greater length in June 1984 when he told a delegation from Japan that 'socialism' could now be understood in terms of the Marxist emphasis on the development of the forces of production and that 'poverty is not socialism, and even less is it communism' (1993g: 64).

Going on to locate this version of socialism in the CCP's narrative of national salvation since the Opium War, the problem of social polarisation could be dismissed as something that would be solved by the principle of distribution according to work done. With it not being possible to realise communist society in the immediate future, socialism's task was to develop productive power more quickly than capitalism could do.

The way was thus paved for the Central Committee to resolve on the formula of describing the socialist economy as 'a planned commodity economy based on public ownership' when it convened for its plenary session in October 1984. It is after this, in 1985, that Deng makes his first overt reference to 'global' processes, when he tells a delegation from the Japanese Chamber of Commerce and Industry:

> From the economic point of view, the two really great problems confronting the world today, strategic problems with a global nature, are: first, peace, and second, economic development. The first involves East-West relations, while the second involves North-South relations.
>
> (1993a: 105)[1]

Perhaps the best example of just how far elements of the leadership were prepared to go in setting up science as a source of political authority in this context, is the way in which Central Committee member Wan Li told the 1985 national education conference that, although China needed people like Marx, it also needed its Newtons, Watts, Eddisons and Einsteins. He even went so far as to compare those in the Party bent on ideological retrenchment to the Vatican, referring to Copernicus, Bruno and Galileo as examples of scientific heroes who were condemned for seeking truth, yet who were proven right by scientific progress (Wan Li 1985). Yet even an advocate of technological revolution like Wan Li was still working very much within the old dilemma of finding a balance between Western functional knowledge and Chinese orthodox essence. While he had been a pioneer of agricultural reform in the late 1970s, since the early 1980s he had been head not only of the State Council's Small Leading Working Group for the Construction of the Computer Network, but also the committee in charge of the 'Five Stresses, Four Beauties and Three Ardent Loves Movement'.

Deng Xiaoping himself stressed the linkage between science and technology and national power when he told the 1985 national education conference that if a country of 1.2 billion could get its education right, its human resources would be unbeatable by any country (Zhou Zhiping *et al.* 1993: 10). In doing so, he was revealing the high expectations that were being placed on the ability of education to maintain the CCP's ideological balance between patriotism and opening to the outside world. The education system was thus put at the cutting edge of the reform process in May 1985, when the Central Committee issued a resolution that explained the problems that would arise in the 1990s if something was not done to remedy the shortage of a whole range of technical and administrative personnel who understood the culture of modern science (CC 1985). To solve the problem, it proposed freeing local initiative and allowing the education system to respond more effectively to the needs of the economy and society. Management would be devolved to local government and to educational institutions themselves, with the introduction of a 'school presidential responsibility system'. Party committees would be confined to supervising the implementation of Party and national policy rather than being involved in day-to-day management. Universities were also to be encouraged to become more involved with manufacturing, scientific research and social development.

Encouraging diversification of sources of finance in order to save central government revenue and develop an education market was another issue raised by the Central Committee. This was to be achieved by encouraging employers to support students, and allowing institutions to accept self-paying students outside the quotas laid down by the national plan. To attract such students, institutions would be allowed to adjust their specialist services, fix their own curricula, and produce and select their own teaching materials. They would have the right to accept commissions, and to collaborate with other institutions. They would have the right to administer the grant received from government, to use the money they earned for themselves, and to develop their own international exchanges.

Driven by economic imperatives, such reforms obviously created the risk that central control over key areas of the education system would be weakened. Ideology was not absent from the document altogether, however. The themes that Deng had been developing since the late 1970s were present in the form of lamentations over the way that students had come to lack a spirit of sacrifice for the sake of a wealthy and strong motherland, and that the teaching of Marxism had become insufficiently lively and active. Yet advocates of faster reforms remained confident that this kind of disillusionment could be dealt with through a process of listening and persuasion. As Wan Li put it to the national conference, 'If we have created a socialist system which has abolished the exploitation of class by class, if we are the communist party that serves the people, are we still afraid of people raising reasonable ideas?' (Wan Li 1985: 265).

This tone was developed further when the Central Committee expressed concern not so much over the failure to instil Marxist orthodoxy in the young, as with the inability of education to raise students capable of living independently and with the ability for critical thought. Many courses were out of date, teaching methods were arcane, and pragmatism was not being stressed. There was too much narrow specialisation, a departure from the needs of the economy and social development, and a falling behind in the development of a contemporary scientific culture. The view that ideological retrenchment meant rejecting foreign influences was denounced as 'leftism', especially since China now faced the challenge of an international technological revolution.

Sautman (1991) describes this reformist current in education as amounting to a form of 'depoliticisation' and 'deideologisation'. The sidelining of ideology by the changing nature of the education system can certainly be seen in the fact that between 1985 and 1987, the ratio of published articles concerned with natural sciences and technology compared to those concerned with social sciences and humanities was 6 to 1 (Xiao, C. 1992: 164). If, however, the managerial and economic reforms are understood as legitimated by the broader patriotic ethics attached to 'reform and opening', then it may be more accurate to say that a new form of legitimacy was being articulated rather than a departure from ideology altogether. Indeed, Sautman himself acknowledges that the turn in CCP ideology represented by the education reforms amounted to what he calls an ideology of 'authoritarian modernization', the roots of which go back through the Kuomintang period under Chiang Kaishek and all the way to the late Qing dynasty (Sautman 1991: 685).

Perhaps 'techno-nationalism' is the best term for the new ideological direction represented by the emerging discourse on science and technology. This term was originally applied by Richard Samuels to the Japanese strategy of linking economic development with state security through a process of indigenisation, diffusion and nurturance of foreign technology across industrial sectors. Adam Segal has applied it to China, claiming that the state has forsaken many of the institutions normally associated with techno-nationalism by scaling back central planning and support for large state-owned enterprises, while embracing actors who were previously ideologically suspect. Technonationalism thus becomes a strategic context within which policy is oriented towards autonomy and independence from other states through policies that can be either state-owned or non-governmental enterprises (Segal 2003: 166–8).

Segal's main task, however, is to look at the economics of high technology enterprises in China, rather than the ideological implications of techno-nationalism. For the CCP political elite, however, managing the political impact of deepening integration with the international technological revolution has been a major challenge under 'reform and opening'. While Deng Xiaoping could look forward to a future when Party conferences and committees would be dominated by welleducated technocrats in their forties, he also consistently warned that the technologically sophisticated cadres of tomorrow would have to be innoculated against infection by evil foreign influences through educating them in the correct virtues of 'socialist morality, love for the socialist motherland and a sense of national dignity' (1984g: 247). By the end of the 1990s, the particular form of Chinese techno-nationalism had become quite explicit in Jiang Zemin's elevation of scientific and technological personnel to the status of a revolutionary vanguard leading the nation to wealth and power under his ideology of the 'Three Represents'. To understand how Chinese nationalism has been developed in the global era, it is therefore necessary to explore further how attitudes towards technology emerged out of the politics of the 1980s.

The genesis of techno-nationalism

The broader political ramifications of this raising of science and technology to the centre of the CCP's nation-building programme can be seen in the way that the new ideological consensus was challenged in the mid–1980s, leading to the downfall of Hu Yaobang in January 1987. In terms of elite Party politics, the context for this was set in 1985 when the balance of power at the top swung in favour of Hu Yaobang after the ending of the campaign against 'spiritual pollution'.

With key positions in charge of ideological development occupied by relatively liberal figures, the following year a campaign to 'Let a Hundred Flowers Bloom a Hundred Schools of Thought Contend' was launched. Within this, science and technology continued to be used as part of the attempt to break down ideological ossification. A major theme in the launching of the campaign was the presentation of the father of China's nuclear weapons programme, the United States-trained Deng Jiaxuan, as a model patriot. Timed to coincide with a meeting of scientists to debate academic freedom, the weekly Party magazine, *Outlook* (*Liaowang* 14–7–86: 13), published an article praising Deng's selflessness and tireless devotion, and claiming that his achievement of creating China's first mushroom cloud in October 1964 represented, 'the spiritual flower in full blossom of the Chinese nation'. 'The intellectuals of China', claimed the magazine, 'are the pride of the Chinese people, for tens of thousands of them like Deng Jiaxian are struggling hard, not for their own gains or game, but for the development of China.'

In the climate of experimentation that followed, avant-garde cultural movements flourished under what came to be called a 'culture fever', which eclectically combined native and foreign influences. Within this atmosphere, debates began to openly focus on some of the most sensitive issues for the Party leadership. Particularly prominent was the argument over whether Marxism is compatible with the kind of 'humanism' that gives pride of place to the development of the full potential of the individual, that had been rumbling on since the late 1970s. Dozens of collections of essays on the subject were published in Beijing, Shanghai, Nanjing, Guangzhou and Chengdu. Wang Ruoshui's 'In Defense of Humanism' became a best-seller in Guangzhou bookshops. On 23 December, the largest conference yet on humanism and the philosophy of man was held in Guangzhou.

The leading Marxist historian of Chinese art and ideas, Li Zehou, also published a series of articles between mid-1986 and early 1987 which took the development of ideology under Hu Yaobang's leadership to its next logical step by claiming that the West was now being taken as 'substance' and China as 'function' (*xi ti zhong yong*). As Li explained, this idea had in fact become common-place in formulae such as 'sinification of Marxism', 'the Chinese-style road to modernisation', 'Chinese-style socialism'. Speaking as a Marxist, Li could claim that it was absurd for a historical materialist to deny that Western science and technology is the 'substance' of modernity. To argue the opposite would be to commit the same error as nineteenth-century

Confucian reformers who failed to realise that objects such as ships and trains were manifestations of the cultural substance of modern society. In the present, if modernisation was not to equal Westernisation, local cultures would have to perform the 'function' of adapting science and technology to local conditions, as evidenced by the case of Japan (1996a).

Finding the right 'function' for Chinese culture to effectively adopt Western learning and adapt it to China's national condition (*guo qing*) would not be easy, acknowledged Li. The sinification of Marxism had already provided an example of how a revolutionary party could achieve power in a peasant society, but it had also proved a bitter lesson of how Marxism could be 'feudalised' in such a process. The only way to avoid such mistakes was to put more effort into understanding Chinese history and tradition. Rather than smashing tradition, the task now was how to creatively adapt tradition and build its culture on the base of large-scale industrial production. While Li admired post-modernism for its compatibility with traditional Chinese humanism, he rejected its suitability for a society that was still trying to modernise (1996b: 213–17). Although Li still believed that world cultural development takes place according to universal principles and rejected cultural relativism, he could still argue that it takes on different forms in different places (1990: 429–30).

Far more problematic for the unfolding discussion of socialism, though, was the way in which equating science and technology with patriotism inevitably gave scientists a new kind of authority. This was seized on and advocated by professor Fang Lizhi, the well-travelled vice-president of Hefei University of Science and Technology in the capital of impoverished Anhui province. Sometimes referred to as 'China's Sakharov', Fang had already had his passport confiscated after he criticised a deputy mayor of Beijing for taking a free trip to the United States to attend a conference on nuclear accelerators, about which he knew nothing. Fang's views on CPC ideology, however, went straight to the heart of the function-essence dichotomy. This is because he questioned the whole principle of proletarian leadership by drawing the implications of Deng Xiaoping's views on science to their logical conclusion. As Fang explained, when Deng had declared the political rehabilation of scientists and technicians at the national science conference back in 1978, he had explained that according to Marxism, science and technology should be categorised as a productive force in society (*kexue jishu shi shengchanli*). Yet his intention had only been to reinstate scientists and technicians as part of the proletariat, after they had been reduced to the 'stinking ninth' category of intellectuals by

Mao. For Fang, however, it was not enough to raise intellectuals to the 'third' grade, behind workers and peasants. Given that Marx had said that the industrial workers were the most positive force for change, and that science had been categorised as a productive force, it only followed that intellectuals were the most advanced element of the proletariat (Fang 1985: 7).

Fang also angered the Party leadership due to the way in which he advocated 'complete westernisation' (*quanpan xihua*), along with two other influential critics, the writer and veteran CPC member Wang Ruowang and the investigative journalist Liu Binyan. The basic position adopted by these figures was that it made no sense to argue that Western science and technology could be imported, while calling capitalist theory and ideology 'pollution'. As Wang Ruowang put it to a meeting in Shanghai, 'Bringing in their technology and not bringing in their thought is the same as bringing in hardware with no software – empty'. What China had been landed with instead was a kind of socialism that was coloured by feudalism, and four decades of socialism had achieved nothing to be proud of (Anon. 1988: 135–40).

This increasingly open discussion of the tensions between 'reform and opening' and the Party's version of socialism finally transgressed the limits of acceptability when demonstrations began at Fang Lizhi's university (which had sent more than 100 research graduates abroad since the beginnings of 'reform and opening') and spread to Shanghai, Tianjin and Beijing. The main demand at Hefei was for increased student representation in university political committees. As the movement widened, posters appeared urging students to 'fight for true freedom and democratic rights', criticising 'fake democracy' and calling for student-led action against the bureaucracy (*Independent* 19–12–86). Official sources claimed that students beat up 31 policemen and broke into municipal offices during a large demonstration in Shanghai on 19 December. During a meeting with Shanghai mayor Jiang Zemin on 20 December, the demands of the students were for recognition of the legality of the movement, a promise of no reprisals, a free press and free elections (*Guardian* 22–12–86).

The Party leadership appears to have been concerned all along to avoid these demonstrations evolving into a contest for the patriotic mantle. This was partly because the previous year, between September and December, students had taken to the streets to protest over a range of issues, from bad campus food and accommodation to inflation and growing corruption (Whiting 1989: 76–7). They had chosen to make their presence felt in a way that would not allow accusations that they were being unpatriotic, by conflating such issues with protests against the import of Japanese goods following the visit of Japanese Prime Minister Nakasone to the Yasukuni Shrine in Tokyo, which contains the remains of Class A war criminals from World War II. Their demonstrations had thus coincided with the commemorations of key events in the historical struggle with Japan, starting with the 18 September 1931 invasion of Manchuria and culminating with the anniversary of a patriotic student demonstration on 9 December 1936, when students had demanded the formation of a united front between the Nationalists and Communists to oppose Japan.

This linkage of various issues of contemporary dissatisfaction with anti-Japanese patriotism created a difficult problem for the Party leadership. Putting a high value on developing economic relations with Japan, Hu Yaobang had adopted a consistently pro-Japanese policy which had come to a head with a welcoming party for a visit by Prime Minister Nakasone in November, attended by more than a thousand Chinese and Japanese youths. Fearing a repeat of the previous year's anti-Japanese demonstrations, the State Council convened a meeting of the Party's Youth League and cadres addressed university meetings from Lhasa to Beijing to drum up support for the Party's policies. The most highly publicised of such meetings was held in the CCP's Zhongnanhai compound adjacent to Tiananmen Square in the last week of November, where 80 'veteran comrades' joined 120 university students and teachers to commemorate the fiftieth anniversary of the 9 December Movement.

When he addressed the ceremony to mark Nakasone's visit, Hu Yaobang implicitly addressed the use of anti-Japanese sentiments by demonstrators when he called for the integration of patriotism with a far-sighted internationalist spirit, arguing that 'If Chinese young people think merely of the well-being of their own country and . . . are indifferent to promoting unity, friendship, and cooperation for mutual benefit with young people in Japan and other countries, they are not sober-minded patriots' (Xinhua 8–11–86; Whiting 1989: 151). When vice-minister of the State Education Commission, He Dongchang, answered questions from foreign reporters when demonstrations occurred on 30 December, he adopted a slightly different strategy, by confirming that the majority of those taking part were both imbued with patriotic motives and supported the ongoing reforms. The authorities would thus adopt a policy of patient persuasion and education (*Ta Kung Pao*, 1–7 January 1987). The official media began to put the disturbances down to a small number of trouble-makers and criminals with ulterior motives. A cautious approach was taken to the demonstrations, as the authorities agreed not to punish anybody at Hefei and accepted the need for more representation for the students.

When a demonstration in Tiananmen Square on 2 January forced the release of students detained the previous day, however, the authorities looked dangerously impotent as the issue of patriotism was put at centre stage. The demonstrators who marched arm-in-arm in Beijing as they demanded the release of their detained comrades revealed how necessary it had become to legitimate political action through claiming to be both a socialist and a patriot, as they sang the Internationale and chanted 'patriotism is no crime' (*Independent* 2–1–87). The growing challenge to the leadership was quite evident, moreover, in the shape of a big character poster that appeared on the Peking University campus telling the government to take note of the fall of the Marcos regime in the Philippines, while another appealed to the spirit of revolutionary martyrdom when it proclaimed 'By shedding our blood, we can awaken the Chinese masses' (*FT* 2–1–87). Especially problematic for the leadership was the way in which the demonstrators tried to align themselves with factions in the Party, with a long banner written on perforated computer paper unfurled during the march to Tiananmen Square claiming to be supporting Deng Xiaoping and the Four Modernisations (*Observer* 4–1–87).

Fighting 'bourgeois liberalisation'

The most important action taken by the Party to regain control was the removal of Hu Yaobang, who resigned his post as Party general secretary on 16 January, admitting mistakes on 'major political issues in violation of the party's principle of collective leadership' before a meeting of the Politburo. Fang Lizhi was also removed from his post and expelled from the Party, along with Wang Ruowang and Liu Binyan. This purge was accompanied by the launching of a campaign against 'bourgeois liberalisation', a concept defined in a *People's Daily* editorial on 1 January as 'repudiating socialism while advocating capitalism'. Special attention was also paid to repudiating 'complete Westernisation'. As a 'commentator' article in the *People's Daily* on 12 January explained, 'Any Chinese person who respects history and respects the truth, any Chinese person who has national self respect and self confidence, can definitely not agree with the argument for "complete Westernisation"'.

Although it could be admitted that mistakes had been made since the establishment of the PRC, the achievements were said to be far more substantial. Those who were worried that criticising 'complete

Westernisation' would have a negative impact on the policy of opening to the outside world, moreover, should remember that the strategy of building 'socialist spiritual civilisation' was resolutely in favour of importing the advanced technology, know-how and culture from the capitalist countries. But it was also resolutely opposed to the introduction of the wicked, exploitative aspects of capitalism. According to this circuitous logic, therefore, it was the advocates of 'complete Westernisation' who were the real opponents of the policy of opening to the outside world.

Despite these attacks on the views of leading dissidents such as Fang, Wang and Liu, the articles that appeared in the *People's Daily* at this time also attempted to keep the campaign from spreading to the general public or beyond the ideological and political fields in the way that the campaign against spritual pollution had done before. Equally important, attempts were made to delink the protests from factional politics when an editorial in *Peking Daily* on 5 January rejected the claim that the demonstrators were supporting socialism and the leadership of the CCP. Deng Xiaoping's support for the campaign against bourgeois liberalisation was also emphasised when a speech he delivered to senior Party figures was widely disseminated via CCP committees and the media.

Yet the attempt to limit the campaign to internal Party politics reveals how difficult it had already become for the leadership to manage the use of patriotism as the main claim to legitimacy under 'reform and opening'. While the authorities had been concerned to dissociate anti-Japanese sentiments from complaints over economic issues and corruption before the demonstrations had grown, once the movement had been reined in, all of these issues were deployed to discredit Hu Yaobang. He was accused not only of having opposed the campaigns against 'spiritual pollution' and 'bourgeois liberalisation' and failure to adhere to the Four Cardinal Principles, but also of taking unauthorised actions regarding foreign policy, such as inviting 3,000 young Japanese to visit China (Goldman 1994: 208–10; Whiting 1989: 150–2).

The demonstrations also reveal the difficulties of balancing domestic patriotism with the development of the United Front policy towards Taiwan and Hong Kong, as accusations were made that the demonstrations had been provoked by agents from Taiwan. When Deng Xiaoping had addressed the Sixth Plenum of the Twelfth Central Committee as early as 28 September 1986, he had specifically singled out Hong Kong and Taiwan as the sources of opinion against the Four Cardinal Principles and advocating taking the capitalist road, and warned that the struggle against 'liberalisation' would have to go on for ten or twenty more years (1993h: 181–2).

More broadly anti-Western tendencies are also revealed in the way that the trigger for the 19 December demonstration in Shanghai appears to have been attempts made by police to stop Chinese and foreigners from dancing together at a concert given by the US pop group *Jan and Dean*. Top leaders attending a tea party for traditional story tellers on 21 January also launched attacks on Western intellectual subversion. Wang Zhen, a member of the CCP's Central Advisory Commission, a haven for retired leaders, poured scorn on those who 'advocate national anihilism [sic], debase and negate China ... and call for complete westernisation', which he condemned as an idea of 'bourgeois liberalisation'. Bo Yibo, another Party veteran who had been active in persuading anti-Japanese demonstrators to call off their protest in late 1985, attacked 'the sort of talk and deeds that advocate bourgeois liberalisation and wholesale Westernisation and are tantamount to negating the socialist system'. A leading article in the *Peking Daily* on 4 February warned that if American-style democracy was adopted in China, it would bring with it AIDS, homosexuality, armed robbery and 'other disgusting things' (*Times* 5–2–87).

Of more significance for the way in which the Party developed its strategy for dealing with dissent in the long term, though, is the nature of the positive measures taken to combat 'bourgeois liberalisation'. While liberal newspapers began to be closed down, the education system became the central battlefield as the leadership criticised the reforms for having allowed 'the invasion of higher education by bourgeois liberalisation' (CC 1987: 302). A widespread press campaign to strengthen the teaching of Party principles and Party history on university campuses was undertaken. Recalling the frosty reception he began to receive at academic gatherings, Li Zehou remembers how it even became difficult to wear a Western-style jacket.

Rather than see the events of 1986 and the downfall of Hu Yaobang as a resurgence of 'leftism', however, it is important to realise that a consensus continued to be maintained over the areas of policy-making that were at the forefront of exposing society to external influences. Deng Xiaoping's support for the campaign against bourgeois liberalisation was a key factor in maintaining continuity. Even vice-premier Li Peng declared after a tour of the Anshan steelworks in the northeast, once seen as the model of socialist industrial organisation, that foreign funds should be used to develop the iron and steel industry. He summed up the paradox of the technocratic vision of revolution when he reiterated a call made by Zhao Ziyang to 'adhere to reform, speed up transformation and always keep Anshan's revolutionary spirit young' (*CD* 3–1–87: 2). In September, as if to underline the pressing need to maintain an open attitude towards the outside world, China's first e-mail was sent over a local network, the China Computer Technology Net, to a German university and finally to the International Science Net. It was titled 'Crossing the Great Wall to the World'.

Continuity can also be seen in education policy. When Deng called on the education system to create citizens and cadres with the 'Four Haves' in a February 1987 speech on history teaching, he was careful to explain that this was not only for the sake of opposing 'bourgeois liberalisation', but also to purge the influence of the Cultural Revolution on the young. Reasserting a theme he had consistently deployed since opposing Mao's followers in the late 1970s, he looked not to class struggle to fill the ideological gap but to the CCP's historical narrative, stressing that ideology had to be taught in the context of China's struggle to throw off the yoke of imperialism from the Opium War onwards, delivering the message that only socialism can save China and prevent it reverting to a condition of semi-colonisation (1993i: 204–60). In foreign policy, too, economic imperatives meant that the appeal to patriotism could not be allowed to stimulate the kind of belligerent attitudes towards foreign influences that had occurred during the anti-spiritual pollution campaign. Deng made this clear in July 1987, when he announced that he hoped for at least seventy years of peace in which China could reconstruct and become a prosperous nation (1993d: 248–50).

Rather than a resurgence of 'leftism', therefore, it is more accurate to see the anti-bourgeois liberalisation campaign as another attempt to restore discipline inside the Party. Refuting the suitability of liberal-democracy and Western culture for China was certainly not new, and was held to be compatible with market-orientated economic reforms so long as disciplinary problems could be dealt with through supervision by the Party and state. This was the message of the *People's Daily* editorial on 5 January 1987, which not only attacked those in the Party held to be tolerating 'bourgeois liberalisation' but also announced the strengthening of the streamlining and restructuring of the Party leadership system, including measures such as the demotion of cadres at the county level and above who were assessed as incompetent, very much in line with Deng's 1980 calls for political reform. As for those who continued to exert a decisive influence on policy-making, it is something of a misnomer to apply the label 'leftist' to a supporter of tightening up Party discipline like Chen Yun, given that he had not supported the Cultural Revolution and had paved the way for Deng Xiaoping's political rehabilitation. Deng Liqun might be called a 'leftist' due to the way in which he still saw class struggle as a central principle of socialism, yet his influence was on the wain as he failed to secure a position on the Central Committee when the Thirteenth Party Congress met in October and November 1987.

The clearest indication, however, that the campaign did not signal the resurgence of 'leftism' is that Hu Yaobang was replaced by Zhao Ziyang as General Secretary of the Party. Having served as Premier during the years of 'reform and opening', Zhao's appointment signalled continuity with the economic and administrative reforms of the past, but not necessarily with Hu's stance on ideological issues. When Zhao reported to the Sixth National People's Congress in March 1987, he thus acknowledged the need for slower economic growth combined with political stability and pledged a resolute fight against 'bourgeois liberalisation'. But he also criticised bureaucracy, praised the success of the market-led reforms for having improved the supply of consumer goods, defended the factory manager responsibility system, and highlighted the need to implement a civil legal code.

Consolidating techno-nationalism at the Thirteenth Congress

Rather than thinking in terms of 'Left' and 'Right', it is better to understand the initiatives taken after the dissent and demonstrations of 1986–7 as an attempt by the Party leadership to try again to develop patriotism in a way that would allow the appropriation of policies designed to bring about 'modernisation'. This can be seen in the way that the symbolic gestures indicating ideological continuity after the fall of Hu Yaobang were accompanied by the further development of globally orientated industrial initiatives associated with techno-nationalism. The '863 Plan'[2] that had been launched in March 1986 to take the PRC into the top ranks of world science and technology by focusing on research and development in a number of high-tech fields, was maintained and expanded. In 1988 the 'Torch Plan' was launched to raise funds and encourage the linkage of enterprises with the development of science parks and high-technology development zones. A strategy was also put in place to transform the largest SOEs into very large business groups by encouraging them to grow outside the central plan.

Developing patriotic ideology in a way that could accommodate such policies was a key task for the new technocratic personnel who were rising up the Party hierarchy and would eventually form the core leadership in the 1990s. Most significant among these figures was the entrance of future CCP General Secretary Jiang Zemin into the Politburo, and his transfer from the post of mayor of Shanghai to Party Secretary for the city. Li Tieying, another technocrat who had studied in the Soviet bloc and was to play a key role in education and ideology policy over the next decade, became the youngest member ever of the Politburo (excluding the Cultural Revolution period) at the age of 49. Li Ruihuan, the mayor of Tianjin who had graduated in building, also joined the Politburo, and would later play a key role in shaping ideology after he defused tension in Tianjin during the spring of 1989 through negotiations. Even Li Peng, who rose to the Standing Committee of the Politburo and was later to be blamed for ordering the bloodshed in Tiananmen Square as Premier in 1989, was an engineer by training.

Born between 1926 (Jiang Zemin) and 1936 (Li Tieying), this cohort was well placed to act as a bridge between the older generation of revolutionaries and the successor generation that had to be picked from those who had come to maturity after 1949. The promotion of such figures at this point in time put them in position to become part of a 'transitional' leadership in the project to steer the economy from the plan to the market. This was certainly the direction maintained by the policies approved by the Thirteenth Party Congress. Central to the justification of these was the promotion of the concept of the 'primary stage of socialism'.

The concept of the 'primary stage of socialism' was enshrined as a principle of the party's basic ideological line by Zhao Ziyang's address to the Thirteenth Party Congress. Deng Xiaoping had already been promoting its basic principle since he had explained that socialism is the 'primary stage of communism' in his talk with the Japanese delegation in June 1984. He revived the idea in August before the Thirteenth Congress when he told a delegation of Italian communists that economic development would have to be achieved in three steps. The first of these was to be completed by the end of the twentieth century when the basic problems of food and shelter had been solved, with the third taking another thirty to fifty years after that (1993j). According to Zhao's report, Chinese society had become 'socialist' in the 1950s with the transformation of the private ownership of the means of production, but another 100 years from that time would be required to accomplish the 'socialist modernisation' of the productive forces. The forward-looking orientation of the concept as well as its nationalistic overtones was emphasised when he explained how growing wealth and industrialisation would be acompanied by 'a great rejuvenation of the Chinese nation'.

What the 'primary stage of socialism' offered the population of the PRC within their lifespan, therefore, was a vision of modernity presented in terms of industrialisation and national rejuvenation. The socialist principles of equality or social welfare were missing and modernisation was to be achieved not through class struggle, but the vigorous expansion of the 'commodity economy', raising labour productivity and completing the Four Modernisations. All of this would require reforming 'such aspects of the relations of production and of the superstructure that are incompatible with the growth of the productive forces' (Zhao 1987).

If socialism is taken to mean a leading role for the state and the public sector in economic development, then Zhao's ideas may have met the mark. He insisted that encouraging a degree of wealth inequality though higher incomes for the owners of private enterprises that did not come from their own labour would not be like the exploitative relation between capitalists and workers because the conditions of wage labour would still be constrained by the limits of the powerful public sector and by state policies and laws. Yet the promotion of egalitarianism was not high in Zhao's mind as he pointed out that more important than requiring 'absolute perfection and egalitarianism' in a socialist society was the development of diverse sectors of the economy and diverse forms of distribution, and 'with the objective of common prosperity in mind, to encourage some people to become well-off first, through honest work and lawful business operations'.

The reform of the 'relations of production' that was being advocated clearly meant a move towards a greater role for market mechanisms. Again, Deng had prepared the ground for this when he had told members of the Central Committee on 6 February 1987 that the market could be used under socialism, so long as it was used in the service of socialism and was good for developing the forces of production. Japan and the United States both used a degree of planning in their economies, he pointed out (Deng 1993k). Although Zhao Ziyang was not so bold as to propose moving towards a 'market economy' when he addressed the Thirteenth Party Congress, he presented the compromise formula of the 'socialist planned commodity economy' instead. He tried to soothe fears that this meant a departure from socialism by emphasising the small size of the non-state sector, claiming that although there were already some 12 million individual businesses and private enterprises in 1986, employing about 18 million people, this accounted for a mere 0.3 per cent of industrial output value and 16.3 per cent of total retail sales. To encourage expansion, policies and laws were to be drawn up to protect the legitimate interests of the private sector. Space was also to be created for new types of ownership by expanding the whole concept of 'public' ownership beyond ownership by the whole people to include ownership by collectives, and enterprises with shares pooled by different localities, departments and enterprises.

The state, though, was not to be made redundant in the process, but was to continue to guide the general direction of the economy through macroeconomic legal, economic and administrative measures. It would become more efficient in these tasks through reforms that would shift the functions of governmental bodies from direct to indirect control over enterprises. Administrative organisations would be streamlined through merging or dissolution, while supervisory, auditing and information organs would be reinforced. Administrative legislation would be tightened up and responsibility systems established at every level to improve efficiency.

The public-owned sector of the economy would also remain import-ant because large and medium-sized enterprises were to remain mainly under public ownership, but the property rights of small state-owned enterprises were to be sold to collectives or individuals. Efficiency would be improved through increasing the incentives for managers to respond to macroeconomic change and to become more entrepreneur-ial, by legally defining their responsibilities under the management responsibility system. They would also be encouraged to raise capital by developing the various experiments in shareholding that had already begun to emerge.

The role of the Party was also to be reformed by limiting its activities to the role of political leadership, in terms of formulating political principles, indicating the correct political direction, making major pol-icy decisions and recommending cadres for key posts in organs of state power. Within enterprises, party organisations were to limit them-selves to a supervisory role and to supporting the directors and man-agers, who should take responsibility for overall leadership. Within government, all Party secretaries who had no government posts but were involved in government affairs would be removed, and Party departments that duplicated government ones would be eliminated.

Finally, Zhao gave some idea of what he understood to be rep-resentation of the people. For him, scrutiny by the public was an important element in ensuring that the Party and state functionaries were performing their jobs properly. His conception of democracy, therefore, was very much in the 'mass line' tradition of 'from the masses, to the masses', rather than the liberal ideal of individual fulfilment through political participation. It meant developing channels through which the voices and demands of the people could be easily and frequently transmitted to the leading bodies, while places should be available for people to offer suggestions or pour out any grievances they might have.

To consolidate a consensus in the Party over the right balance between ideology and economic reform, Zhao summed up the Party line that had been developed since the 1978 Third Plenum with the formula of taking 'economic construction' as the 'centre' and the Four Cardinal Principles, and 'reform and opening' as the 'two basic points', which came to be summed up as the slogan 'one centre and two basic points' (*yi ge zhongxin liangge jiben dian*). In some respects, this was an attempt to resuscitate the original spirit of 'reform and opening' created by the 1978 Third Plenum, with its stress on the Four Modernisations, 'democracy' and 'seeking truth from facts'. It might also be seen as a new formulation of the old '*ti-yong*' dichotomy. In this respect, the nationalistic aspects of the Party line are illustrated when Zhao Ziyang pledged to the Congress that the party would '. . . struggle to take economic construction as the centre, uphold the Four Cardinal Principles, uphold reform and opening, independence and self-reliance, and work hard to build our country as a wealthy, democratic, civilised socialist country'.

That the Congress promoted Deng's 1983 'Three Faces' slogan leaves little doubt about the global orientation of the leadership that emerged at that time, despite the campaign against bourgeois liberalisation that had been launched. The need to adhere to the open policy was explained in terms of the fact that 'Economic relations between states today have become increasingly close, and no country can possibly advance behind closed doors' (Thirteenth Congress: 26). The strategic plan for economic development was drawn up specifically to deal with the dual tasks of 'concentration on the traditional industrial revolution and trying to catch up with the new worldwide technological revolution' (Thirteenth Party Congress: 61–2). It contained measures to vigorously develop export-oriented industries and products by using competitive products and raising quality, and by extending the open policy into the interior areas by expanding horizontal economic ties. A general development plan was to be drawn up for the existing SEZs, open cities and regions, and the announcement was made that Hainan Island, China's second biggest island after Taiwan, would become an SEZ and raised to the status of a province. It was expected that the policies adopted in Hainan would be even more open and flexible than those in the existing SEZs, making it a test bed for the world's most effective methods.

In order to achieve the economic goals for the end of the century, the Thirteenth Congress held that it was necessary to give top priority to the expansion of scientific, technical and educational undertakings and to open wider to the outside world to constantly expand economic and technological exchanges and cooperation with other countries (Thirteenth Congress: 62–3). The Central Committee proposed that the State Council should draw up a medium- and long-term programme for the development of science and technology. Stress was to be laid on promoting the modernisation of technology and equipment of industries devoted to large-scale production and effecting a noticeable change in the technology of principal sectors of the economy. Qualified personnel were to be organised to start high-tech research and development, especially in the fields of microelectronics, information, bioengineering and new materials. The reform of the scientific and technological management system was to be accelerated with emphasis on incentives to achieve a closer integration between science and technology and the economy, stepping up the expansion of a technology market and the commercialisation of technological achievements. Advanced technologies were to continue to be imported from abroad, to be integrated with and absorbed into native research.

The basic thrust of enhancing national power in a global economy was thus maintained by the Thirteenth Congress. This had the virtue of being able to consolidate the leadership on the foundations of theories about how China might be able to transform itself in ways that would enable it to survive in the emerging global economy while maintaining the semblance of 'socialism' in the sense of a lead role for the planned and publicly owned economy. As with Deng's January 1980 justification of reform and opening by presenting it as a way to oppose international hegemony, now he could explain to members of the preparatory committee for the Hong Kong Basic Law, in March 1987, that China's reforms would have to continue if the nation was to overcome its underdevelopment in an international economy dominated and controlled by international monopoly capitalism (1993l: 218).

The ideological developments and personnel changes that took place at the Thirteenth Congress show, therefore, that the fall of Hu Yaobang signalled neither a movement towards a kind of xenophobic introversion nor a wholesale opening to the world. Instead, the Congress marked a significant step towards the formation of an outwardly orientated authoritarian developmental state legitimated by a call for patriotic nationalism that was ultimately to be consolidated by the Fourteenth Party Congress in 1992.

By the mid-1980s, Deng's relatively positive view of the international situation (1993m) also made it possible to square this emphasis on economic reform and openness with the Party's mission to defend the nation by calling for a smaller and more professional fighting force, both by cutting military personnel and forming a new relationship between the defence and civilian industrial sectors. A new military doctrine of 'taking the path of building an elite army with Chinese characteristics' (*zou you zhongguo tese de jingbing zhilu*) thus emerged from an enlarged meeting of the CMC in 1988. Doubts about the capabilities of the PLA had certainly been reinforced by its poor performance during the invasion of Vietnam, yet the spectacular success of the campaigns by the Israeli army in Lebanon and the Royal Navy in the South Atlantic in 1982 also illustrated the need for radical reforms of both military structure and defence doctrine. It is not necessary to argue that maintaining the low-intensity conflict with Vietnam was a deliberate ploy to justify military modernisation in order to see that a border clash with Vietnam in January 1987 and a naval clash with Vietnam over the Spratly Islands in 1988 created important conditions for the strengthening of a more technocratic type of nationalism. The patriotism of Chinese troops who were reported to have killed 200 Vietnamese combatants attacking an area of Yunnan province in January 1987 (*Xinhua*, 7–1–87) may have provided a useful contrast to the actions of the students demonstrating in support of Hu Yaobang.

The road to Tiananmen

The attempt of the Thirteenth Party Congress to square the circle between technological and economic development and loyalty to the Party may have made some sense in terms of general ideology. But pressing requirements of development meant that theory was increasingly divorced from practice when it came to making policy. Nowhere was this more evident than in the field of education, where the Thirteenth Congress recommended meeting the demands of development by upgrading the status of vocational education and on-the-job training, and creating a social environment in which knowledge and educated people would be respected (Thirteenth Party Congress: 64–5). Early in 1988, Education Commissioner Li Peng confirmed that the reforms proposed for the management of higher education would go ahead (Li Peng 1988).

This growing divorce of ideology from policy was made embarrassingly clear by an incident that became known as the 'Shekou storm', so-called because it occurred in the industrial district of Shekou in the

Shenzhen Special Economic Zone, bordering Hong Kong (Xu 1995). It began when the local branch of the Communist Youth League tried to bring a fresh approach to ideological education in the SEZ by inviting 'experts' on the subject from Beijing to hold a symposium on 13 January 1988. When one of the experts, Qu Xiao, complained that a small number of people in Shenzhen were 'gold diggers' who had gone there to tap the wealth created by others, and accused them of being opposed to the spirit of 'opening up, bringing up new things, and devoting oneself' that was advocated by the SEZ authorities, members of the audience protested that it was gold diggers who had opened up the American West and that making money for oneself was also a way of contributing to the national economy.

In the debate that followed, young people ridiculed propaganda claiming that Shenzhen was taking the 'socialist road with Chinese characteristics'. Others pointed out that there were no 'Chinese characteristics' in Shenzhen, given that the architecture, streets, urban structure and management of enterprises was all based on foreign models. Patriotism in the shape of buying domestic products was also criticised, as members of the audience pointed out that it was reasonable to buy items like motor cars from abroad if China lacked the knowledge to make them. One man summed up the tone of the meeting when he exclaimed, 'We are here to make money. There are no such things as ideals and making contributions to the state! Propaganda work in the newspapers carries little truth' (Xu 1995: 543–4).

Shekou showed that the Party leadership was seriously failing in its task of instilling loyalty in the student population, as the 'fourth generation' began to displace the 'scarred generation' of the Cultural Revolution. It also revealed the fundamental contradiction within an ideological formula that called for self-sacrifice while policies were being initiated such as the expansion of the SEZs. After all, even Deng Xiaoping himself had taken to complementing his calls for self-sacrifice with the promise of future material well-being (1993n).

The Education Commission attempted to address this growing division between ideology and practice by giving more substantial guidance on the content of ideological education, with a greater emphasis on nationalistic themes. In a circular issued in August 1988 it was explained that students should learn the 'idea of the country' (*guojia guannian*), how to have an 'ardent love of the rivers and mountains, the culture, the people and the long history and splendid tradition of the motherland, the great achievements of the building of socialism, respect for the brother nationalities, and strengthening the unity of the nationalities' under the heading of 'patriotism and internationalism'. Students were to develop their nationalism by learning a 'patriotism' that was defined as 'contributing to the wealth and power of the motherland and the welfare of the people; correctly knowing the glorious tradition of the thought and culture of the Chinese nation (*minzu*), opposing the influence of corrupt bourgeois thought; putting the interests of the country above all else; respecting the policy on nationalities, upholding the unity of the nationaltities and the unification of the motherland'.

Such guidance was reinforced by the Central Committee when it issued a circular in December 1988 that defined the purpose of moral education as being 'to turn the whole body of students into ardent patriots with social morality and civilised habits'. Within this, patriotism was to take the leading position in allowing students to understand the splendid history and revolutionary tradition of the Chinese nation (*zhonghua minzu*), the suffering of the Chinese nation over the past hundred years, and the heroic struggle of the Party in leading the people against imperialism and feudalism.

Marxism was not forgotten in these educational prescriptions, merely redefined in purely ideological terms which were compatible with the emphasis on patriotism. In January 1989, Li Tieying (who succeeded Li Peng as education commissioner when the latter was promoted to Premier in April 1988), thus told a meeting on moral education in schools that Marxism should be used to prevent the influence of 'corrupt capitalist thinking' and 'semi-feudalist and semi-colonial thinking' (Li, T. 1988). According to Li, this would allow patriotic education to amount to more than the promotion of empty slogans influenced by rigid 'Left' thinking, because good citizens could be made out of the young by instilling in them a consciousness of the state (*guojia yishi*), of the nation (*minzu yishi*), and of civics (*gongmin yishi*). The ideological void would be filled by making patriotism the starting point for teaching 'ideals' (*lixiang jiaoyu*), with the raising of patriotic sentiments, national self-respect and confidence at the fore. In this way, students would be instilled with a strong national consciousness and a spirit of sacrifice for the country and the nation. 'Socialism', it should be noted, was ranked last when Li Tieying asked teachers to promote 'love of the motherland, love of the people, love of the workers, love of science, love of socialism'.

Attempts by the leadership to assert the Party's monopoly on patriotism since the fall of Hu Yaobang thus remained based on the hope that the loyalty of the rising generations could be maintained as the country moved towards integration into the world economic system, so long as they could be made to understand China's national condition. If they could just be given a sufficient quantity of revolutionary history, then they would realise the necessity of building 'socialism with Chinese characteristics', and that 'socialist democracy' means stability while any other kind of democracy leads to Cultural Revolution-style chaos and instability (Deng 1993n).

Yet this atttempt by the Party to reassert its monopoly on patriotism made it even more important for dissenting voices to shape the emerging nationalist discourse during the events that led up to the Tiananmen massacre of 4 June 1989. This can be seen quite clearly in cultural events like the six-part television documentary series *River Elegy* (*He Shang*), which was broadcast in 1988. Written by Su Xiaokang, the son of a member of the Communist elite who had grown up in a Marxist household and then been sent to a village in Henan during the Cultural Revolution, this expressed a widespread frustration with the futility of an inward-looking obsession with a past civilisation symbolised by the yellow earth of the loess plateau and by the entrapment represented by the Great Wall. Yet such a production was nationalistic, too, in the way that its call to turn towards the blue ocean and absorb the spirit of science and democracy was aimed at achieving a rejuvenation of the nation. While images of the West were presented as the model for China's future, the West also was portrayed as made up of hostile powers that had attacked, exploited and humiliated China.

As Suisheng Zhao points out (1997: 727–9), even the most notable anti-traditionalists of the time remained deeply nationalistic at heart in the years running up to Tiananmen, yearning for the re-creation of China's past greatness. The challenge for China was not to become Western, but to revitalise itself to compete with the West. Such a deployment of patriotic themes goes back at least as far as the May Fourth Movement of 1919, when students had taken to the streets to express their outrage over the transfer of German concessions in China to Japan at Versailles. In 1989, claiming the patriotic high ground was seen as essential when demonstrators took to the streets. When it appeared that a division over how to deal with the demonstrations had opened up in the leadership after Zhao Ziyang failed to state the need to 'oppose bourgeois liberalisation' in a speech he made to commemorate the anniversary of the May Fourth Movement (Oksenberg *et al.* 1990: 244–512; Nathan and Link 2001: 110), tens of thousands of students responded by issuing a declaration that identified themselves with the patriotic movement of 1919. This articulates the linkage between science, democracy and nationalism as follows:

Fellow students and countrymen, what the spirit of democracy means is that people should pool their ideas and think together, and that every person's abilities should be fully developed and his or her interests protected. What the spirit of science means is that people should respect rationality and build the nation through science. Now more than ever, we need to sum up the experience and lessons of the many student movements since the May 4 Movement, to turn democracy and rationality into a kind of system and procedure. Only thus can the ideas first raised by the May 4 Movement become further institutionalised, the spirit of the movement develop, and the hope of a strong and prosperous Chinese nation become a reality.

(Coalition of Students)

In identifying with the calls for 'Mr Science and Mr Democracy' to save the nation that had been made by the May Fourth Movement, the protestors were also appropriating an historical theme that had been deployed consistently by Deng Xiaoping since the late 1970s. Like *River Elegy*, the demonstrators were not rejecting the Party's call for patriotism, but appropriating it for their own political projects, which varied from moderate calls for reform to an insistence on the spilling of blood to create revolutionary martyrs. The hunger strike that began in Tiananmen Square on 13 May demanded not only immediate dialogue with the government, but also 'A fair and unbiased acknowledgement of the legitimacy of the student movement by labeling it both "patriotic" and "democratic"', as the manifesto of the hunger strikers put it (Nathan and Link 2001: 155). Ultimately, while the values of the students were expressed in terms of democracy, science, freedom, human rights and the rule of law, their strategy was to imply that one could be 'patriotic' without being opposed to 'bourgeois liberalisation'. The resulting salience of nationalist themes in the democracy movement shows how, in times of political reform such as the late 1980s, it is imperative for political dissident actors to be able to legitimate their actions as not amounting to traitorous activities likely to derail the process of nation-building (Kelly and He 1992: 33–4). It is in this way that the need for the Party leadership to reclaim the nationalist mantle became central to the politics of legitimacy that emerged in the 1990s.

Conclusion

A number of observations can be made concerning how nationalist discourse developed in the first ten years of Deng Xiaoping's leadership.

First of all, while patriotism has always been an element in CCP ideology, under 'reform and opening' it became increasingly prominent as the leadership went further than before in denuding socialism of notions of egalitarianism and class struggle. Second, following the negative consequences of the campaign against spiritual pollution, the nationalistic themes that can be used to cultivate patriotism had to be presented in ways that were compatible with the growing realisation that economic development depended on access to international investment, know-how and technology. Within the debates that followed, science and technology began to take on a new political status as the means for national salvation. When the consequent liberalisation of central control led to calls for increasingly radical political change from both inside and outside the Party, the Thirteenth National Congress attempted to arrive at a compromise between maintaining cultural orthodoxy and appropriating the foreign. This represents something of an alternative from either ideological ossification or 'complete Westernisation', insofar as it encouraged participation in the global scientific, technological and economic revolution under the leadership of the CCP. While learning from global developments was thus encouraged, the highest ethic remained that of increasing China's national power and preventing 'bourgeios liberalisation'. In this way, the three major tasks on which the legitimacy of the CCP depends could be achieved.

At the same time, the frequent mass campaigns and demonstrations that took place in the 1980s indicate just how difficult it is for China's political elite to deploy nationalism for the purpose of instilling social solidarity in a time of radical change while preventing it from becoming a destructive mass movement. This pattern of the political elite resorting to patriotic themes, only to be confronted by xenophobic crowds on the streets of Chinese cities, can be seen repeating itself over the years that followed as probably the most important dynamic of nationalist discourse. Below it will be argued that this tension continued to exist at the heart of CCP ideology after the events of 1989, when the political elite articulated a new patriotic orthodoxy which only encouraged the further appropriation and contestation of nationalist themes by wider social circles. It is important to bear these dynamics in mind when exploring how globalisation impacted on nationalist discourse in the 1990s as the Party leadership tried to establish continuity after the domestic upheavals of 1989 within the transformation of the international situation that occurred after the Cold War. This process will be explored in the next chapter.

2 After 1989
Nationalism and the new global elite

After the events of June 1989, the credibility of the CCP's claim to be a socialist organisation leading the nation to salvation was challenged not only by the social and ideological dislocation created by economic reform, but also by the diplomatic and economic sanctions imposed by the G7 states and the European Union. Over the years that followed, the articulation of 'socialism with Chinese characteristics' began to take on added significance as the Party had to achieve the tasks set for it by Deng Xiaoping in the context of unassailable American military predominance, the liberalisation of international trade and financial markets, and the challenge of the information revolution.

Yet the emerging post-Cold War order also presented opportunities. The demise of the Soviet Union removed the most serious military threat from China's northern border, allowing a redeployment of forces to the southeastern coast opposite Taiwan. Domestically, the poor condition of the Soviet successor states could also be held up as an example of what would happen if the CCP lost power. The defeat of Iraq in the first Gulf War could also be used by advocates of radical reform to underline the importance of linking technology with national defence if the task of opposing hegemonism was to be successful. The prospect of the transformation of the General Agreement on Tariffs and Trade (GATT) into the WTO and the liberalisation of financial markets held out the possibility of greater access to FDI and foreign trade. The spread of the Internet and global media under commercialisation presented the promise of e-commerce and more efficient e-governance by integrating China's provincialised domestic society and linking its economy with world markets.

Deng Xiaoping thus drummed up confidence in the reform process by insisting that China should maintain the policies agreed by the Thirteenth Party Congress and proceed with opening up to the outside world, even establishing a number of new Hong Kongs to act as windows on the world. In order to meet the challenges of the post-Cold War era, though, the post-Tiananmen CCP leadership had first of all to rebuild the fragile consensus over ideology among the political elite that had existed before 1989. In the process, the movement from socialism to patriotism was accelerated as many of the themes associated with globalisation discourse were incorporated into the Party line.

Jiang Zemin's patriotic turn

The crisis of June 1989 had seriously strained the fragile *modus vivendi* over the meaning of 'socialism' that had held among the Party elite over the previous ten years. With Deng Xiaoping never having satisfactorily defined 'socialism', senior figures now criticised the degree of attention that had been paid to the privatisation of the state-owned sector, the pursuit of material wealth and the neglect of ideological strengthening. Even articles in the Party-controlled Beijing press pointed out that there might be some truth in the dissident argument that the introduction of market mechanisms into the economy would undermine the rule of the Party and fuel 'bourgeois liberalisation'. Deng's proposition that it is hard to distinguish between socialism and capitalism was condemned for being a betrayal of Marxism, the CCP and the struggle of the masses to build socialism (Ma and Lin 1998: 183–4).

What the older generation of leaders feared most after the demonstrations of 1989 was a Cultural Revolution-style mass movement from below. Their criticisms of the now disgraced Zhao Ziyang did not amount to a complete rejection of Deng's line but were more of a call for greater emphasis on its moralistic and disciplinary elements. Writers and critics of the older generation (some of whom had been inactive since the Yan'an period) attacked leading figures of the liberal and avant-garde cultural movements that had flourished in the late 1980s. The cult of Mao Zedong as the model of selfless morality that had been presented in the 1981 *Resolution on Party History* was revived. Similarly, artists and writers were called on to serve the workers, peasants and soldiers according to the principles of Mao's 'Yan'an Forum Talks on Literature and Art', drawn up during the war against Japan and promoted again by Deng Xiaoping himself when he had addressed the Congress of Writers and Artists in October 1979 (Barme 1999: 20–37).

When the Central Committee met for a plenary session on 23–24 June, laments went up over the way in which values of arduous struggle, selflessness, and helping people in need, 'which make up the exalted character of a Communist and are also the traditional virtues of the Chinese people', were now regarded as out of date (Nathan and Link 2001: 433–6). When Jiang Zemin was appointed to the post of General Secretary by the meeting, he sympathised with these anxieties by stating that it had been wrong to assume that a rise in living standards was enough to create social stability and the right conditions for political reform (1998i: 347). He also agreed that the growth of consumerism, short-termism, selfishness and the worship of foreign things was leading to a widespread trend of 'looking to money in everything' at the expense of the state and the nation – a popular pun on the Chinese wording of the speech that marked Deng's consolidation of power in December 1978 (Deng 1984b). Jiang also began to express his views about the political role of education, elaborating on the need for the young to be taught more about the 'national condition' (*guo qing*). By this he meant teaching the history of the last 100 years, the necessity of socialism, current economic conditions, economic resources and population, and the 'excellent tradition of the Chinese nation'. He explained that this was necessary because, while the young supported 'reform and opening', many of them were still labouring under the illusion that Western material civilisation could be transferred to China over night (1998l: 347).

In November that year, Jiang went on to tell newsworkers that they had a responsibility to stimulate a spirit of nationalist pride, self-confidence and activism, and to educate society in patriotism, socialism, collectivism, self-reliance, hard struggle, and nation-building (1998b: 354–5). The Education Commission accordingly sent out instructions (EC 1989) for patriotism to permeate the entire curriculum, being taught not only in special courses but also in subjects like language, history and geography. 'Communism' was still to be taught, but reduced to the stories of revolutionaries who illustrated the virtues of self-sacrifice for the interests of the collective and the need to always put the state before the individual. In an April 1990 report, the commission again stressed the anti-democratic and anti-Western aspects of this patriotic campaign by emphasising the need to defend education from foreign and domestic opponents of socialism, insisting that the battle against 'bourgeois liberalisation' and 'peaceful evolution' would continue for a long time and would become very heated. Schools would have to oppose these forces and learn from the experience of 1989 by studying ideology, making moral and political education the priority, and shedding the idea that the only purpose of study is to get into university.

With 1990 celebrated as the 150th anniversary of the Opium War, the new leadership was presented with something of a golden opportunity to alert the population against the foreign plot of 'peaceful evolution' by teaching them about the poverty and backwardness of 'semi-colonised' and 'feudal' old China, and the glorious achievements that had been made since the founding of 'New China'. In this way, the Education Commission explained, they would come to realise that 'without the CCP there is no New China, only socialism can save China, only with socialism can a Chinese "way" (*dao li*) be developed; to have faith that China can support socialism, and that China can sufficiently develop socialism' (EC 1990: 387–8). In a July 1990 speech to mark the end of an exhibition on China's revolutionary history, Jiang Zemin himself presented the Nanjing massacre as a valuable example that could be used to stir up popular anger, recommending the production of special text books for this purpose. In the same speech, he stressed how important it was to draw attention to negative examples of people who collaborated with foreign powers or worshipped foreign things and lacked all trace of 'nationalist fibre' (Jiang 1998c).

Just as Deng had responded to the 1979 Beijing Spring by asserting the need for the young to be made to understand that Western material civilisation could not be transplanted onto Chinese soil overnight, in 1990 Jiang chose the anniversary of the patriotic May Fourth Movement to decry critics of the Party because: 'They don't even want a national character or individual character, so what qualifications do they have for talking about patriotism, democracy and human rights!' Faced by the problem of what socialism had come to mean, Jiang finally took Deng Xiaoping's thinking to its logical conclusion, announcing that 'socialism' and 'patriotism' are 'by nature the same' (*benzhi shang shi tongyi de*) (1998a: 360–1).

Forging the new technocratic consensus

The challenge for Jiang Zemin was very much like that faced by Zhang Zhidong at the end of the Qing dynasty and Hu Yaobang in the early 1980s, namely to craft patriotism in a way that would both please those in the leadership who longed for a return to the values of the 'days before and after Liberation', while also appealing to those who were more interested in the pursuit of technological and economic modernisation. This latter constituency was likely to be alienated by the measures taken after Tiananmen to deal with the immediate causes of social unrest, such as slowing the rate of economic growth and investment in order to reduce inflation and freezing aspects of education reform that had begun in 1985. Yet it is something of a misnomer to describe the key figures in the post-Tiananmen leadership as 'leftist'. Their technocratic nature is exemplified by a figure like Ding Guan'gen, who was appointed head of the United Front Department and head of the Party's propaganda work in 1990. Like Jiang Zemin, an alumnus of Shanghai's Jiaotong University, Ding's previous career had been in the railway industry.

Even Premier Li Peng, while announcing a raft of measures for economic retrenchment in his 1990 report to the National People's Congress (1990), accepted the need to maintain 'reform and opening', albeit with a stress on the Four Cardinal Principles and a protracted struggle against 'bourgeois liberalisation' (Li 1990: 16–17). This was in the context of his announcement of the closure or merging of 70,000 corporations (24.5 per cent of the country's total), the severing of links between corporations and Party and government organisations, and the preferential allocation of funds, materials and transportation services to large and medium-sized SOEs that produced high-quality, readily marketable goods (Li 1990: 25). Meanwhile, strategies like the '863 Plan' and the 'Torch Plan' and efforts to transform the largest SOEs into very large business groups not only survived the downfall of the pre-Tiananmen leadership, but were expanded. In December 1991, some 55 burgeoning enterprise groups were selected for membership of what came to be called the 'national team', and by the mid-1990s this had grown to 120 large enterprises being prepared for competition in the global market (Sutherland 2001: 67–139).

A number of ideological strategies could be adopted to shape patriotism in ways compatible with such policies. Li Ruihuan, for example, now a member of the Standing Committee of the Politburo, diverted the atavistic patriotism of the Party elders towards the positive theme of a 'Chinese rejuvenation' (*zhenxing zhonghua*), a term originally coined by Sun Yatsen. Within the context of elite politics, Li Ruihuan's promotion of 'national culture' (*minzu wenhua*) and 'cultural flowering' (*fanrong wenyi*) was more useful for restraining the purges that were being undertaken by the Ministry of Culture and the Department of Propaganda by focusing their work on a campaign against pornography that had already been in progress for some time. The mission to combat 'bourgeois liberalisation' could also be balanced with a call to oppose the 'ossification' (*jianghua*) of neo-Maoist dogmatism (Barme 1999: 29). This strategy was similar to the way in which Hu Yaobang had moderated the meaning of patriotism in order to deflate the anti-spiritual pollution campaign by limiting its scope to a rectification of Party work.

A similar strategy can be seen in the approach of Education Commissioner Li Tieying to education reform in the context of the patriotic education campaign. When Li (1990) addressed a conference on the implications of the outcome of the Fourth Plenum for higher education in 1990, he certainly repeated the reduction of socialism to patriotism, opposition to the worshipping of foreign influences and the need for Party leadership. But he also emphasised the importance of realising the Four Modernisations and creating a 'Chinese rejuvenation'. He then went on to advocate a number of managerial reforms that were consistent with the original 1985 plans for education, reiterating the importance of staying open to the outside world and engaging in international student exchanges. Addressing the Education Commission's national work conference the following year, Li (1991) again reminded his audience that China would not only have to oppose the Western strategy of 'peaceful evolution' in the last decade of the twentieth century, it would also have to deal with the challenge of the world technological revolution.

Whatever their various motives, the location of figures like Li Tieying and Li Ruihuan, along with Ding Guan'gen and Li Peng, at the top of the Party had an important impact on the way that themes such as the technological revolution and 'cultural renaissance' were deployed by Jiang Zemin to legitimate the new leadership. This can be seen quite clearly in the way that Jiang was careful to add that, 'Of course, there cannot be the creation of a new "Left" atmosphere either', when he explained his ideas on patriotic education to Li Tieying and Party Secretary of the Education Commission, He Dongchang (1991), in an open letter in *People's Daily*. Before the Central Committee had issued its 'Outline for Implementing Patriotic Education' in August 1994, patriotism had thus already been modified and described as the 'great power pushing forwards our country's social history'. Its basic principles were to establish Deng Xiaoping's project of building 'socialism with Chinese characteristics' and the facilitation of 'reform and opening' (CC 1994: 920).

Any initiatives taken by Deng himself would of course have a decisive impact on the interpretation of his legacy. Given his age and failing health, the views he promoted at this time have to be understood as shaped by a number of constituencies upon whom he relied, or who were close enough to influence him. High among these was the 'imperial bodyguard' under the Sichuanese brothers, Yang Shangkun and Yang Baibing, who held power over the Central Military Commission and the Central Party Secretariat (Nathan and Link 2001: 456). Aware of the technological backwardness of the armed forces following the spectacle of United States power in the Gulf War, such military personnel were sympathetic to the view that success in the reform process was essential if the PLA was ever to become a professional fighting force.

Then there was the Shanghai Party, the rival power base from where Deng could launch an ideological campaign in much the same way that Mao Zedong had launched the Cultural Revolution nearly three decades earlier. The mayor of the city, Zhu Rongji, an alumnus of the science and technology-based National Tsinghua University in Beijing, had served as deputy secretary of the Shanghai Party under Jiang Zemin. His managerial outlook is summed up by the way he described Shanghai as the 'model executive area' for the planned economy. Although he had been labelled a 'rightist' in the 1950s, he had displayed unwavering loyalty to the Party, remarking that 'If a mother beats her child by mistake, how can the child hate its mother?' (Gao and He 1996: 83–6). While Zhu's appointment to the Standing Committee of the Politburo at the Fourteenth Party Congress, and to the Premiership in 1998, is often described as the formation of a 'Shanghai faction', such an alliance had to be acceptable to a broad section of the Party elite if it was to be effective.

While Zhu came to be known as an economic reformer, one of his sponsors was in fact Song Ping, then head of the Central Party Organisation Department and soon to labelled by radical reformers as a 'leftist'. Song (b. 1928) was older than Zhu, but he too was a Tsinghua alumnus. Song is said to have been impressed by Zhu's participation in the 'red student movement', and the two had worked together in the 1950s in the northeast bureau of the Party and on economic planning. Given such personal relationships, Yuan Ming, a former deputy head of the theoretical research office of the Central Party School, has described members of the 'Shanghai faction' as forming a bridge between the extremes represented by the economic planner Chen Yun and the advocate of market mechanisms, Deng Xiaoping (Yuan, M. 1992).

Deng was also under the influence of his immediate family, and ultimately their control, as he increasingly relied on them for physical support. His daughter, Deng Nan, became one of the most powerful figures in the country because she could control access to Deng, and eventually even had the privilege of interpreting his increasingly unintelligible utterances. Her positions as Director of the National Science and Technology Committee of the State Council and Deputy Director of the Central Committee's Social Development Science Research Committee clearly identify Deng Nan with techno-nationalism. Being the descendant of a Party leader also makes

Deng Nan representative of what has come to be called the 'princeling party' in Chinese discourse. Jiang Zemin's son, Jiang Mianheng, similarly boasts a long list of directorships of Internet firms, and his appointment as Vice-President of the Chinese Academy of Sciences was to make him something of a spokesman for the electronics industry.

Dropping any pretensions to communism, the 'princelings' have tended to be sympathetic to the idea of 'neo-authoritarianism', floated before Tiananmen by various academics and personal assistants of Zhao Ziyang. Drawing on the theories developed by Harvard political scientist Samuel Huntington, from Latin American case studies, they could argue that China had to go through a period of economic modernisation under an authoritarian state before democracy would be possible. Looking to societies like the Asian Tigers as the model for development, they claimed that Confucian collectivism, the family, hard work, frugality and a hierarchical, patriarchal power structure are the values that underpin prosperity. Although 'neo-authoritarianism' had been proscribed, its central themes had been given a new degree of credibility by the collapse of the Soviet Union, and reappeared in September 1991 with the publication of an article under the auspices of *China Youth Daily* (*Zhongguo qingnian bao*). This urged the leadership to base its claim to power on nationalism and draw on traditional culture to develop its ideological vision to legitimate the state, given that Marxism-Leninism could no longer mobilise the population (Zhao, S. 1997: 733).

Towards 'Deng Xiaoping Theory'

The first step in the consolidation of a post-Tiananmen ideological consensus between these various constituencies took place when Deng Xiaoping retreated to Shanghai in the winter of 1990/91. While there, he collaborated with the editorial team of the city's *Liberation Daily* (*Jiefang ribao*) to produce a series of articles under the pen-name 'Huang Puping'. These remarkable texts, which might be taken as the start of Shanghai's stunning rise to become an icon of globalisation, regretted that the city had not been made one of the first SEZs and urged the population to restore the city's role as a financial centre and to take a more active role in regenerating the Yangtze delta. They sent shockwaves throughout the country when they directly addressed the debate on the nature of socialism by restating the view that market mechanisms should play a more important role in the economy and called on the people of the city to be more daring in creating an open environment suitable for an advanced international city, a 'socialist Hong Kong' (Ma and Lin 1998: 171–3).

Given the emphasis on patriotism in the ideological discourse of the time, the Huang Puping articles adopted an ingenious strategy for capturing the ideological high ground by combining modernising themes with the narrative of national salvation. This can be seen in the way that the first article in the series appeared under the title 'Be the "Lead Ram" for Reform and Opening'. This is a reference to the traditional Chinese twelve-year cosmological cycle, according to which 1991 was the 'Year of the Ram'. The last such year just happened to be 1979, which the article claimed to be the start of the era of 'reform and opening', described as 'the only road for a strong state and wealthy people' (*qiang guo fu min*). Just as convenient, though, was that the longer sixty-year cosmological cycle happened to have begun in 1931, the year that Japan invaded northern China. The writers could thus neatly contrast the situation at that time with expectations for the end of the next sixty-year cycle in 2051, when 'socialist China will have reached the glorious period of a semi-advanced level. Our per-capita income will have reached US$4,000, which will have put the "comprehensive national power" of our big country of over a billion people at the forefront of the world'.

The use of nationalist themes to legitimate a radical reform agenda became fully systematised and took an authoritative form the following winter, when Deng Xiaoping made his 'Southern Tour' of the cities of Wuchang, Shenzhen, Zhuhai and Shanghai in January and February 1992. This was a crucial event for political developments, because the speeches made by Deng on these visits were used to sway the outcome of the Fourteenth Party Congress in October, when Jiang Zemin announced that the spirit of the Southern Tour was to be taken as the basic line of his work report and to arm the whole Party in carrying out its responsibilities under the formula of 'Comrade Deng Xiaoping's Theory of Building Socialism with Chinese Characteristics' (Jiang 1992: 1–2). The canonical status of the Southern Tour within Deng's ideological heritage was further consolidated when it became the final chapter of the third volume of his selected works, published in October 1993 (Deng 1993o).

The symbolic significance of using the 'Southern Tour' to settle the ongoing debate over the nature of socialism lies partly in its similarities with the journeys that China's emperors used to make when they inspected conditions in the provinces in centuries past. It also has a more recent historical resonance, though, in the way that it parallels Deng's termination of the campaign against 'spiritual pollution' by visiting the SEZs in Guangdong and Fujian in February 1984. In 1992 the Southern Tour was again used as an opportunity to articulate anew the themes that had been developed during the period of 'reform and opening', establishing new boundaries for the discussion of the relationship between socialism, nationalism and globalisation. Within this discourse, the aims of the Party remain the three tasks of economic development, national unification and opposing international hegemony that were established in 1980. Yet the spectre of the world technological revolution finally allows Deng to present his view that socialism means no more than raising national production as the final decision in the ongoing debate over how to distinguish whether a policy has a 'socialist nature' or a 'capitalist nature' that had raged since Tiananmen.

One crucial political implication of this development of ideology is that Deng created a new orthodoxy according to which the status of the rising professional classes could be established as 'revolutionary'. This was because 'revolution' (*geming*) had become synonymous with 'the liberation of productive forces', and science and technology had become 'the primary productive force' (Deng 1993o: 377–8). Thanking workers in science and technology for the glory of their contributions to the nation, he called on everybody to remember the age when the physicists Qian Xuesen, Li Siguang and Qian Sanqiang had been able to produce the 'two atomic bombs and one satellite' (377–8).

The rationale presented in Deng Xiaoping's Southern Tour text for faster growth and greater openness to outside influences is thus part of a political strategy to ensure the continuation of the Party's monopoly on power. Deng's reduction of socialism to the liberation of productive forces is the logical outcome of his view that Party rule would not have survived Tiananmen if the population had not experienced a rising standard of living throughout the 1980s. The alternative, he warns, would have been a civil war similar to the conflict of the Cultural Revolution. Although the notion of egalitarianism is not entirely absent from the speech, it is clear that the measure of efficiency is to be the national interest rather than the interests of any particular class. Even when Deng explains that socialism aims to prevent exploitation and polarisation and eventually to build common prosperity, he claims that this is to avoid a polarisation between the coastal and interior regions that could have a negative impact on national unity rather than being due to an ethical commitment to egalitarianism (373). Such caution is necessary because his vision of rapid development inevitably means encouraging some areas of the country to develop more quickly than others. Guangdong is thus to be allowed to catch up with the

Four Tigers within twenty years, while less developed areas will have to wait until the end of the century to reach such a level through the transfer of technology and revenue from the more advanced regions.

Rather than be concerned over Marxist orthodoxy, Deng thus admonishes the Party not to behave like a 'woman with bound feet'. If socialism is to achieve a comparative advantage over capitalism, it should 'boldly absorb and borrow all the fruits of civilisation created by human society, absorb and borrow all the advanced ways of enterprise and management that reflect the rules of production that modern society has created in all the countries of the world including the advanced capitalist ones'. To meet this challenge, he urges boldness in experimenting with measures such as the introduction of stock markets and the expansion of foreign investment. So long as 'our heads are clear', he explains, there is no need to be timid, because state control can quickly be exerted again after a year or two.

This departure from socialist ideology should not, of course, be mistaken for a commitment to political liberalisation. Instead, the displacement of egalitarianism and the elevation of science are the conditions for formulating an ideology appropriate for an authoritarian developmental state. The economic models closest to hand are neighbouring countries like Japan, South Korea and 'some in Southeast Asia'. Although, as Deng points out, the comparatively rapid development of these neighbours presents a bleak comparison with China's own condition, their experiences show that it is possible to go through periods of over-heated growth without being overly concerned about social stability. The concentrated power of the one-party system is what will make it possible for China to go through its own stage of rapid economic growth. Deng left little doubt that his formula had come closer to the thinking of Lee Kuan Yew than Karl Marx when he cited Singapore as a model to be emulated in the search for the right relationship between ideology and economic development (Deng 1993o: 377–8).

That Deng's openness to foreign ideas and practices should not be confused with political liberalisation is made clear by the way in which the first chapter of the last volume of his selected works is his statement to the Twelfth Congress, in September 1982, where he warns that learning from abroad must not involve subordination to any foreign power or permit 'rotten thinking' to be imported and spread a bourgeois lifestyle (1993c: 1–4). He explains further in May 1985 that succumbing to foreign cultural influences not only poses a threat to unification with Taiwan, but to the unity of the Chinese mainland itself. The reason for 'reform and opening', moreover, is not the promotion of the rights of individuals or minorities, which should be firmly subordinated to the rights of the majority and interpreted in China's own context (1993p: 124).

The inclusion of Deng's speech to the Second Plenum in 1983, in which he warns about the general lack of enthusiasm for socialism and the Party, the growing interest in individualism and Western 'modernism' (*xiandai pai*) and the commercialisation of culture, shows how these themes remained as relevant to the technocratic leadership that was moving towards a market-based economy in 1993, as they had been for ideological 'conservatives' ten years before. The same is true for the inclusion of Deng's September 1986 call for the struggle against 'bourgeois liberalisation' to carry on for another twenty years. In the Southern Tour text, he could take this further by adding that the consolidation of the socialist system will require fighting bourgeois liberalisation through 'our own few generations, more than ten generations, or even tens of generations' (1993o: 383). The condition for success in this venture is that the CCP must hold political power and defend national integrity through a policy of 'grabbing with two hands', with 'one hand reforming and opening, one hand striking hard at all kinds of criminal activities' (1993o: 379).

This, then, is the formula according to which China can preserve its sovereignty while reaping the benefits of the international economic system. Indeed, the most pronounced difference between the third volume of Deng's selected works and the two that came before lies in the amount of material that is devoted to international affairs. No less than 97 of the 119 texts are concerned with diplomacy, international relations and changes in the global environment. The result is a complex narrative that characterises the emerging post-Cold War international situation as one of developed states encouraging small wars between developing states. In this situation China is the victim of two new cold wars, one between the North and the South and the other being the war against socialism, while the G7 states are presented as the old imperial powers (Deng 1993q). Bent on replacing the superpowers as the international hegemon, they have imposed sanctions on China under the pretext of promoting democracy and human rights, but in reality to pursue their own interests under the pretext of putting 'human rights' (*ren quan*) above 'state rights' (Deng 1993r).

The overall effect of the ideology in the third volume of Deng's selected works is thus to modernise the narrative of the CCP as the only organisation that can save China from the continuing aggression of the old imperialists, taking the nation forward into the global era under the protection of a strong state. Continuing this will only be possible if China becomes one of three or four poles of global power, as Cold War bipolarity gives way to a multipolar international order. The outcome to be avoided at all costs is the emergence of an unbalanced United States, at liberty to fight a 'smokeless war' against socialism in its determination to stop China developing to a level where it might become a rival. The neo-liberal belief that China can be transformed through market mechanisms is thus condemned as a policy of 'peaceful evolution', amounting to nothing more than a conspiracy to bring about chaos in the socialist states (1993t: 325). The result is an intensely state-centric vision of foreign policy. As Deng reminds a visiting Richard Nixon: if chaos is to be avoided, international politics will have to be conducted according to the pursuit of national interests while refraining from interfering in the internal affairs of other states (Deng 1993u). Moreover, the imposition of sanctions can be transformed into a positive force to mobilise the population behind the Party as Deng insists that China cannot afford to appear soft when subjected to international pressure, and must be prepared to resist invaders (Deng 1993v).

The significance of this ideological formula in Deng's Southern Tour can be seen in the way that all of its themes were deployed when Jiang Zemin took another step towards the creation of a market economy when he reported to the Fourteenth Party Congress in October 1992. Under the rather oxymoronic theory of the 'socialist market economy' (*shehui zhuyi shichang jingji*), the state was to withdraw from central planning and rely on macroeconomic controls to regulate an economy that would increasingly be disciplined by market principles. There would be losers as well as winners, as enterprises would feel the pressure to become more efficient and active, with only the fittest surviving. On this road to 'socialism with Chinese characteristics', however, the ideological prescription was still to avoid copying foreign models. Moreover, although the end goal was still supposed to be socialism, it would be a long wait, because the 'primary stage of socialism' would last for at least another hundred years. To achieve this, international peace and an 'independent and self-reliant' foreign policy also had to be maintained, so that opening up to the outside would allow absorption of the advanced fruits of the civilisation of all countries, including the advanced capitalist ones, for developing socialism.

Jiang could also reiterate Deng's principle that the criterion for judging policy was whether it was 'good for socialist production and good or bad for increasing the comprehensive national power of the socialist state, good or bad for raising the standard of living of the people'. Science and technology had become the 'primary productive force', and reform had become 'a kind of revolution and a kind of liberation of productive forces'. The political guarantee for building socialism remained adherence to the Four Cardinal Principles, yet these were to be 'filled with new content' from the process of reform and opening and modernisation. While he accepted that poverty was not socialism, it was not possible for everybody to become wealthy at the same time. So some areas and people should be allowed and encouraged to get wealthy first, pulling up others behind them. Opportunities to build socialism through bursts of rapid and efficient development should be 'grasped', with each spurt lasting a few years and leading to new stage of development. In the process, the life and death of the Party would be determined by its work style and its links with the masses. National unification remained an objective, through the cultivation of links with patriots overseas and promoting the formula of 'one country, two systems'.

Just as with Zhang Zhidong's attempt to preserve Chinese '*ti*' by using Western '*yong*', many of the themes deployed in Jiang's speech to the Fourteenth Congress appear to be contradictory from the perspective of theories that assume globalisation will weaken nationalism and the authoritarian state. Yet the proliferation of dichotomies does make sense as an attempt to create the limits of a discourse that can accommodate a range of political constituencies within boundaries that do not permit any challenge to CCP rule. The concept of the 'socialist market economic system' is such a dichotomy, which leaves space for the arguments of both those who advocate planning and public ownership and those who want more rapid introduction of market mechanisms.

Accepting that patriotism means loyalty to the CCP is the minimum requirement for participation in this debate. In his comments on the Southern Tour, Jiang could thus call on cadres to focus on Deng's call for a policy of 'grabbing with two hands', in terms of constructing a flourishing spiritual civilisation based on academic freedom and work in the arts and media, while at the same time hardening the policy of eradicating all 'evil phenomena'. In January 1993, after consolidation of the reform process, he places more emphasis on the propagation of traditional Chinese culture and modern and contemporary Chinese history, strengthening selfless morality to enable cadres to pass the test of 'money, power and beautiful women', strengthening education in Marxist dialectical materialist method, and strengthening education in unity (Jiang 1998f: 393).

By the end of 1993, Jiang could describe Deng's theory of 'socialism with Chinese characteristics' as the 'continuation and development of

Mao Zedong Thought, Marxism for the present age, the great banner for our socialist venture and the mighty spiritual pillar of the revival of the Chinese nation (*minzu*)' (1993g: 411). Taken together, Deng Xiaoping's Southern Tour, the Fourteenth Party Congress and the third volume of Deng's selected works provide the core themes around which the post-Tiananmen CCP leadership has built its legitimacy. They present an interpretation of reality in which the CCP is presented as the party of national salvation, implementing a market-orientated economic reform process within a multipolar post-Cold War international situation, harnessing the forces of technology to ensure the survival of the Chinese nation-state in a globalising world (Jiang 1998h: 408–9).

Teaching the nation

In 1987 Fang Lizhi had been expelled from the CCP for claiming that 'reform and opening' had given intellectuals the highest political status because they represented the most advanced forces of production. The difference between Fang's views and the treatment of 'science and technology' in Deng Xiaoping's Southern Tour is that Fang had seen the prospect of a revival of nationalism as promising a return to 'feudalism'. He lauded science for the global community it created, approved of its integration into Western democratic societies and approved of internationalist-minded scientists like Albert Einstein, even though he saw that their ideals were unlikely to be realised (Fang 1986: 32–3). Moreover, he did not think that economic development was the criterion of an advanced society, which had to be measured above all by its intellectual achievements.

Internationalism and democracy had become the antithesis of Deng's thinking on science, however. Instead, the linkage between science and the nationalist narrative had become so strong for him that he could go so far as to explain that the defeat of imperialism and feudalism could only be described as 'revolutionary' because it liberated the productive forces of the Chinese people. Whether a policy is socialist or capitalist in nature had come to depend not on the way in which it impacted on class relationships, but on whether it measured up to the 'Three Benefits' (*san ge liyou*) of whether it is 'good or bad for benefiting the development of social production in socialist society, good or bad for benefiting an increase in the comprehensive national power of the socialist country (*guojia*), good or bad for benefiting the rising living standards of the people' (Deng 1993o: 372).

This political role of science and technology was reflected when the

Central Committee and State Council issued a resolution on speeding up the development of science and technology soon after the passing of a new Election Law in 1995. From then on, the slogan 'science and education rejuvenate the country' (*ke jiao xing guo*) would be used to explain the Party line of putting economic development first, that had been established back in 1978 (CC 1995: 1344–5). The way in which the forces of globalisation had been appropriated within nationalist discourse is illustrated by the way this resolution stated that 'Strength in science and technology has already become an important factor in deciding the comprehensive national power and international status of the country' (CC 1995: 1343–4).

The articulation of 'socialism with Chinese characteristics', as a version of patriotism that can incorporate many of the themes of globalisation, is more than just rhetoric; it can be demonstrated by looking at how the patriotic education campaign was adapted to respond to the broader economic demands being made on education. As a member of the Education Commission explained, if each of the 200,000 village enterprises that had come to play a crucial structural role in the Chinese economy were to be given just one trained manager and an engineer, an economist and an accountant, then no fewer than 800,000 people would have to be trained. Some 100 million agricultural workers would have to find work in other sectors as farming became more efficient, yet some 35.9 per cent of agricultural workers were either illiterate or semi-literate. Population increase alone meant that 20 million extra people per year would have to be educated. Meanwhile, demand for highly qualified personnel in manufacturing, law, medicine and the cultural field would grow, too (Li, K. 1993).

The line that emerged from the Fourteenth Party Congress meant that in addressing these problems, schools would have to make moral and ideological education compatible with an increasingly market-based socioeconomic system, if Jiang Zemin's vision of a 'personnel great power' (*rencai qiangguo*) was to become reality (Xu and Lin 2002: 408). In practical terms, as Li Keming pointed out, the 22.3 per cent (4.3 million) of children who did not even go into secondary education and the 60 per cent of the remainder who did not graduate to high school were unlikely to stay on when the emphasis was on 'cultural' education rather than the kind of vocational training that was responsive to the needs of the local economy and society.

The broad guidelines for remedying these shortcomings in the education system in ways that would not erode the authority of the Party had already been set out in the Central Committee's 'Outline of the Reform and Development of China's Education' in February 1993.

According to this document, the rationale for reforming education is to win the world competition for economic and national power, which has become a competition in science and technology and over national (*minzu*) quality. Having set education policy in a global context, however, the targets established by the document are very pragmatic. In some respects, the Outline was more ambitious than the 1985 education reforms, in terms of the aim to extend nine years of compulsory education to all areas of the country and a strong emphasis on vocational education. Employers and work-based education, for example, would play a key role in raising the educational standards of those already in work. At the high-school level, there would be a movement away from 'cultural education'. An expansion of places at technical colleges and vocational courses would take place. Higher education would also become more responsive to local social and economic needs, meeting the demands of local farms and enterprises.

At the highest level, around 100 key point universities and a group of key point technical colleges would be equipped to meet the challenges of world scientific and technological development by the beginning of the twenty-first century. World-class research would be developed by establishing a group of key point laboratories and engineering research centres. Opening to the outside world was also to be increased through more academic exchanges, borrowing from the successful experiences in developing and managing education of other countries. Students who studied overseas would be encouraged to return, cooperation with foreign universities would be strengthened, and personnel would be trained and research carried out in collaboration with foreign institutions.

More politically significant is the degree of decentralisation proposed when the 'Outline' grapples with the problem of reforming management in step with the overall development of the 'socialist market economy'. Central to this is the enduring problem of how to strike a balance between achieving coordination at the national level while not stifling local initiative. The general thrust of the proposal is for a decentralisation of management, with the province, autonomous region or directly administered municipality having the power to decide on issues such as student numbers, teaching plans, the selection and compilation of teaching materials, the duties of teachers and individual salaries. Central government would maintain overall control of the curriculum, standards, staff qualifications and basic salaries at the macro level through instruments such as the law, finance, regulations and information services. It would also play a direct role in running parts of higher education deemed to be strategically important for national economic and social development. The role of the Party in schools would similarly be limited to decisions regarding major issues, while executive personnel would be left alone to carry out their daily duties. In junior and middle schools, the Party organisations would still provide core political leadership, but not be involved in management.

Ideological education is not absent from the 'Outline'. Given the importance of the patriotic education campaign, though, it is significant that this is relegated to the fourth section of the report. Its content is largely familiar, including reminders for schools to raise socialists with the correct ideals, morals, culture and discipline for building 'socialism with Chinese characteristics'. It is also significant that the 'Outline' calls for education in national defence to be strengthened, with a continuation of the system of students at high school and above taking part in military training (156). Yet it is also important to note that the 'Outline' puts just as much stress on the need to make the content of education relevant to social needs and the development of modern science and technology. Teaching materials should thus not just reflect the civilisational achievements of China and the world, but also the latest developments in science and culture. Localities should be encouraged to produce materials suitable for the specific conditions of schools in their rural areas. Technical and vocational schools should gradually produce materials compatible with the area they are supposed to be teaching.

Ultimately, the use of the education system to disseminate the orthodoxies of Party ideology was being limited by the demands of economic modernisation and professionalisation. Moreover, the role of the Party and the state was being weakened by the need to pay for an expansion of the system through the diversification of sources of finance. As the 'Outline' explained, to date this had been woefully inadequate. In future, schools would have to make up the difference by not just looking to local and central government, but also by raising income from school enterprises and seeking donations from enterprises, individuals, from Hong Kong, Macao, Taiwan, the overseas Chinese, and even friendly foreign individuals and organisations.

The Education Commission's 'Outline' thus set out a bold reformist agenda for education that encapsulates much about the endurance of the *ti-yong* dichotomy in Chinese political discourse. As Li Tieying remarked on the 'Outline', what was being called for was a 'liberation of thought' and a reform of all ideas and systems not appropriate for the demands of modernisation, an opening up to the outside world and the bold absorption of and borrowing of the fruits of human society. Yet, while speeding up reform and opening and building socialism with Chinese characteristics, there also had to be a strengthening of Party leadership, upholding the socialist direction of education, and the strengthening and improvement of ideological work. As he reminded his audience, Deng Xiaoping had remarked at the time of Tiananmen that great mistakes had been made for a time in ideological education, and that this should never occur again (Li 1993: 27).

The resulting 1995 Education Law thus makes clear that teachers are supposed to produce personnel who can both contribute to economic development and 'uphold the guidance of Marxism-Leninism, Mao Zedong Thought and the theory of building socialism with Chinese characteristics'. Balancing the old '*ti-yong*' dichotomy of using foreign learning to preserve Chinese essence, these new personnel are supposed to continue 'the excellent historical cultural tradition of the Chinese nation (*minzu*), [and] absorb all the excellent results of the development of human civilisation'. The mission of teachers and schools is to 'develop education, raise the quality of the whole nation (*minzu*), and facilitate the building of socialist material and spiritual civilisation' (NPC 1995: 1293–4).

To illustrate the patriotic education that this entails, it is worth looking at the kind of teaching materials that have been produced since the passing of the Education Law.[1] As recommended by the Education Commission, school textbooks across the entire curriculum and at all levels are used to deliver patriotic education. Language (*yuwen*) textbooks produced in Beijing in 1997 for junior school classes, for example, teach Putonghua Mandarin through the use of vocabulary and phrases such as 'I love Beijing, I love Tiananmen, I love the five star red flag', 'I am Chinese', 'I love the motherland', 'My motherland is China' and 'The five star red flag is our national flag'. Social paradigms are presented by learning sentences such as 'father is in the PLA', 'mother is a nurse', 'the workers work, the peasants plant the fields, the PLA defends the motherland'. National symbols illustrate these lessons, such as Mao Zedong's portrait hanging over the Tiananmen Gate, at the centre of which flies a national flag, a water colour showing young pioneers saluting the national flag, the national emblem, buildings and places of national significance such as the Great Wall, and PLA figures and political leaders from the past doing good deeds.

Stories from the civil war are also introduced as the language course progresses. One tells of a fifteen-year-old girl communist fighter who is imprisoned in a temple, beaten and threatened with torture if she does not reveal her comrades when her village is occupied by the KMT in 1947. She prefers to impale herself on a knife rather than give away information, leading Chairman Mao to write the couplet, 'A great life, a glorious death'. Among the new words that are conveyed by this story are 'turncoat' (*pantu*), 'kill' (*sha*) and 'dagger' (*zha*). The role of the CCP as saviour of the nation is also woven into the course material in the form of stories about heroic figures, such as the execution of CCP founder Li Dazhao, Zhou Enlai working overnight, the 'poem of the revolutionary martyr', the Long March, Chairman Mao announcing the founding of the PRC, and the heroic exploits of a soldier in the Korean War.

Similar patriotic themes are also dispersed throughout 'Thought and Value' (*sixiang pinde*), a kind of civics course that promotes selfless virtues such as hard work, study, respect for parents and teachers, discipline and thrift. Here junior school pupils are presented with the story of a peasant boy who leads a children's anti-Japanese resistance unit and is executed by the Japanese along with the rest of his village rather than give away information. The association of the CCP with patriotism is also stressed right from the beginning, with the first lesson being on the subject of the 'Beloved Leader', telling the story of how an elderly man comes home with a portrait of Chairman Mao and explains to his grandson how grateful he is to the leader for having improved his standard of living. This is followed by a photograph of Mao, Zhou Enlai, Liu Shaoqi and Zhu De at an airport, an exercise of practising singing 'The East is Red', and simple lessons on national anniversaries used to mark the establishment of the CCP, the PLA and the PRC, and the special flags used to mark these occasions.

Such patriotic themes and icons are gradually combined with themes more closely associated with globalisation discourse as the curriculum becomes more advanced. Exercises in the junior school textbook for 'Thought and Values', for example, begin to associate Mao, Zhou, Liu and Zhu with the development of technology. The focus is increasingly forward-looking, with a general emphasis on the need to study for the sake of the motherland and building socialism in the twenty-first century. The technological achievements of the 'motherland' are also hailed, such as the PRC's first successful satellite launch in August 1992, and increases in industrial and agricultural production. One lesson on 'loving the socialist motherland' uses the story of Deng Jiaxian, inventor of the PRC's first atom bomb, as its subject matter.

Within the context of the concern over immunising the young against foreign influences under globalisation, it is also important to note that special attention is given to maintaining patriotism when abroad. This is conveyed by stories such as those of a young Chinese scientist who threatens to withdraw from an international conference if the PRC flag is not displayed. Another tells of a delegation of school children who get off their bus to salute the PRC flag when they see it being raised by a hotel worker in New York. A lesson under the title 'Study for the Motherland' tells how a Chinese woman reading engineering in Germany receives the highest merit for her thesis after studying without a break for seven days a week, and having chosen all her topics to fulfil the needs of her country. Perhaps most importantly, having achieved such success overseas, she still returns to China because all of her study was 'not for myself, but for my motherland'.

As the discussion of the political system is introduced, nationalistic themes are again deployed. The nature of 'democratic' decision-making is explained by the way in which Mao Zedong chose the national flag by having a conference on the matter, listening to dissenting opinions, discussing them, and making a final decision based on the whole body of opinions. The lesson is illustrated by a painting of Mao and Zhou looking at a design of the flag, surrounded by various dignitaries.

Other nationalistic themes that are introduced across the curriculum at junior level include the patriotism of the Chinese overseas, illustrated by the story of an ethnic-Chinese Singaporean returning to the motherland to establish a school in Xiamen. The issue of Taiwan is also introduced through the tale of Zheng Chenggong, the national hero who expelled the Dutch from the island, which has been 'Chinese territory since ancient times'. Such themes are further developed and reinforced at middle-school level, where the textbook for 'Thought and Politics' (*sixiang zhengzhi*) starts by explaining that the first quality of a good Chinese citizen is ardent love of the motherland. The first three sections of the first volume cover 'The Interests of the Motherland are Paramount', 'Ardently Love the Socialist Motherland' and 'Develop Thought that is for the Service of the People'. Again, the subject is widened to greater China, the civil war, Taiwan and national humiliation by the United States. As an aside to the United Front, the paragon of virtue is presented here in the form of a KMT general who opposes Chiang Kaishek's anti-CCP policies and is sent into exile in the United States. There he takes to wearing a placard on his chest saying 'I am Chinese', after he is snubbed at the post office for being just that.

The general narrative is one of China having moved from darkness to light under the PRC. Within this story, maintaining the tradition of opposing division and upholding the unity of the motherland that was established when Qin Shi Huangdi united China in 221 BC is the duty of all Chinese. The fact that these territories include various non-Han nationalities is not a problem, because all those living in the territory of the motherland have been turned into a cohesive force through a common economic life and linked cultures. It is explained that, without unification, there would be no world-famous Chinese ancient civilisation and no long-term independent development of the Chinese nation, no 9.6 million square kilometres of Chinese territory and no 'great family' of the 56 nationalities. History shows that when China is united, it is rich and powerful, which is why the constitution says that Chinese citizens are obliged to defend the unity of the motherland. Unification, moreover, is proclaimed to be the historical trend and the common wish of the sons and daughters of China (*zhonghua*). In recent years, continues the narrative, the common efforts of people on both sides of the Strait have led to a situation in which all are looking forward eagerly to unification.

Personnel power: from 'Deng Xiaoping Theory' to the 'Three Represents'

A key function of this kind of patriotic education is to win loyalty to the Party from the growing number of professional personnel upon whom 'building socialism with Chinese characteristics depends'. By 1995, Jiang Zemin could claim that there were already 18 million personnel working in science and technology (1995a: 1392). Deng had given such personnel and their enterprises a key role in his Southern Tour, during which he had marvelled at the speed of scientific and technological advance over the previous two decades and insisted that every business should establish a clear target that would help China to secure a world-class position in high technology.

There followed a dramatic expansion of interfaces with foreign scientific and technological activity and know-how through mechanisms such as the creation of science parks in cooperation with Russia and Singapore, the establishment of special high-technology industry zones, and the creation of research and development bases in China by cooperation with foreign high-tech firms such as IBM and Microsoft. By 1997, the Torch Plan had approved 12,606 projects in the areas of new materials, microelectronics and information, energy, biotechnology, and electromagnetic devices (Segal 2003: 31–2). Chinese scientists were also encouraged to collaborate in international initiatives, such as the Human Genome Project, work on global climate change, and the Euratom project. By the start of the twenty-first century, it could be claimed that since 1978 no fewer than 320,000 Chinese had gone abroad to study, more than twice the number who had done so in the hundred years before that. Around 110,000 of these had come back to China, and the government was taking measures to attract more to return through local initiatives such as creating special industrial parks to act as 'incubators'.

While many young Chinese with a higher education had sought refuge abroad after the events of June 1989, the dependency of the Party on the new generation of scientists, technicians and managers was so great that a policy of encouraging them to freely enter and leave the country had been adopted and publicised. As Jiang Zemin told a meeting of ethnic Chinese experts at the Third Symposium of China-America Engineering Technology: 'There are Chinese people working and living in many countries in the world. They work hard and are richly creative, with their achievements in many areas gaining attention. This brings great pride to the Chinese nation' (Xu and Lin 2002: 408). By increasing the incentives for such people to move to China, along with foreign expertise, attracting some 440,000 foreign experts to China each year and sending 40,000 overseas, the aim is to create a 'personnel great power' (*rencai qiangguo*) (Xu and Lin 2002: 408).

As Jiang Zemin explained, however, members of the new professional class being created by such exchanges had to be reminded that they were the key force for realising the aim of 'national rejuvenation through science and education'. Their historical mission is to divert their entire strength to building socialist material and spiritual civilisation. While upholding the Party line, they should be imbued with the glorious patriotic tradition of China's intellectuals. In the present stage of history, they will have to protect the leadership of the CCP and devote their ideals and expertise to the great task of the 'socialist modernisation of the motherland' (1995a: 1392–4).

Such rhetoric might appeal to senior managers who have risen to their positions under the Party's tutelage, making their loyalty to the CCP more secure. As Peter Nolan points out, a figure like Zhou Guanwu, who spearheaded the attempt to transform Beijing's Shougang steel corporation into the world's largest steel producer, was once the leader of a guerrilla unit in the anti-Japanese struggle. Not surprisingly, members of his management team saw themselves as 'commanders' in the industrial battlefront of steel-making, and developed a 'mobilizatory, quasi-military and highly disciplined style of getting things done' (Nolan 2001: 669–70). Yet this blurring of the lines between CCP organisation and industry is not only the case in heavy industry. Even a key sector of the new economy such as information technology is seen as having a strategic role in 'building socialism with Chinese characteristics', both because China's leaders believe it can help 'leap frog' industrialisation and also due to fears over information security (Hughes 2003). A typical example might be Eastcom, a 'private' telecoms firm that grew out of the Equipment Supply Office of Zhejiang Posts and Telecommunications Bureau and went on to become a leading player in the mobile communications market. Seven of its directors are over 50 years of age, four over 45, and only two below the age of 35. The CEO and chairman of the board of directors, the 58-year-old Mr Shi Jixing, has been distinguished with the Model Worker Medal for Zhejiang Province (*www.eastcom.com*).

Another good example is *Legend*, China's largest PC manufacturer and a member of the 'national team' of enterprises that have been groomed for global competition. The founder of this firm, Liu Chuanzhi, is a graduate of Peking University who received his original training at the Military Telecommunications Academy in 1961–67 and was selected from the cadre section of the Chinese Academy of Sciences (CAS) to establish the firm in 1984. Hosting the ambition of becoming the world's biggest PC manufacturer, this firm has come a long way since it was established in 1984 with funding from CAS, allowing it to win a domestic monopoly on the technology for inputting and displaying Chinese characters and the credibility that allowed funds to be raised in Hong Kong to enter the international OEM market in 1988. In return, the firm has played a leading role in building the infrastructure that makes possible the state's plans for e-government and e-commerce. When *Legend* launched its global Internet strategy in 1999, it chose the ancient capital city of Xian for the opening ceremony, indicating its commitment to the project of linking the whole of China to the rest of the world. Re-branded for global markets as 'Lenovo', *Legend* made international headlines when it spearheaded the emergence of Chinese multinationals onto the global stage with a US$1.75 billion bid for IBM's PC unit in December 2004, making reality out of Jiang Zemin's December call for investors to follow a twin strategy of 'welcoming in' (*yin jinlai*) and 'going out' (*zou chuqu*) (PDC 2002: 191), which became formal policy in 2000 to take full advantage of WTO membership.

By March 1998, Liu had been appointed to the National People's Congress. His 'Three Factors of Management', namely 'organise the troops, fix the strategy, lead the team' (*zuzhi tuandui, ding zhanlue, dai duiwu*), is characteristic of the language imposed on his generation by decades of political sloganeering. He also complains about the loss of the ideals of honesty, hard work, thrift and patriotism in his firm since it started to recruit personnel from sources other than the

CAS in 1988. He is not at all happy about the way in which members of the new generation of employees have become so interested in seeking personal glory, are accustomed to good work conditions and are fully aware that they can take up other job opportunities if they are not satisfied with the treatment they receive (Song, H. 2002: 200). Given that *Legend* has entered into a partnership with AOL-Time Warner to provide Internet services in China, the national loyalties of its staff present a real test of whether two decades of patriotic education have succeeded in inoculating the rising professional generation against 'spiritual pollution'.

The need to articulate an outward- and forward-looking patriotism has thus become stronger, reaching a turning point when the final vestige of the CCP's commitment to public ownership was dropped in Jiang Zemin's report to the Fifteenth Party Congress in September 1997. With Deng having passed away on 19 February, Jiang not only raised the newly christened ideology of 'Deng Xiaoping Theory' to the same status as 'Mao Zedong Thought' at the Congress, he also explained that the definition of 'public ownership' could include collective ownership and share holding by members of the public. The acquisition of SOE stock by private shareholders thus became a form of 'socialism'. While Jiang acknowledged that many workers would suffer as smaller and less efficient SOEs were sold off or dismantled, he insisted that 'Basically, what is beneficial to economic development is good for the long-term interests of the working class.'

To strengthen the legitimacy of the leadership as he made this departure from the last vestige of socialist principles, Jiang presented this message within the full panoply of the CCP's narrative of national salvation. Proclaiming that all the Party congresses of the twentieth century had understood that 'Our party shoulders a sacred historical responsibility for the fate of the Chinese nation', he made a favourable comparison of the present situation with that of China at the time of the Opium War and the near extinction of the Chinese nation at the hands of the Eight Armies, a coalition of imperial armies that had invaded China to suppress the Boxer Rebellion in 1900. After that crisis, the Chinese nation had two responsibilities: first, to achieve national independence and the liberation of the people, then to build a prosperous and strong country with common wealth for all the people. The conclusion to be drawn from the last hundred years was thus that: 'Only the Chinese Communist Party can lead the Chinese people to national independence, the liberation of the people and the victory of socialism'.

Unification and foreign policy interrupt

The development of a an outwardly orientated, elitist nationalism driven by the need to achieve the task of economic construction could only work, however, so long as the tasks of national unification and opposing 'international hegemony' did not impinge on domestic politics too much. As the sanctions imposed after Tiananmen crumbled, the transfer of Hong Kong approached in 1997, and Taiwan came to the negotiating table at Singapore in 1993, this was a feasible prospect. Yet the impact of events in both of these areas of policy-making in the late 1990s meant that more than the sweeping narrative of the leadership would be required to ensure the patriotic loyalties of the rising professional class to the CCP leadership.

The first challenge to the leadership's patriotic credentials was presented by the crisis in the Taiwan Strait that began in the summer of 1995, when ROC President Lee Teng-hui was granted a visa to visit the United States, and culminated in a military stand-off with the United States Navy in the run-up to the island's first presidential election in March the following year. While this triggered the first wave of popular nationalism in the 1990s, it is notable that Jiang Zemin attempted to keep the focus of ideological debate on domestic problems. At the end of 1995, he thus opened up discussion of the right way to address the social and political problems generated by the development of the 'socialist market system' by presenting a speech to the plenary session of the Central Committee in which he listed twelve major relationships that had to be properly managed by the Party. These are the relationships between: reform, development and stability; speed and efficiency; economic construction, population, natural resources and environment; different levels of industry; the eastern and the western regions; the market and macroeconomic controls; public ownership and other forms of ownership; the distribution of income between the state, enterprises and individuals; opening to the outside and self-reliance; the centre and the provinces; national defence and economic construction; and building material and spiritual civilisation (Jiang 1995a). The issue of Taiwan was not mentioned, even though the crisis was well under way by that time.

Despite the sanctions taken by Beijing against the United States around the time of the election in Taiwan and the strong anti-Americanism that was developing in popular books such as *China Can Say No* (Song *et al.* 1996), both Washington and Beijing made efforts to repair their relationship. In October 1997, Jiang Zemin thus made the first visit to the United States by a Chinese head of state since 1985, during which billions of dollars of new business was cleared for US companies, including a deal for the sale of 50 Boeing aircraft worth about US$3 billion. When President Clinton returned Jiang's visit with his own trip to China in June 1998, deals for some US$1.4 billion worth of US goods and services were signed. With Beijing holding the value of the Renminbi Yuan during the Asian Financial Crisis and providing vital support for the Hong Kong dollar, US Secretary of State Madeleine Albright had a strong case to make when she urged Congress to renew China's MFN status in July 1998, putting global economic stability before pressure on China to make political reforms. It is also important to note that at the centre of these attempts to take nationalism out of PRC-US relations was a major concession to China over Taiwan, when Clinton made a significant shift in Washington's policy in the form of a verbal announcement of a 'Three No' policy for Taiwan: 'No one China, one Taiwan; no Taiwan independence; no Taiwan membership in international organisations requiring statehood'.

The patriotic rhetoric of the leadership was also called into question by a perceived failure of the government to react to atrocities against ethnic Chinese Indonesians during riots that swept Jakarta on 13–15 May 1998, in the wake of the Asian financial crisis. Particular indignation was caused by reports that ethnic Chinese women of all ages had been subjected to gang rape, often in front of their families. When Chinese citizens showed their concern by holding demonstrations in various Southeast Asian states, Hong Kong and Taiwan, and as far away as Australia and the United States, mainland China was the stark exception. It was only after news filtered through to mainland China via the Internet that students began to use the new medium to organise a march to the Indonesian embassy in Beijing (Hughes 2000).

Of particular importance for the formation of elite nationalism is the way in which the Internet began to be used as the medium for such news to be disseminated. The expansion of the Internet was driven largely by the government's own drive to 'leapfrog' industrialisation by informatising the economy and administration (Dai 2003). Yet it was already showing fewer signs of leading to the kind of social liberalisation expected by many pundits outside China and more of a tendency to mirror and magnify existing nationalistic sentiments in the online population. The heated nature of the nationalist emotions that were spreading at the time is encapsulated by the message left by one correspondent, who asked:

My mother country, do you hear the crying? Your children abroad are crying out. Help them. I do not understand politics and do not dare talk about politics. I do not know what it means to say 'we have no long-term friends or enemies, only long term interests', and I do not know what these interests are . . . I only know that my own compatriots are being barbarously slaughtered, they need help, and not just moral expressions of understanding and concern. My motherland, they are your children. The blood that flows from their bodies is the blood of the Han race. Their sincerity and good will also comes from your nourishment. Help them . . .

These nationalistic feelings encouraged numerous Internet users to call into question the CCP's patriotism, ridiculing Beijing's strong stance on non-intervention by asking how the Arab states would react if China started to kill its Muslim citizens, pointing out how France and the United States had intervened in Rwanda, and describing how the British and Americans always stand together. The PRC, by contrast, had not even used its seat at the UN to promote sanctions against Indonesia and had actually taken part in securing International Monetary Fund (IMF) aid for that country, while straining under its own domestic problems. Even Taiwan had taken a stronger stance towards Jakarta, responding to public outrage by suspending a supply of 200,000 tons of rice. Perhaps most significant for the evolution of nationalist politics inside mainland China, though, was the inevitable links that were drawn between Beijing's conservative foreign policy, the patriotic rhetoric of Jiang Zemin, and the CCP's monopoly on power. 'It is quite simple', pointed out one correspondent, 'You can demonstrate against the atrocities in Indonesia, but as soon as you demonstrate a bit about democracy, freedom, lack of human rights, government incompetence, official corruption, then how can the CCP and the "collective leadership around the core of Jiang Zemin" accept it?'

The largest foreign policy challenge for the leadership, however, was presented by the destruction of the Chinese embassy in Belgrade on 8 May 1999 (Beijing Time), during which three embassy personnel died and more than twenty were injured. This took place as many in China were already seeing evidence of Washington's conspiracy to fight Deng's 'smokeless war' against the Chinese political system and way of life. The belief that anti-Chinese forces were on the rise in Washington had been reinforced by the trial of the Taiwanese-born scientist Wen Ho Lee in the United States on espionage charges. In January 1999, accusations that large numbers of Chinese visitors to the United States were engaged in the illicit transfer of militarily sensitive high technology to China were also made in a report by the Select Committee on US National Security and Military/Commercial Concerns with the People's Republic of China, under Congressman Christopher Cox. In foreign policy, Washington's increasing practice of humanitarian intervention around the world seemed to be consolidating what Deng Xiaoping had condemned as the doctrine of 'human rights above sovereignty' and the use of force to spread Western values (Chu and Wang 1999). Such suspicions were further heightened when the Pentagon's 1997 Quadrennial Defense Review presented a strategy in which Washington would use a window of opportunity before 2015 in which it would have unrivalled power to 'shape' the international strategic environment. The air raids launched against Iraq by the United States and the United Kingdom under the Desert Fox campaign of December 1998, and opposed by France, Russia and China at the UN Security Council, confirmed the dangers posed by US unipolarity. NATO's intervention in Yugoslavia and its eastward expansion were seen as part of a grand strategy to control the Balkans and dominate Europe.

Closer to home, Washington was seen to be encouraging Japan to develop a more active defence policy and the signing of the Joint US–Japan Security Declaration in April 1996 was seen as an expansion of the scope of Japan's security commitments to include the Taiwan Strait. Despite the efforts made by Beijing and Washington to restore stable relations after the Taiwan Strait crisis, by the end of 1998 reports were already spreading in the dissident overseas Chinese press that Jiang Zemin was coming under intense pressure from the military to take a stronger line against the United States and Japan. This criticism reached a new peak when Jiang became the first head of state to visit Japan in November 1998, only to suffer serious humiliation when he failed to satisfy expectations at home that he would secure a new apology for the invasion of China and Tokyo's confirmation of Washington's 'Three Nos' policy for Taiwan. In December 1998, the Hong Kong-based journal *Zhengming* claimed that more than fifty retired generals had signed a petition demanding that the CCP Politburo review and explain its policy towards the United States and Japan and demanded that Jiang should lodge strong protests and take sanctions against Washington and Tokyo over their interference in the unification of China. The report claimed that a study session for high-ranking cadres held by the CMC in November had turned into major criticism of Central Committee regarding policies towards the United States and Japan and weakness in Taiwan policy.

This situation was particularly sensitive for Premier Zhu Rongji, whose main priority in relations with Washington was to secure agreement on the terms of China's accession to the WTO. Zhu responded to pressure from the military at a special briefing for high-ranking officers held by the CMC in November. He was reported to have received a standing ovation for interpreting Deng Xiaoping's foreign policy line as meaning that hegemonic politics have to be opposed and that normal relations with the US depend on America's adherence to the principle of non-intervention, upholding the principle of independence. Compromises would not be entered into with the Western powers in exchange for temporary benefits. Zhu also insisted that the leadership would demand that Japan should amend portions of the US–Japan security agreement where it threatened to interfere with Chinese territory, would oppose the revival of Japanese militarism and its designs on Taiwan. Demands would continue to be made for Japan to admit to the destruction and damage it caused during its invasion of China, and to make a correct summation of such historical incidents. Zhu also insisted that the Central Committee was committed to accelerated development and enhancement of military readiness, high-tech defence and armaments, with the doctrine of preparing to fight against a high-tech partial encroachment in an anti-Chinese war remaining unchanged and being given top priority.

The nature of the legitimacy crisis that Zhu had to deal with is summed up by the claim made in *Zhengming* (December 1998: 9–11) that at a dinner with PLA leaders and retired generals after the CMC briefing, he assured his audience that:

> Should the leadership one day stray from Comrade Deng Xiaoping's theories and line toward the US and Japan – becoming an appendage of American hegemony, discarding the territory and sovereignty of the motherland – the entire population and the military are charged with the responsibility of defending national justice, to overturn and overthrow such a corrupt, reactionary ruling party and government!

Whether or not such reports are accurate, this was the context of opinion and perception within which Premier Zhu Rongji visited the United States on 6–14 April, with the aim of signing an agreement on the terms of China's WTO accession. That NATO had begun the bombardment of Serbia on 24 March, made the journey even more sensitive. On 20 April, however, Zhu returned to China without President Clinton's signature on the WTO agreement. It did not go without notice that there were no representatives from the National People's

Congress to meet him, as protocol demands. The NPC, under the chairmanship of the conservative and technocratic Li Peng, then became a major source of the attacks on Zhu that ensued (*Zhengming*, June 1999: 10–11).

Zhu Rongji was thus in a vulnerable position due to the interplay between domestic politics and foreign policy even before the destruction of the Chinese Embassy in Belgrade. When that crisis broke out, hundreds of thousands of people protested in cities across China, attacking the US Embassy in Beijing with stones and eggs. US Ambassador James Sasser was trapped in his embassy, guarded by US Marines, as enraged students yelled 'kill Americans', hurled rocks and tried to storm the compound. Over the following days, students in Beijing shouted slogans like 'get out American pigs' and burned the American flag. In the central industrial city of Nanjing, they staged a sit-down protest outside a Kentucky Fried Chicken restaurant and plastered posters on windows saying 'Strike the US Economy', and trade unions marching past the US consulate in the southern city of Guangzhou chanted 'Stop American mad dogs from biting'.

The powerlessness of the powerful

The most notable characteristic of the reaction of the leadership to this crisis is that the vital task of trying to maintain public order was given to the rising star of the Politburo, Vice-President Hu Jintao. It was Hu that made a carefully balanced televised speech on 9 May, while Jiang Zemin did not respond in public until four more days had passed. Moreover, Hu's speech on this occasion encapsulates how the ideological formula of Deng Xiaoping Theory could be applied by acknowledging, on the one hand, the right of the Chinese people to express their fury and ardent patriotism, while on the other insisting that the protests should be carried out within the law and that there should be vigilance against those who might take advantage of the opportunity to disrupt social order.

The only concrete actions that Hu could offer on behalf of the government, however, were official protests and the demand for an emergency meeting of the UN Security Council. Aside from saying that the government reserved the right to take further unspecified measures, Hu's message for the future of foreign policy was that the government would not be moved from its line of independence, self-sufficiency and peace, resolutely upholding national sovereignty and the dignity of the nation, opposing hegemony and power politics. In a note of reassurance for those who might doubt the continuation of the domestic reforms, Hu insisted that the basic line of 'reform and opening' would continue and that the rights of overseas Chinese and foreigners in China would be protected. The key political message was summed up in Hu's last paragraph, where he appealed for the nation to unite around 'the Party Centre with Jiang Zemin at its core' and to 'hold high the great banner of Deng Xiaoping Theory, the spirit of struggle, united as one, taking the great project of building socialism with Chinese characteristics forward into the twenty-first century'.

The Belgrade Incident thus illustrates how difficult it had become for the Chinese leadership to match its patriotic rhetoric with rising domestic expectations for the country to 'say no' to the United States. The relationship between foreign policy and domestic politics had not only been complicated by factionalism in the Party, but also by the development of alternative channels for the formation of public opinion. Not only did books such as *China Can Say No* and the genre it established show the significance of a commercial publishing sector, but the Internet was also coming into its own as a venue for discussion. While American foreign policy since the end of the Cold War had encouraged the spread of the Internet to authoritarian states in the hope that it would bring about liberalisation, it was already clear in 1999 that public use of the new technology to air anti-American emotions was far more popular.

Faced by accusations of weakness, the Party organs could only go along with the tide of nationalistic anger. The *People's Daily* thus claimed that NATO had purposely 'spilled Chinese blood', and the Xinhua news agency quoted a prominent Chinese scientist who was sure that the attack had been elaborately planned. On 6 May, as the crisis in Kosovo began to unfold, all of the large papers in Beijing published a long article entitled, 'The Chinese Academy of Sciences and "Two Missiles, One Satellite": A Remembrance', by Zhang Jinfu, former Party Secretary of the Chinese Academy of Sciences. It gave a detailed recounting of the process that took place in the year that China developed the atomic bomb, a missile and a satellite. Discussing this article after the embassy attack, scientists at CAS expressed that they could quickly produce whatever national security required. On 10 May, as the demonstrations continued to grow, involving over a million people in the major cities, two satellites were launched on the Long March 4B rocket, the first of the year and reportedly arranged by the top leadership to demonstrate to the US China's potential capacity to launch international missiles. The following day, Foreign Ministry spokesman Zhu Bangzao announced that China had reached certain decisions according to the spirit of the Chinese government statement and in consideration of the current situation: to postpone high-level military contacts between the armed forces of China and the US; postpone PRC consultations with the US in the fields of proliferation prevention, arms control and international security; and suspend dialogue with the US on human rights.

Ultimately, however, despite these gestures of defiance, the crisis of 1999 showed the limits of China's capabilities to oppose American power. With Hu Jintao having established the basic framework of expressing patriotism within the limits established by Deng Xiaoping Theory, Jiang Zemin finally elaborated more on the nature of nationalism when he gave an address to the nation on 13 May to mark the return of the dead embassy workers to China (Jiang 1999a). Reiterating that the government had lodged the strongest possible protest with the United States and reserved the right to take further measures, Jiang acknowledged that the protests inside China were an expression of the 'great patriotic spirit and solidarity' of the Chinese nation and their determination to uphold peace and oppose hegemony, and that 'The Great PRC could not be bullied!' Having stressed the legitimacy of nationalistic emotions, Jiang then went on to describe how the post-Cold War international situation was still developing towards multipolarity, although the situation was still not peaceful, as more countries were becoming alarmed over the way that the United States used its economic and technological power to interfere in the domestic affairs of other states. Humanity was thus at a crucial point in establishing peace and development, so all peaceful nations should unite to oppose hegemony and struggle to build an ethical and rational international order. What China was supposed to do to further this, however, was confined to Jiang's insistence that the path of taking economic development as the central task that was established by Deng Xiaoping should be followed. This meant that:

> The whole Party and people of all nationalities in the country should take the great indignity and heated patriotism they feel towards the barbaric actions of NATO and turn it into a powerful motivating force, with one heart and one ethic and hard struggle to incessantly increase our country's economic power, defence power and national solidarity.

Only socialism could guarantee the right conditions for this to take place, explained Jiang, because reform and opening is the 'road to a great power'. While maintaining independence and self-sufficiency, continuing economic and technological exchanges on the basis of equality, 'ceaselessly promoting modernisation by combining the best of Chinese tradition with the best of the world's civilisations'. Naturally, in the process it was essential that all should be vigilant towards those inside the country who might take advantage of the situation to create social disorder. A peaceful foreign policy based on principles of independence and self-sufficiency and cooperation with all states would be developed according to the Five Principles of Peaceful Coexistence and under the leadership of the CCP.

The correct interpretation of the speeches made by Jiang and Hu was explained in some detail in a *People's Daily* article on 27 May 1999 under the title 'Come Together under the Great Banner of Patriotism' (Huang 1999). This reiterated the stress on continuity with the reform programme and identified the leadership with the patriotic emotions of the public by agreeing that the bombing of the embassy had revealed that the doctrine of 'human rights before sovereignty' is nothing more than a new kind of imperialism, shattering any illusions that intellectuals might have held about the US. But its real message was to restate Deng's view that 'Only development is hard reason'. As the article explained, only the strong can avoid being humiliated by foreigners, so 'we must transform our anger into strength, build the economy, this is the lasting guarantee of being able to hold the ground of not being defeated'. After all, went the argument, it is only economic power that enables the United States to punish those who do not bend to its will. Chinese history since 1840 has taught us that only the strong can avoid humiliation. What was important in the immediate present, therefore, was to resolutely uphold social stability and the great unity of the nationalities, because 'Without a solid Great Wall, where is there a secure home?' The answer to the crisis, therefore, was to 'resolutely take economic construction as the centre, comprehensively strengthen national defence and the armed forces'. Technological education was to be used to 'revive the country', and technology would defend the country, but only if a high point of scientific development could be reached in the coming century. The only way to achieve the strength to face this complex situation was to follow the Party centre with Jiang Zemin at its core.

Maintaining this balance between patriotism and the priority of economic development became increasingly difficult, however, as foreign events continued to unfold. When, on 9 July, Taiwan President Lee Teng-hui announced in an interview on German radio that from then on the relationship between the two sides of the Taiwan Strait should be considered a 'special relationship between two states', the nationalistic fervour reached a new height. Reports began to appear in the overseas Chinese press indicating that the foreign policy line established by Deng Xiaoping was being tested by elements in the military. Zhang Wannian, Vice-Chairman of the Central Military Commission, was supposed to have stated on at least two occasions that China faced the possibility of a 'New World War', which would have represented a major departure from Deng's principle that a world war was not likely in the near future. According to the reports, Zhang also argued that it was impossible to establish a strategic partnership with the United States while it was implementing hegemonism and gunboat diplomacy, and that the military considered US hegemonism to be the main enemy of the people. The attack had generated bitter hatred of the enemy and spurred the military to step up modernisation to fight a high-tech war against the United States, predicated on fighting a war in the Taiwan Strait and opposing an offensive war mounted by United States and Japanese forces that would involve a war of resistance, attrition and destruction that would expand into a world war and with nuclear conflict hard to avoid. Given such sentiments, it is not surprising that when Lee Teng-hui was asked by the *Voice of Germany* whether Taiwan would share the fate of Hong Kong and Macau, he explained, 'The crucial question is the Chinese mainland's overemphasis on nationalism and its failure to implement democracy.'

Facing the past: facing the future

The numerous crises of 1999 had a special poignancy because this was also the year that marked the 50th anniversary of the founding of the PRC. The predicament that the sponsorship of nationalism had created for China's leaders at the end of the millennium is symbolised by a front-page editorial that appeared in the PLA newspaper, *Jiefangjun bao*, on 16 August, which denounced Lee Teng-hui and warned that 50 years ago an outmanned and outgunned PLA defeated the nationalist army. Taiwan could spend 'mountains' of US dollars modernising its military, but its forces would never have the morale to fight for a '1000 year sinner' and 'splittist' like Lee. The PLA, insisted the article, is 'willing to lose thousands of troops, but will not lose a single inch of Chinese territory'. Meanwhile, American and Japanese defence officials were busy signing a memorandum of understanding on joint research into a ship-based theatre missile defence (TMD) system. The PLA staged a massive show of force in Beijing with a dress rehearsal for the 1 October National Day parade.

When Jiang Zemin delivered his National Day address to the nation (1999a), the ideological formula that Deng Xiaoping had put in place since the late 1970s was reiterated. Jiang recalled how Mao Zedong had announced the birth of the New China 50 years before, after which the Chinese people had stood up, followed by Deng Xiaoping who had set China on the road of 'reform and opening'. Practice had shown that only socialism could 'save China', establishing independence after a hundred years of bloody struggle. Looking ahead, Jiang laid out a vision of the Chinese people devoting their strength and bravery to standing up in the 'world's forest of nations', showing again how they could use their intelligence and ability to contribute to world civilisation. Deng's three major tasks remained firmly in place, as he explained that all of China's nationalities would work together to build a new stage in the development of 'socialism with Chinese characteristics'. At the same time, they would strive to achieve complete national unification, and adhere to an 'independent and self-reliant' foreign policy based on the Five Principles of Peaceful Coexistence to stand with friendly countries in opposing hegemony and promoting multipolarity and a fair and rational international economic system. Ultimately, under the 'great banner' of Marxism-Leninism, Mao Zedong Thought and Deng Xiaoping Theory, 'a wealthy, strong, democratic and civilised modernised socialist China must appear in the Orient'.

It is as part of this strengthening of the nationalistic rhetoric of the Party leadership that Jiang Zemin finally made his own contribution to the Party line in the form of the 'Three Represents', which proposes that the CCP represents the development of advanced productive forces, represents the taking forward of China's advanced culture, and represents the fundamental interests of the great majority of the Chinese people. Based on a set of ideas that Jiang first unveiled in February 2000 during a tour of Guangdong province, this formula was installed alongside Mao Zedong Thought and Deng Xiaoping Theory in his report to the Sixteenth Party Congress in November 2002. It thus constitutes the ideological heritage within which China's new generation of leaders has to articulate its policies. In this sense, its real significance is that it formalises the status of the rising class of professional personnel as a revolutionary vanguard in the Leninist political hierarchy. The breadth of this new class can be seen in the way that Jiang told the Sixteenth Congress how the new 'builders of socialism with Chinese characteristics' that had emerged from the process of social change had come to include 'entrepreneurs and technical personnel employed by non-public scientific and technological enterprises, managerial and technical staff employed by overseas-funded enterprises, the self-employed, private entrepreneurs, employees in intermediaries, free-lance professionals and members of other social strata'.

The kind of dilemma faced by the founder of *Lenovo* when dealing with the self-interest of his younger professional employees had thus been resolved. As Jiang told the Sixteenth Congress, the CCP should unite with all people who 'make the motherland prosperous and strong'. People should not be judged by how much property they own, but by their 'political awareness, state of mind and performance, by how they have acquired and used their property, and by how they have contributed to the cause of building socialism with Chinese character-istics through their work'. In the 'primary stage of socialism', it is no longer necessary to pay even lip-service to a class analysis of society, because 'In building socialism with Chinese characteristics, the fun-damental interests of the people of the whole country are identical, on the basis of which interest relations and internal contradictions can be adjusted.' While the world situation is thus moving towards 'political multipolarization and economic globalization' amidst twists and turns, it is the representatives of the advanced forces of production that will work with the CCP to bring about 'a great rejuvenation of the Chinese nation on its road to socialism with Chinese characteristics'.

3 Globalisation and its discontents

While there have been winners as the CCP leadership has embraced globalisation, the departure from the planned economy has also eroded the security provided for workers in the state sector and imposed new demands on those who have traditionally been seen as the guardians of ideological orthodoxy, such as 'intellectuals' and educators. The discussion of the emerging CCP orthodoxy that this has generated has undoubtedly become more pluralistic due to the creation of new outlets for expression, such as a more commercialised publishing industry and the Internet. Yet it is Party orthodoxy that remains the main subject of such discussion and thus determines its permissible limits.

Mainstream Chinese social scientists find it useful to understand the increasingly pluralistic debate over fundamental issues of ideology as structured around a discourse between various schools of thought, such as the 'Right' and the 'Left' (Ma and Li u1998), and more recently 'neo-authoritarianism', 'liberalism' and the 'New Left' (Xiao 2003). Any classification of those taking part in this debate according to such categories should be undertaken with caution, however, given that such labels are deployed as strategies within Chinese political discourse. What can be demonstrated, though, is that the CCP's post-Tiananmen emphasis on patriotism requires that nearly all such schools strive to achieve legitimacy by appropriating the nationalistic goals established by the CCP. It is not surprising, therefore, that a vast number of themes have been associated with the 'new nationalism' of the 1990s. However, rather than reduce such schools to a single ideology called nationalism, the significance of nationalist discourse has to be understood by looking at the divergent political strategies that are being pursued.

Nationalism as political strategy

One such strategy is to use certain themes to promote the rise of the new political and economic elite, which the CCP leadership sees as central to the success of building 'socialism with Chinese characteristics'. This strategy can be seen in what is probably the first monograph to undertake an explicit discussion of the relationship of 'nationalism' (*minzu zhuyi*) to policy-making under 'reform and opening', namely the 1994 book *Viewing China Through the Third Eye* (1994), by Wang Shan, a deputy director of the Beijing Opera Academy. In the range of constituencies attempting to influence the post-Tiananmen ideological consensus, the views in this work come closest to the wholesale departure from socialism in favour of the elitist authoritarianism supported by the 'princelings'. It has, in fact, been claimed that the work was sponsored by Chen Yuan and Pan Yue, the sons of Party elders Chen Yun and Liu Huaqing, commander of the PLA Navy.

A central theme of the *Third Eye* is the fear that the movement away from central planning and public ownership could lead to social disintegration, a topic that was being widely discussed after the events of 1989 and the collapse of the Soviet Union. In this respect, Wang is openly critical of both Deng Xiaoping and Jiang Zemin for failing to respond effectively to the weakening of the state generated by 'reform and opening'. The main threat that Wang identifies for China arises from the internal migration of peasants to urban areas. This allows Wang to appropriate certain authoritarian elements from Mao Zedong, whose confinement of the peasants to the people's communes Wang approves of, and also to deploy themes from Deng Xiaoping to propose an authoritarian ideology that will be more effective than Jiang Zemin's misplaced belief that stability can be maintained by advocating selfless morality and socialist ideals (80). Deng gave up such a belief, argues Wang, when he began to promote the idea of the 'primary stage of socialism', effectively renouncing his dream of a return to the China of 1956 (114–15). Jiang's task was thus to become more like Mao and Deng in order to consolidate his power and force through market reforms against a wall of opposition by rising above factional struggles and mobilising patriotism (202–3).

This concern with strengthening the state is not sufficient on its own to classify a work as nationalistic, however. To understand why nationalism is relevant to Wang Shan, it is necessary to see it as part of his strategy to persuade Jiang Zemin that he will have to side with the rising enlightened urbanised elite (*shehui youxiu pingji*). It is here that

Wang specifically cites nationalism as one element of a new ideology. Combined with Social Darwinism and Marxism, it is part of the perspective that Wang calls the 'Third Eye'. While Social Darwinism may have become politically incorrect since its adoption by Hitler, he insists that it remains valid in a world characterised by a growing population struggling for resources, with cross-border flows of information acculturating, destroying and rejecting 'backward nations' for the sake of the overall improvement of the human race. By combining Social Darwinism with nationalism and Marxism, a guide will be provided for China to compete with India and Russia by following the developmental models of South Korea and Japan. The alternative is to be left like 'a piece of plump meat surrounded by wolves', namely Japan, South Korea, Taiwan and the rising states of Southeast Asia (275–90).

To clarify that the revival of nationalism in the 1990s has little to do with 'leftism', it is important to realise that Wang's commitment to the market is firmly aligned with the elitist nationalism emerging within the post-Tiananmen Party orthodoxy. In comparison, the most notorious 'leftist' document of the early 1990s, an anonymous pamphlet circulated under the title 'Various Factors Influencing the Country's National Security' (Anon. 1995), is relatively conservative when it comes to deploying nationalist themes. Commonly called the *Ten Thousand Word Letter*, this text appeared the year after Wang's book and is widely assumed to be the work of Deng Liqun, the architect of the anti-spiritual pollution campaign who had lost his last official post in 1992. Much of it is taken up with an impressive array of statistics and reports illustrating the decline of CCP power, the erosion of public ownership and the spreading of social problems.

If the *Ten Thousand Word Letter* can be said to deploy nationalistic themes, this is most evident in the way that it reasserts the conservative elements of Deng Xiaoping by claiming that the domestic forces of 'bourgeois liberalisation' regrouped after 1989 and in 1992 triumphed over the Four Cardinal Principles. Working with the support of foreign states, these forces are said to be bringing about the 'peaceful evolution' of the political system by eroding the belief in Marxism and the Four Cardinal Principles and denuding the Chinese people of their public property. Echoes of the xenophobic campaigns of the 1980s can certainly be seen in the way that the *Ten Thousand Word Letter* pours scorn on the proliferation of bars, night clubs, golf courses, saunas, massage parlours and brothels, and the impact of culture from Hong Kong, Taiwan and the West, the widespread use of Cantonese, playing the lottery and fashions such as wearing the Stars and Stripes. If this is 'leftist', though, it has little to do with the kind of radicalism of the Cultural Revolution, and it is a relatively constrained and inward-looking kind of nationalism.

What texts like *The Third Eye* and the *Ten Thousand Word Letter* show, however, is that at the centre of what Chinese political discourse presents as a contest between 'Right' and 'Left' is a competition to see who can most successfully appropriate elements from Deng Xiaoping to articulate the right kind of patriotism for the new leadership. Within this debate, nationalism is in fact deployed most assertively by some of those who argue most vociferously in support of market-orientated reforms and see the poltical situation as being generally benign. The best example of this is the March 1996 response to the *Ten Thousand Word Letter* that emerged in the form of a letter to the National People's Congress under the title 'Reform and Opening Cannot be Permitted to be Shaken: A Critique of Deng Liqun's "Ten Thousand Word Letter"' (Fan 1996). The author, Fan Liqin, is again linked with the princelings, having worked with Deng Xiaoping's son, Deng Pufang, at the National League for the Disabled during the 1980s. Both had been disabled by Red Guards during the Cultural Revolution (Shi 1997: 5–6).

Fan is similar to Wang Shan insofar as both see the creation of a stable and large bourgeois class as the future guarantor of social stability and development. Much of what he says in this respect is again a restatement of some of the central themes in Deng Xiaoping. Stability and unity are to be preserved by maintaining the large SOEs, while collective, individual and private enterprises are to be developed apace. Macroeconomic controls should be used to influence the market rather than state planning. People with knowledge, ability and 'connections' (*you guanxi de ren*) should rightly be encouraged to get rich before others. Intellectuals should be recognised as part of the proletariat, and science and technology should be seen as the 'first productive force'. Capital, personnel and technology should be imported when useful, and the door should be open for people to travel in and out of the country as they wish. Where Fan Liqin departs from Wang Shan, however, is in his very positive appraisal of 'reform and opening'. Whereas Wang sees the reforms as destabilising society, Fan follows Deng Xiaoping in attributing the ability of the CCP to avoid the fate of its counterparts in the Soviet Union and Eastern Europe to the rise in living standards that they have made possible. The relations between the classes are in fact at their best ever, and the state can serve all the people by maintaining domestic order, opposing foreign invasion and preserving national independence, unity and sovereignty (66).

More important for the articulation of nationalist discourse is the way in which Fan's essay and the *Ten Thousand Word Letter* both attack their opponents by linking them with the foreign threat, despite the intense antagonisms that exist between these two texts in all other respects. In the *Ten Thousand Word Letter*, 'bourgeois liberalisation' is said to be present in those who deny the validity of Marxism, those who advocate learning about the West, the revival of Confucianism, and the use of 'post-modernism' and 'mass culture' to change social consciousness. It is evident in scepticism about the possibility of developing a new kind of selfless person. It can be seen in the selection of cadres on the basis of their professional and technical experience rather than political orientation, while Marxist theoreticians are confined to the Party School and research organisations. Ultimately, anybody showing such signs of 'bourgeois liberalisation' has to be seen as a threat to national security because they are unlikely to support the government and serve the motherland in any conflict with the United States.

For Fan, though, the enemy within is a curious alliance of 'rightists' and 'leftists' who thrived under Zhao Ziyang and developed links with Deng Liqun in order to secure positions in think tanks and research institutes and with extremist forces in the United States. This poses a threat to national security because, since Tiananmen, the Gulf War and the transformation of the Soviet Union and Eastern Europe, foreign powers have come to believe that they can completely destroy the socialist states, including the PRC, and control the world because they no longer need China to balance Soviet power. Yet, argues Fan, their misguided beliefs about the spread of liberalism are merely creating disasters from Bosnia to Chechnya, while the imposition of sanctions on China is causing them great losses, and their policies are disrupting stability and development in Taiwan (101–5).

Given Fan's deployment of the foreign threat to justify the movement towards the market, it is remarkable that the only author who specifically advocates the need for the leadership to turn to 'nationalism', namely Wang Shan, stresses that the foreign threat should *not* be used as an excuse for the failure to address domestic problems. He points out, for example, that the Eighth Party Congress, in 1956, was able to adopt a line that was more democratic than that of the Third Plenum in 1978, despite the proximity of the Hungarian and Polish crises and the Korean War (92–3). Similarly, the United States is presented not so much as an international bogeyman as an infantile nation motivated to help the people of China by a combination of misguided intentions (4–7). Wang ridicules Washington's policies not because they pose a danger to Chinese security but because they do not promote the national interests of the United States. Instead, sanctions have merely consolidated support for Party rule by humiliating the population and discrediting the student movement, while the country has not been stopped from continuing to develop into an engine of world growth (9–11).

When Wang does talk about the foreign threat, it is actually to support his much more extensive argument about the dangers posed to stability by mass movements from below, warning that failure to cope with the growing differentials of wealth produced by 'reform and opening' could create the kind of social instability that is used by Western powers as a pretext for intervention (23–4). Although he starts the book by warning that the Western powers tend to use their previous experience of Hitler and their fear of weapons of mass destruction falling into the wrong hands as reasons for intervening in the domestic affairs of other states (7), the function of this is to warn the leadership to be cautious about the way in which they portray the rising power of China. He thus goes on to explain the need to reassure concerned states by continuing with economic reform and following this up in the future with political reform. If the leadership resorts to appealing to the extreme emotions of the lower orders of society instead, then this will only lead to the kind of division and crisis that occurred in 1989 (292). The urbanised economic elite thus leads the nation to salvation as market-based reforms are introduced into the advanced parts of the economy, while socialism is used to maintain stability in other areas, avoiding domestic divisions that might give foreign powers a pretext for intervention (293).

Similarly, the focus of the *Ten Thousand Word Letter* on the enemy within means that it is relatively constrained in what it has to say about the international situation. Even a second *Ten Thousand Word Letter* under the title 'Preliminary Investigations into the Internal and External Situation and Main Threats Affecting Our Country's Security over the Next 10–20 Years', which focuses more specifically on the international situation, draws on the contents of Deng Xiaoping to portray a relatively positive international scene. According to this, there is little immediate prospect of a nuclear war, America's ambitions for world domination are seen to be constrained by a trend towards multipolarity, Russia is unable to rebuild its hegemonic power, and Japan is still a long way from becoming a major military force. Meanwhile, the Western powers find it hard to act militarily as they are riven by contradictions over economic interests and regional leadership issues, while the states of the South are uniting in opposition to their intervention and control. At the same time, the national power of the PRC is increasing rapidly and its regional power and mutual relationships are on the whole favourable (Anon. 1996).

It is the pro-market, reform-orientated Fan, on the other hand, who spends the most time on linking his opponents with foreign enemy forces by cultivating an image of the West as a threat in his analysis of the international situation. Arguing that the hegemonistic aggression of the West has been proven by American opposition to Beijing holding the 2000 Olympic Games, he then reminds the 'descendants of the Yellow Emperor' that it cannot change its basic nature of striving to preserve the superiority of the white race and to prevent China from becoming a great country with world influence. While he too ridicules American policy as 'infantile' and misdirected, Fan goes further than Wang Shan or the *Ten Thousand Word Letter* in stressing the dangers of American aggression, warning that the US Congress is becoming increasingly bellicose as it recovers from the trauma of Vietnam. He is confident, though, that American power can be balanced by a Russia increasingly ready to use its nuclear arsenal against the United States as its conventional forces deteriorate, and a China that is very different from Iraq. Citing Mao Zedong, he reminds his readers that although China's nuclear arsenal is not big, 'If I have six nuclear bombs, that is enough' (103–4).

Having denegrated his enemies, Fan is then free to establish his own political allegiance to the leadership. He announces that the machinations of the West are as mistaken as trying to stop the Sun from rising in the East, since Deng Xiaoping has discovered that reform and opening is the road to becoming a strong and great country. It is a road that has been carved from China's own great territory, represents the interests of the majority of the people, and stimulates the creativity and activity of all the nationalities, classes and outstanding personnel of the country. It is a road that faces the world, moves towards the world and opens up to the world. It is the road of scientific development, of self-reliance and self-development. This road does not just reflect the demands and aspirations of the CCP, but of China's struggle since the Opium War. It is a revolution that includes politics, economics and culture, and its scale exceeds that of the reforms carried out by Peter the Great and the Meiji Restoration. It will go down in history along with the name of its architect (119–21).

Globalisation and political change

The above deployment of nationalism behind diverse political strategies shows how the debate on the nature of socialism after the Fourteenth

Party Congress involves an unravelling of the patriotic rhetoric of the CCP leadership. This also occurred as academics explored the kind of nationalism that was most appropriate for China in the wake of the collapse of the Soviet Union and the disintegration of Yugoslavia, often using it as a critical tool for persuading the CCP to undertake systemic political reforms. In the process, the concept of globalisation began to be introduced into political debate as a way to argue for certain types of political change.

After the Fourteenth Party Congress, the collapse of other communist states had certainly become a well-established theme for academics to warn the CCP about the pressing need to accompany economic reform with significant political change. This can be seen by the proceedings of a conference on China's modernisation held in April 1994 in Beijing under the auspices of the newly established journal *Strategy and Management*, which brought together many of the country's most influential social scientists. One theme that emerged in the debate was the need for 'ideological regeneration'. As Kang Xiaoguang, a member of the 'National Condition Study Group' at CASS, pointed out, the rapid fall of the CPSU and the Romanian leader Nicolae Ceauşescu showed how a great empire can collapse in a very short period of time if its ideology fails to legitimate political power. For Kang, it was thus important to promote a regeneration of ideology that would allow China to 'stand up in the world of nations' and cure the decadence of the spirit. Allowing everyone to just follow their own feelings in a country of over a billion people, he warned, would lead to the end of the state (Kang 1994: 10–12).

From the perspective of nationalism as a political strategy, it may be possible to view this theme of ideological regeneration as particularly suitable for Chinese academics whose political role is being challenged by the rise of the new technocratic elite. Peking University sociologist Sun Liping (1994) was quite open about this when he located the root of political instability in the nature of a political system in which the power of the leader is unbalanced and policies are determined by a coterie of advisors who spend their time engaged in factional struggles. The solution is to reconstruct a social elite that can mediate between the state and the public as capital flows out from the state sector of the economy. 'Intellectuals', he warns, are thus left facing the choice of moving towards either democracy or nationalism to reconnect with the masses as their own social position is eroded by the rise of a new business elite.

Another theme that was frequently used in the debate on China's modernisation was the need to strengthen the capacity of the state to gather revenue. The most important advocates of this theory are the political economists Wang Shaoguang and Hu Angang, who have forcefully argued that the introduction of market mechanisms has weakened the ability of the state to accrue resources. Rather than being categorised as 'nationalists' within Chinese debates, such figures tend to be seen as members of the 'New Left'. This term, which probably only began to be used in 1994, is again highly problematic. It is useful, however, for distinguishing young, overseas-educated intellectuals from figures like Deng Liqun on the old 'Left' in the debates on the nature of socialism under 'reform and opening'. These younger figures tend to focus on the lack of democratisation and high degree of corruption engendered by the penetration of transnational capital into China and the selling off of nationalised industries. They thus stand in opposition to the 'liberal' faith in the market as the guarantor of individual freedom. Some of them go so far as to advocate a revision of the legacy of Mao Zedong's later years, seeing even the Cultural Revolution as a valid way to resist the resurgence of a class-based society under globalisation. Yet they are different from the old Left in the way that they are influenced by the New Left in the West, especially in the way that they turn to critical theorists like Habermas and the Frankfurt School to critique capitalist culture.

The broader political implications of the sceptical appraisal of economic globalisation by members of the New Left are thus highly complex. For example, an academic like Professor Xiao Gongqin of Shanghai's Fudan University, who took part in the debates on 'neo-authoritarianism' in the late 1980s and early 1990s, echoing the warnings made by Hu Angang and Wang Shaoguang over the softening of the state, has ended up advocating a revival of Confucianism. As an attempt to influence Party thinking, this kind of strategy makes good sense. It neatly fits into the orthodox categorisation of 'broad' (*guang yi*) nationalism that is a 'natural resource' that the state can use to consolidate the community and oppose foreign aggression, as against the 'narrow' (*xia yi*) nationalism that involves separatism and secession. As Xiao points out, Deng Xiaoping himself resorts to combining nationalistic sentiments with socialist modernisation, and slogans like 'one country, two systems' can be seen as a symbol of traditional mainstream culture.

Perhaps the most interesting example of the CCP appeal to tradition cited by Xiao is that of the visit of Li Ruihuan to the tombs of the Yellow Emperor and Yan Emperor in Shaanxi for the Tomb Sweeping Festival in 1994. While Li called the two emperors the 'ancestors of culture' of the Chinese nation, the media went further, explaining how,

'The common ancestors first faced finding a common language, achieved the widest solidarity, then aroused the national spirit, realising the revival of national glory.' Meanwhile, the virtues of a revival of tradition could also be seen at the local and more popular level, as witnessed by the good reception given by the local community and authorities in Heilongjiang province to the promotion by schools of 'Five Hearts Education' based on 'Loyalty to the nation, love for fellow students, love of the family' (Xiao 1994a).[1] For Xiao Gongqin, this kind of 'broad' nationalism can become a spiritual force for the modernisation of the post-developmental state if it is rooted in the mainstream culture that grows from accumulated collective experiences and is like the 'soul' of the nation. Although Confucianism was condemned as 'feudalism' in the 1950s, a forward-looking version could be useful for establishing the legitimacy of the leadership as it tries to reconcile socialist principles with the market and lacks a foreign enemy that can be used to mobilise nationalism.

Others associated with the New Left take quite a different view of the relationship between nationalism and culture. Wang Hui, a critic who wields great influence as the editor of the leading cultural magazine, *Du shu*, points out the irony of an intellectual elite that is attracted to a kind of cultural conservatism by a fashionable interest in foreign concepts such as 'orientalism' and 'Western cultural imperialism' that had originally been used to critique mainstream culture by ethnic minorities in the United States. Whereas the ideas of 'post-colonial culture' and Samuel Huntington's thesis on the 'clash of civilisations' occupy opposed poles of political discourse in the US, he points out, in China they have somehow been combined into one body of thought based on the foundation of native nationalism. Using China's unusually large reserve of nationalism as a force to oppose the outside world is a recipe for big trouble, warns Wang. What China needs, he argues, is to recover values from modern Chinese tradition that are higher than nationalism, such as the pursuit of an equal and peaceful world that is found in the May Fourth Movement and the thought of Sun Yatsen. When asked to be more specific about what the new values should be for China, however, Wang is at a loss, other than to hope that they will not divide the world into 'East' and 'West', 'us' and 'them', given that many human experiences 'know no boundaries of nation or culture' (Wang Hui 1994).

Other academics in this debate address the issue of cultural development in Weberian terms of creating a new 'Protestant ethic' for China, combining the Party line with acceptance of Western influences and a revival of tradition. In this respect, the *ti-yong* tradition is alive and kicking, at least for a writer like Li Fan (1994), who sees 'tradition' as useful for satisfying the 'irrational' (*fei lixing zhuyi*) demands of the people, while the use of Western ideas is necessary for economic management. Yet, ultimately, there is still a democratic message behind such formulae. As Fan points out, only this kind of syncretic ideology can create the conditions for the CCP to change from being a revolutionary party into a governing party that allows the freedom of thought and expression, the expansion of the democratic system, and the establishment of a new policy-making process.

Oblique criticism of the Party line can also be seen in the argument in favour of a 'pragmatic nationalism' (*wushi minzu zhuyi*), which is necessary as China becomes more integrated into the international market and the economic role of the state is limited to ensuring the accumulation of wealth through unfettered exchange (Rong Jingben 1994). That this can be used as a device for mounting an oblique criticism of elements of Jiang Zemin's patriotism can be seen in the way that 'pragmatic nationalism' is contrasted with the parochial nationalism of a dictator like Syngman Rhee in South Korea in the 1950s, who appealed to anti-Japanese sentiment and national unification while neglecting the true causes of economic development and abusing his power for personal profit while maintaining a closed-door policy that suppressed the entrepreneurial spirit (Yin Baoyun 1994). In contrast, when Park Chung Hee came to power, he freed entrepreneurs from suppression by the centralised bureaucracy and used them as a tool to join the international market. He adopted an export-oriented industrialisation strategy that encouraged the population to compete with Japan in the international economy, making nationalism a major force for promoting development. Apart from 'patriotism' (*aiguo zhuyi*), Park's nationalism had no clear ideological content. Shortly after he came to power, he made his bureaucrats learn foreign words like 'budget' and 'efficiency', instead of slogans like 'fight communism', 'political platform' and 'unification'. While officials may not have appeared to be as politically moral as before, in terms of following rules and regulations they respected the national interest and contributed to South Korea's economic take-off.

Perhaps the outer limit of this use of globalisation discourse to hollow out Jiang Zemin's patriotism can be seen in the contribution to the debate on nationalism made by the former advisor to Zhou Enlai and Deng Xiaoping on foreign affairs, Li Shenzhi, who had resigned his post as Deputy Director of CASS in 1989. Li barely disguises his disdain for the parochial elements in Jiang Zemin's thinking, appealing instead to Deng Xiaoping's global vision to refute the argument that

China can challenge US power without jeopardising its own inward investment and wealth creation. For Li, to be truly patriotic is to want to be a key player in shaping the rules of world development. Exploiting the country's rich nationalist resources to pursue the road of chauvinistic nationalism is 'definitely not the road to China's fortune', he warns.

At the other extreme is the younger writer Wang Xiaodong, an editor of *Strategy and Management* who had studied for several years in Japan in the early 1980s. For Wang, Li Shenzhi's positive view of globalisation is highly dangerous because it overlooks the way in which its dynamics are determined by the Western powers and especially by the United States. Rather than see the obstacles to China's engagement in international society as arising from domestic 'conservative forces', he claims, it is better to argue for a national leadership under an 'enlightened nationalism' (*mingzhi de minzu zhuyi*). The fact that nationalists had won a majority in the December 1993 Russian parliamentary elections had shown that a great nation cannot be humiliated without a protest. Echoing the vision found in the *Third Eye*, Wang concludes that the emergence of an enlightened nationalist who can preserve the nation's interests and stop the masses looking to 'extreme nationalism' for simple answers has become imperative for China (Wang/Shi, 1994).

These debates that took place before the 1995–6 Taiwan Strait crisis thus illustrate how themes associated with nationalism and globalisation can be deployed behind a large array of political strategies. The spectrum stretches from Li Shenzhi's appeal to globalisation as a way to argue against a defiant nationalism that will jeopardise the reform process, to Wang Xiaodong's insistence that globalisation makes a stronger sense of nationalism essential for China's survival. In this respect, Wang Xiaoding is certainly right when he points out that no fully formed ideology is shared by the intellectuals who are commonly lumped together as 'nationalists', advocating as they do a range of solutions to China's problems ranging from authoritarianism, democracy, government intervention, complete liberalisaton of the market, a return to a tradition and a rejection of tradition (Wang 1999: 132).

Within this range, Wang Xiaodong himself is probably the most radical thinker because he does not draw back from approving of the patriotic elements of the Party line that ultimately led to a more defiant attitude towards the United States. Moreover, out of all the thinkers taking part in the *Strategy and Management* debate, he is the only one who sees nationalism as an end in itself. Even when he goes on in later works to argue that a strong nationalism is the precondition for building democracy in China, he remains somewhat less than convincing because he spends far more time on excoriating 'liberals' who see globalisation, the market and the importation of Western models as the solution for China's social ills (Fang and Wang 1999; Wang 2005). Perhaps most significant of all is that Wang may be the most sensitive to changes taking place in popular political culture before the Taiwan crisis, given that one of his jobs was to take opinion polls for the newspaper *China Youth Daily*. A survey of international security in East Asia by the Director of the Second Division of the Department of Strategic Studies at the Academy of Military Science that was published in the first issue of *Strategy and Management* does not even mention the issue of Taiwan (Tian 1993).

China Can Say No

The train of events that culminated in a stand-off between the United States and PRC navies in the run-up to Taiwan's March 1996 presidential election, however, brought the linkage between national unification and CCP legitimacy that Deng Xiaoping had established in January 1980 to the fore of discussion amongst sections of the urban population. This was facilitated in large part by the way in which the views of previously unknown writers were brought to the attention of the wider public through an expanding, commercialised publishing industry. The most sensational work to be produced at this time was the best-selling collection of essays that appeared under the title *China Can Say No* (Song *et al.* 1996), authored by a number of writers whose formative experiences were mainly in the 1980s. Public attention was also gripped by the publication of *Behind the Demonization of China* (Li *et al.* 1996), produced by eight graduates of top Chinese universities who had either been awarded doctorates in the United States or were in the process of studying for them. This sets out to correct misunderstandings of the United States by describing the way in which its government, media and academia work together to construct a thoroughly evil portrait of China.

Both of these works have taken on a strong significance in the narrative of the rise of 'popular nationalism' in the 1990s due to the new and open defiance they display towards the United States. While *Behind the Demonization of China* makes for interesting reading, it is also significant for the way in which it presents solid evidence that foreign travel is as likely to lead to a sense of festering resentment as it is to a cosmopolitan outlook. Within China's domestic discourse on nationalism and globalisation, however, *China Can Say No* is more significant for what it has to say about the fundamental lack of confidence in China's ability to be a major power that goes back for over a century. While the text was viewed with alarm outside China due to the defiance and disgust it expresses towards the United States, Japan and even the United Kingdom, its domestic message is more significant for the way in which most of its contributors accept that their country is only at the beginning of its possible climb to world power and feel that it is being held back as much by attitudes inside China as by foreign forces. As one of the authors puts it, before the Chinese can say 'no' to America they have to learn how to say 'no' to themselves about slavishly following all things foreign (Song Qiang).

Another contributor, Tang Zhengyu, expresses views that share much in common with the defiance of Wang Xiaodong, complaining about the lack of self-confidence symbolised by the proliferation in Chinese streets of phenomena such as signs advertising 'China's Long Island' and the 'Manhattan of the East'. Like Wang, though, Tang also links nationalism with democracy, arguing that remedying this situation will require not just maintaining economic growth but also the building of a strong civic consciousness for the Chinese nation. In making this argument, Tang also rejects 'extreme nationalism' in favour of adopting the kind of measures used by Canada and France to defend themselves against the hegemony of Hollywood, such as taxing the consumption of American culture to provide funds to subsidise native arts and imposing quotas on the dissemination of American (and English) culture. The ambiguity within this thinking is revealed, however, when Tang then describes Chinese solidarity in terms of the story of the African ants that can only cross a river by rolling into a ball and sacrificing themselves for the survival of the colony.

That the articulation of nationalism in this text is far more ambiguous than has been portrayed in much of the secondary literature is illustrated above all by the chapter by Gu Qingsheng, who rejects the idea that the Chinese are imprisoned by a 'post-colonial culture' and argues for mixing the best of all cultures available. Wearing a tie, banning smoking in public places, local elections and economic reforms are all as acceptable as going to a neighbour's house to learn how to make dumplings. In other words, international contact for the sake of reform and modernisation does not fall under the rubric of cultural colonisation. For Gu, again, the roots of China's problems lie in the Chinese psyche, and the need to believe that the Chinese are not inferior to other peoples, only that they started out a little later on the road to development. For the present, there is no need to combine the ideas of two thousand years ago with those of the present and future, and no need to adopt the *River Elegy* terminology of 'blue' (outgoing, oceanic) versus 'yellow' (land-locked) cultures. What is important for Gu is to step out into the world with confidence. After all, Americans and Europeans are bound to be presented with a warped vision of China when the Chinese present themselves to the world as a museum piece rather than as a modern state based on a system of law and order. Yet, as with most of the authors, this openness is still wrought with ambiguity when Gu devotes an entire chapter to explaining why people should not fly in Boeing 777s.

A complete reading of *China Can Say No* that does not just focus on its anti-American content thus reveals how the authors try to break away from the increasingly sterile dichotomies of independence versus development, national pride versus self-strengthening, 'essence' (*ti*) versus 'function' (*yong*), and tradition versus modernisation that have bedevilled Chinese political thought for over a century. Ultimately they fail in this endeavour, tending to fall back on crudely xenophobic themes that make for saleable material in a mass market that has been shaped by years of patriotic education.

This growing market for a defiant kind of nationalism presents a difficult situation for a government and ruling party that has made the embrace of globalisation a central principle of its policy-making. Despite the efforts made by Beijing and Washington to repair their relationship after the Taiwan Strait crisis, the Chinese population was becoming better informed about foreign policy issues. As the structure of the culture industry was transformed by the embrace of globalisation, there was increasing evidence to support the growing wariness towards the complexity of the relationship between cultural change and nationalism shown by the New Left.

The liberal dilemma

The way in which the Taiwan crisis of 1995–6 and the Indonesian atrocities of 1998 gave a new poignancy to the debates on nationalism and globalisation proved to be highly problematic for those who were attempting to present the Party line in a way that emphasised the embrace of globalisation as a generally benign force for China and that the priority in foreign policy should be maintaining good relations with the United States. This message had been developed at great length in 1996 by a team of young social scientists at CASS, who produced a book-length commentary on Jiang Zemin's September 1995 speech on the twelve major relationships (Jiang 1995a), which they presented as a personal appeal for a radical movement towards the market, under the title *Heart to Heart Talks with the General Secretary* (Chu *et al.* 1996). According to their narrative of the collapse of the communist bloc, the travails of the Soviet Union could be traced to the sclerosis that set in when Leonid Brezhnev back-tracked on the implementation of managerial reforms in favour of ensuring stability. Standing at the critical juncture of choosing between more reforms or ensuring social stability, they urged Jiang Zemin to emulate Mao Zedong's ability to take decisive action, as when he went against all caution and ordered his forces to cross the Yangtze to defeat the ROC forces in the civil war. This was better than following the model of the King of Chu who has been excoriated by history for accepting to restrain his forces along the river that separated his kingdom from the kingdom of Han. Now Jiang was facing the test of whether he would advance or retreat (17–22).

Acknowledging the warnings of figures like Wang Shan and the political economist Hu Angang that the reforms could lead to the kind of collapse of the state that occurred in Yugoslavia, they rejoin by reiterating Deng Xiaoping's argument that such a fate can only be avoided by continuing to raise economic prosperity. Rather than increasing the capacity of the state to collect government revenue, the kind of liberal policy used around the world since the era of Ronald Reagan and Margaret Thatcher should be adopted, part of which involves making government more efficient by reducing the scope of its operations and the number of civil servants, what the CASS team call 'elite troops reducing the government' (*jingbing jian zheng*). As they point out, when the federal government runs into financial trouble in the United States, part of the solution is to cut the White House staff and even suspend the work of some government offices (155–62). The Thatcherite model of privatisation should be followed when it comes to solving the problem of the SOEs (132).

As an attempt to promote the liberal economic agenda, *Heart to Heart Talks* is far more constrained than Fan Liqin's text when it talks about international relations. Yet it does still deploy foreign policy and unification policy to promote the movement towards the market. This can be seen when the authors argue that speeding up the reforms is the best way to defeat the scepticism of Westerners who are bent on the 'peaceful evolution' and 'containment' of China. Among the strategies that will benefit from the reforms is Taiwan policy, because China's leaders will no longer be in the humiliating position of having to thank their Western counterparts for upholding the 'one China policy' every time they meet them (27).

The vision of Chinese identity in this work is also somewhat similar to that found in Wang Shan, insofar as it is based on the syncretic metaphor of a tree which has Chinese tradition as its roots, Marxism-Mao Zedong Thought, and Deng Xiaoping's theory of building social-ism with Chinese characteristics as its branches, the absorption of the advanced cultures of the nations of the world as the leaves, and 'China's new socialist culture' as the fruit (242). In a somewhat more benign vein than Wang Shan's Social Darwinist vision of progress through competition, however, the authors deal with the issue of main-taining China's identity by citing Bertrand Russell's proposition that historical progress comes from the interaction between cultures. As Mao Zedong had stated, the most advanced Chinese people were those figures who had introduced foreign cultures, from the Qing reformer Liang Qichao to Sun Yatsen. Even Marx and Engels had described how the spread of the market had created a world system in which barriers between nations had been broken down (246–7).

After *Heart to Heart Talks*, the next most systematic liberal attempt to tackle the rise of popular nationalism head-on is the book *Outcry: Five Voices of Contemporary China*, authored by Lin Zhijun and Ma Licheng (1999). Given that both these authors worked for the *People's Daily*, it is fair to call them 'establishment intellectuals'. They had already established their credentials earlier in 1998 by elaborating a version of political history since 1978 under the title *Crossed Swords*, which presents the period of reform and opening as a victory over 'leftists' through the winning of three 'Thought Liberation' campaigns, namely the 1978 campaign against Hua Guofeng, Deng Xiaoping's 1992 Southern Tour, and victory in the debate over public versus private ownership that was consolidated at the Fifteenth Party Congress. It is also interesting to note that Lin and Ma locate themselves in China's modernist tradition by using the term *Outcry*, the title of the first modern/revolutionary text in Chinese literature by the revered dramatist Lu Xun.

Of direct relevance to the development of nationalist discourse is the way in which a section of *Outcry* is devoted to a critique of nation-alism as one of the five main voices of Chinese politics. This is treated in much the same way as the voices of 'dogmatism' (read 'leftism), 'feudalism' and misguided ideas about 'democracy' as being in conflict with the 'mainstream' orthodoxy. Setting themselves in the context of supporting the line of the Party leadership established by Deng Xiaoping and Jiang Zemin, Lin and Ma can thus point with enthusi-asm to the revival of US–PRC relations since the Taiwan Strait crisis and the establishment of a 'strategic partnership' between the two countries. This is in line with Deng Xiaoping's emphasis on restoring relations with the United States after Tiananmen, they point out, and the securing of the 'three nos' statement from President Clinton shows the benefits that have already been accrued. Lin and Ma are also scathing about the over-inflated pride in the rise of Asia and Asian values that can be found in *China Can Say No* and *Demonizing China*. In this respect, they contrast the suffering of ethnic Chinese women and property in Indonesia after the fall of the Suharto regime and the legalised discrimination against ethnic Chinese there with the relative security for Chinese working in the United States, who can even become state governors and university presidents (234).

Lin and Ma are careful to accept that the *China Can Say No* phenomenon is understandable in the context of the Taiwan Strait crisis and to agree that the military exercises by the PLA at that time showed that the Chinese were prepared to make great sacrifices to defend the 'one China' policy and oppose Taiwanese independence. However, they argue that this should not obscure the fact that the kind of anti-American views peddled by the authors of *China Can Say No* are ill-informed and irrational. The kind of popular anti-Americanism that refuses to buy McDonald's hamburgers fails to understand the benefits that foreign investment brings to China. There are, moreover, more Chinese restaurants in America than there are Macdonald's outlets in China they point out. The charge made in *China Can Say No* that the SEZs have become similar to the foreign concessions in old Shanghai is rebutted by the observation that many industries have been saved or created by foreign investment. The claims made about the economic decline of the United States in *China Can Say No*, moreover, are not well founded and the authors exaggerate the importance of those in Washington politics who advocate containing China. Even authors who do have direct experience of living, studying and working in the United States, like those who critique the negative portrayal of China in the American media in *Behind the Demonization of China*, fail to understand that US China policy is the outcome of complex interactions between different interest groups and not a simple conspiracy. While it is reasonable to criticise the American media and academics for misunderstanding China, such authors should know that everyone gets treated like that in the United States, even the President. As for the broadside launched against Hollywood culture in *China Can Say No*, the Fu Manchu syndrome, and accusations that even Bruce Lee is portrayed as intimidated by the opposite sex, the production of Mulan and its favourable criticism in the Chinese press should also be taken into account (219–35).

Within the broader context of Chinese domestic politics, though, the target for Lin and Ma's criticism of nationalism is the 'Left'. They thus portray products such as *China Can Say No* and *Demonizing China* as symptomatic of an alliance of nationalism and leftism which is creating the biggest obstacle to China's opening up and movement towards the world. If the advice of such factions to defy the United States with military force and heroic sacrifice had been followed, they argue, the outcome would have been war. As with Fan Liqin, Lin and Ma cannot accept a class-based vision of international politics, and deploy Deng Xiaoping's 1990 statement that ideological struggle should not play a role in relations with the big powers (Deng 1993s), rebutting claims made about the capitalist class driving American hegemony that are made in *Demonizing China*. They discredit such talk by associating it with the 'proletarian revolutionary diplomatic line' of the Cultural Revolution (229–34).

The misfortune for the authors of *Outcry* is that they finished their manuscript in December 1998,[2] when the linkages between domestic politics and foreign policy were already proving increasingly difficult for both Washington and Beijing to handle. By the time the book had been circulated, the deterioration of relations with Taiwan, Japan and the United States that characterised 1999 did not make for a receptive audience. As the Party leadership attempted to divert nationalistic fervour into support for their own elitist brand of patriotism, only the boldest and most senior figures were able to express their concerns. Most notable in this respect is the trenchant criticism of the ostentatious celebrations to mark the fiftieth anniversary of the establishment of the PRC that was produced in an essay by the 76-year-old Li Shenzhi (1999).

Looking back over all the tenth anniversaries of the founding of the PRC that had taken place since 1949, Li recalled how, as a 26-year-old man, he had been overcome with emotion and unable to find words to express his joyous optimism when Mao had taken the podium in Tiananmen Square. Nobody could have imagined the purges that were to follow. On the tenth and twentieth anniversaries of National Day, Li had himself been suffering 're-education through labour', having been labelled a 'bourgeois Rightist'. On the thirtieth anniversary, in 1979, there had been no celebrations. During the fortieth anniversary, in 1989, Beijing had been under martial law. Now, in 1999, the scale of the parade could only be rivalled by Kim Jong Il in North Korea, given that Hitler and Stalin were dead. As the slogans and media explained, the past fifty years had been the story of one victory after another. Nothing was said about how Mao had turned into a dictator, turned on his own party, about the persecutions and purges, the Great Leap Forward or the Cultural Revolution.

Instead of using this occasion to reassess the past and re-establish the legitimacy of the Party, the leaders had denied the people their collective memory and ability for rational thought by closing the archives and forbidding research. If Japan was to be castigated for refusing to admit to its wartime aggression and atrocities, pointed out Li, shouldn't the Chinese be shamed even more for the mistakes they have committed against their own people? Yet instead of an appropriate retrospective, this National Day festival had seen an exaggeration of China's national power and international influence. Repeating the views he had expressed in his clash with Wang Xiaodong in 1994, Li pointed out that the development of this kind of extreme nationalism in a world of globalisation is extremely dangerous, adding that China's nationalist passions should have been satisfied when the PRC took its seat on the UN Security Council.

If this tenth anniversary of the Tiananmen Massacre had been used as an opportunity to address the plight of the victims, asserted Li, then the faith of the country could have been restored, a new foundation for the reforms established and China's international standing raised. Yet instead of heeding incidents such as the demonstration by the Falungong religious movement in Beijing and the attack on the United States Embassy after the Belgrade Incident as signs that the control of the Party is slipping and its mandate was being lost, the leadership had resorted to a Mao-style cult of the individual. The original aims of the May Fourth Movement to bring science and democracy and liberation of the individual to China had still not been achieved.

Li thus urged Jiang to use his last years in power to move towards democracy. Just as Deng could break his own Four Cardinal Principles during the Southern Tour by announcing that socialism could use the market if capitalism could, Jiang should announce that socialism can use parliamentary democracy if capitalism can. Jiang likes to quote Sun Yatsen's saying that 'The world tide is surging ahead, if you ride it you will prosper, if you fight it you will perish'. Now, however, the world tide is globalisation, the market economy, democracy and improving human rights.

The following month saw the publication of *China's Road under the Shadow of Globalization*, co-authored by Li Shenzhi's nemesis, Wang Xiaodong and Fang Ning. Following the appearance of popular works like *China Can Say No* since the Taiwan Strait crisis, and following so soon after the Belgrade Incident, many of the themes in Wang's earlier texts had become developed to a more extreme degree. What used to be a measured criticism of 'liberals' like Li Shenzhi who look to the West for answers to China's problems had become a torrent of abuse. The producers of *River Elegy* are even condemned as preachers of a kind of 'reverse racism' that puts them on the same level as anxious Italians before the rise of fascism. The criticism of the United States is unrelenting, and the vision of a world in which conflict between nations is determined by a combination of racism and the struggle for economic resources is also more developed.

Yet there is also something new about the way that Wang orientates his ideas towards the changing orthodoxy of the Party leadership. The first inkling of this can be seen when Wang warns that the intention of NATO in bombing the Chinese Embassy in Belgrade is to weaken the Chinese government by making it lose face in the eyes of an angry population when they see it does not have the power to react (Fang and Wang 1999: 6). Of more significance for the use of nationalism as a political strategy in Chinese politics is the way in which Wang focuses so much of what he has to say on discrediting 'liberals' by reproducing some of the well-established strategies of nationalist discourse coined by Deng Xiaoping and appropriated by Jiang Zemin. 'Nationalists', for example, are proclaimed as China's true democrats because, unlike 'liberals', they properly understand the relationship between 'national sovereignty' and 'human rights'. Such a view is clearly derived from the argument that there can be no human rights without state rights that appears in the third volume of Deng's selected works. Similarly, Wang's definition of 'nationalism' is ultimately dependent on the way in which he distinguishes it from the arguments of 'liberals'. These 'liberals' have little in common other than the fact that they are accused of denigrating Chinese culture, a categorisation that can be found at least as early as Deng's 1979 speech on the 'Four Cardinal Principles', which signalled the end of the Beijing Spring Democracy Wall movement.

Wang's vision for the future of China is also compatible with the emerging Party line, insofar as he hopes that China will maintain stability and smoothly realise political reforms so that the state will have more power to deal with corruption, social disorder and inequality at home, and to modernise in a way that will allow China to enter the stage of advanced technology. In foreign affairs, it will have sufficient power to preserve the national interest and will use its power to effectively promote world peace and development. This is contrasted with less desirable scenarios that will prevent the building of a 'strong state', including a weakening of the state through the failure to deal with problems of corruption and social order, the dispersal of economic power, and Soviet and Yugoslav-style disintegration (100–101).

Wang's preference is not really distinguishable from the rhetoric of the leadership. Yet it provides a useful vision under which he can categorise as 'nationalism' a whole range of what he believes to be desirable political forces, ranging from statism and neo-conservatism to democracy. Yet within the broader context of Wang's argument, the real criterion that brings commonality to such themes is that they are distinguishable from the kind of 'liberalism' advocated by Li Shenzhi, to which Wang attributes no special characteristics other than a kind of 'reverse racism' which denigrates all things Chinese and wants to emulate all things Western.

The genius of Wang's argument is thus that he allows democracy to be appropriated by his brand of nationalism, which is becoming increasingly indistinguishable from the Party orthodoxy. The key difference between this and the kind of liberalism advocated by Li Shenzhi is that it places the highest value on nationalism by making democracy merely the best way to build a strong state. As Wang explains, it is the idea of 'building a great China' that motivates China's nationalists to promote democracy more strongly than other people, and the problem is one of how to achieve this scenario without disintegration: 'In this respect, the work of the "nationalists" among China's intellectuals is constructive and thus most likely to be China's future direction' (Fang and Wang 1999: 104–5).

As Wang later elucidated during a lecture at the London School of Economics, democracy is not the issue that distinguishes nationalists from 'liberals'. The real difference is over their respective views of the international system, where Wang sees that liberals fail to grasp the priority of national interests, leading them to stand on the side of the United States when there is a conflict with China. Nationalists, however, are prudent enough to realise that the structure of the international system gives the United States a kind of dictatorial power. Even Deng Xiaoping, it can be pointed out, was wary of American intentions, arguing that the Chinese should 'conceal our abilities and bide our time'. While some nationalists and members of the New Left had been critical of Deng's strategy of putting economic development before building national defence and locating China in the downstream of the international division of labour, his true ideal was to have a wealthy country and strong army, eventually becoming a world power, an ambition that has existed since the Opium War with Britain, regardless of party or belief. Only after the Cultural Revolution did China's elite become divided. But, according to Wang, there is now plenty of evidence to suggest that the post-Cultural Revolution generation do not harbour the resentment that the older elite have towards their own country and will return to the old goals again.

The appropriation of democracy as a theme for nationalist discourse is thus complete, along with technology and authoritarianism. In this respect, when Wang describes nationalism as China's 'sword and shield', this is a truly ingenious play on the Chinese pictogram for 'contradiction', in which these two concepts are combined (Wang in Fang *et al.* 1999: 101). Just as the contradictory themes of the 1990s are brought together under nationalism, Wang makes himself a nationalist icon by locating himself within the discourse that calls for all to 'build socialism with Chinese characteristics'. In the process, the wind is stolen from the attempt to appropriate 'Deng Xiaoping Theory' on the side of 'liberalism' as found in Li Shenzhi. Wang's presentation of nationalism as the true form of democracy (insofar as it embraces the entire nation in the global struggle for technological supremacy) is tailored to fit increasingly comfortably with the official discourse as the new ideological dispensation of the 'Three Represents' emerges and is finally consolidated within the Party line at the CCP's Sixteenth National Congress in November 2002.

Wang's views have thus become increasingly hard to distinguish from Party orthodoxy (Wang 2005). He sees Deng Xiaoping's strategy of 'biding time' until China can move to the high-technology stage of development as risky but reasonable. It is hard to see how his own prescription to use China's national power 'to advance to high-tech development in an unconventional way' is any different from the belief in technological leapfrogging that is expressed under Jiang Zemin's leadership and central to the Three Represents. Wang places more faith in technological solutions than political answers when it comes to solving some of the specific problems of globalisation, such as environmental degradation, although he is prepared to accept the need for a system of global governance that is seen to be fair by a majority of people when technology is unable to solve such problems. As for the widening wealth gap under globalisation, he confines himself to saying that society needs to be able to guarantee a certain standard of living for every person, for all to have full degree of freedom, and for all to use their abilities to the full. As for how to create this kind of society, nationalism remains the key to building a democratic system, rather than vice-versa, while returning to the road of Mao Zedong will remain just an option in the mouths of some disadvantaged minorities and intellectuals so long as economic development continues. As for those peasants on low incomes, they will pragmatically come to the cities to labour in order to improve their lives.

For Wang, with China 'on the express train to globalization', no anti-globalisation movement can form like that in Latin America, or even like those in Europe and the United States. Although incomes are comparatively low, most Chinese people do not feel the need to be dissatisfied with the globalising world order and are content to maintain their present attitude of patiently working and biding their time to greatly improve their lives. This means that they lack sympathy with the problems of the Third World. According to Wang, China's development actually benefits the Third World states anyway, because it raises the price of the commodities and goods they export. Moreover, if China grows more powerful, then the Third World will be able to turn to it to seek support when the United States behaves badly. A balance of power can thus be created which will be beneficial for the democratisation of the structure of international politics, with China eventually having enough economic and political power to manage issues of development that affect the Third World (Wang 2005).

The WTO: contradictions among the people

It was argued at the beginning of this work that the dynamics of the discourse on nationalism and globalisation under 'reform and opening' were established in the late 1970s and early 1980s. This is when Deng Xiaoping used patriotism to establish a linkage between certain areas of policy-making, namely economic development, unification policy and foreign policy. In the decades that followed, political elites had to deploy these linkages to promote certain strategies. This can still be seen in Jiang Zemin's final work report to the Sixteenth Party Congress in November 2002 (Jiang 2002). While the economic aspects of this are concerned with an explanation of the techno-nationalism of the Three Represents, he also devotes an entire section of the speech to national unification, and asserts that the CCP monopoly on political power is still needed to protect the nation by promoting multipolarity and shielding it from the negative forces of globalisation while harnessing its positive aspect behind the project of building 'socialism with Chinese characteristics'. While Jiang accepts that transnational problems of economic integration, the environment, international terrorism and arms proliferation force relations between states to be more constructive, the corollary of this is that states need to be stronger.

Yet in none of these three areas of policy-making has nationalism proven able to resolve the political tensions that arise under 'reform and opening'. In unification policy, Beijing's predicament was all too clearly revealed in the run-up to Taiwan's 2000 presidential election. In Beijing's propaganda campaign against the opposition candidate, Chen Shui-bian, the State Council issued a White Paper that warned that continuing to postpone negotiations on unification could be taken as a reason to use force against the island (Taiwan Affairs Office 2000: 17). When Premier Zhu Rongji was asked about the coming election by the press, he shook his fist and raised his voice in anger, stating 'We trust that our Taiwan compatriots will make a sensible choice', adding that if they did not, they might not 'get another opportunity'. The consequent anger in Taiwan allowed Chen Shui-bian to win the election by the smallest of margins.

In foreign policy, the way that the Chinese leadership was handling the relationship with the United States was put under the domestic spotlight again after the downing of a United States' reconnaissance aircraft on 1 April 2001. 'Put the crew on trial – execute their commander!' was typical of the emotional outpouring on the Internet, and the possibility of war with the United States was raised. The criticism of the government's patriotic credentials was summed up by a message that read, 'Little Japan invades and *they* call it "entering", the US invades and *we* call it "entering"', comparing the official wording with that used by the Japanese to white-wash their invasion of China in the 1930s.

At the centre of the leadership's predicament, however, is a growing discontent over the social dislocation caused by the deepening of market-based reforms and entry to the international economy under WTO membership. It is easy to see why one commentator on the New Left should point out that the use of the term 'liberal' is problematic, given that it has been displaced by 'neo-conservatism' since the era of Reagan and Thatcher (Gan Yang 2003). The advocates of a 'liberal' agenda in China thus face increasingly difficult dilemmas when presented with alternative arguments about the nature of globalisation. While most of the 'intellectuals' who took part in the debates on nationalism before the Taiwan Strait crisis tended to view the *China Can Say No* phenomenon with a degree of disdain, they have found it increasingly difficult to accept a benign view of globalisation. When, in 1997, Wang Hui published a seminal article of the New Left under the title 'Problems Concerning Contemporary China's Ideological Situation and the Nature of Modernisation', he thus spent most of his time criticising 'liberals' and 'neo-Marxists' alike for failing to take their political and economic analysis beyond the nation-state and to grasp the full significance of globalisation. All such schools of thought, he complained, will become redundant if they expect constitutional reforms to balance the alliance between international and domestic capital and fail to see how the realism of Western international relations perpetuates global inequality and replicates it at the domestic level (Wang 2003).

Wang Hui's conception of globalisation also shows an important development for nationalist discourse in China because it identifies the way in which states are becoming stronger as the facilitators of international transactions. According to this view, ensuring that economic liberalisation is balanced by some kind of democracy is thus highly complex, especially when the traditional role of 'intellectuals' as the guardians of social propriety has been transformed as they are expected to professionalise and commodify their role. With the state sector accounting for only around 30 per cent of the economy, moreover, it makes little sense to talk about China's social problems as problems of socialism or to talk in terms of dichotomies of reformers/conservatives, the West/China, capitalism/socialism, the market/planning. Instead, it is necessary to clarify that modernisation is not a technical issue but must be underpinned by a system of values. For Mao Zedong, egalitarianism provided a clear set of values that enabled the mobilisation of society and allowed fundamental historical problems to be solved, such as increasing the revenue of the central state through collectivisation. In this respect, Mao's 'modernist anti-modernism' was like that of the late Qing reformers.

Ultimately, for Wang Hui, China's socialism contains a form of anti-modernism which has to be superseded. Even post-colonialism, he points out, has become a form of nationalism in China that has departed a long way from its original radical critique of the nation-state in the West. While it is fashionable for Chinese intellectuals to criticise Eurocentricy in the West, it is still impossible to find anybody who applies a post-colonial critique to China itself by examining the nature of Han-centrism or sinocentricity. Postmodernism, too, has failed to analyse the relationship between capital and China's socialist reforms. Instead, it is used as a political strategy by alienated intellectuals in the academies to boost their own status by claiming that they are defending popular culture against the market in the name of building the 'socialist market with Chinese characteristics'. In the meantime, neo-Marxists who discuss the commodification of culture under the influence of leftist thinkers in the United States and Europe fail to take into account the existing domination of the media by the state in China.

The hope of many intellectuals that the market will solve China's democratic problems is thus a form of naivety, according to Wang Hui.

What they should be doing is looking at the relationships between the production of mass culture and domestic and international capital. Moreover, those who pin their hopes on the emergence of civil society overlook phenomena such as the merging of the economic and political elites, as represented by the princelings, and their further involvement with the activity of international capital.

Texts such as *Modernization's Pitfall*, by the investigative journalist and Fudan University economics graduate He Qinglian, provide alternative empirical accounts of how the new moneyed, technical and intellectual elite are rising out of the rampant corruption generated by the sale of the SOEs and transforming the class structure of Chinese society. Rather than a middle class emerging to enhance social stability, a pyramidal social structure is said to be developing, akin to that found in Latin America or countries such as Thailand and the Philippines, with a small minority dominating a huge mass of depressed or marginalised strata. Urban landscapes are increasingly characterised by wealthy neighbourhoods often guarded by state-of-the-art security systems, special stores sell high-fashion items to the rich, and class conflict is manifested in terrorist incidents, physical attacks on the rich, stoppages and the sabotage of SOEs.

In March 2000, He Qinglian published a condensed version of her journalistic exposures of corruption and social transformation in a journal article under the title 'China's Listing Social Structure'. She was particularly sceptical about the impact of WTO entry on social stability. Pointing out that membership had not reduced corruption in Latin American and Southeast Asian states, and that American multinationals would soon learn to play by the local rules of the game, she argued that only those who possessed the right kind of knowledge and connections to be useful in a market economy would benefit from the new opportunities, as will richer provinces with adequate resources and capital. The political elite will cooperate with foreign capital, while the intellectual elite will become further divided. Sectors of the economy that have little chance of forming joint ventures with foreign capital will risk being wiped out by competition with multinationals, and small and medium-sized firms that have been kept in business by a high level of public commissions will probably be discarded. In the absence of any policies to balance these consequences, the general result will be further enrichment of the upper class and greater marginalisation of the middle and lower classes. An entirely new social movement that could completely reform ideas and institutions is thus needed to solve China's new problems.

As soon as He's article was published, it was denounced by the Propaganda Department of the Central Committee of the CCP as a 'liberal' document, and all mention of her works was banned. After being placed under domestic surveillance, she sought refuge in the United States. The discourse on nationalism and globalisation thus remains both sensitive and central within the ideological dispensation inherited by the leadership established under the new CCP General Secretary Hu Jintao after the Sixteenth Party Congress.

The fate of He Qinglian is somewhat ironic, given that many of the problems she raises were also being voiced in both academic and Party publications as WTO accession approached. In fact, at almost the same time as 'China's Listing Social Structure' appeared in print, academics at the Institute of World Economics and Politics at CASS issued a detailed sector-by-sector analysis of the impact of WTO entry which contains some startling forecasts (Yu *et al.* 2000). In agriculture alone, 10 million workers would have to be found work in other sectors. In the year 2000, some 7 million workers would lose their jobs in the SOEs and have to survive on an average of RMB170 per month. With the social security system far from complete, supporting these people would place a significant strain on the national finances. Moreover, the wealth gap between town and country would grow and have a negative impact on social stability, as rural incomes would fall by 2.1 per cent over the coming five years, while urban incomes would rise by 4.6 per cent (5–6).

This kind of report is permissible, however. It is even headed with an inscription by none other than Li Tieying, proclaiming that 'Entry into the WTO is the result of our country's unceasing deepening of reform and opening, and the strengthening of our comprehensive national power and raising of our international status'. The reason for this is that its negative findings are couched in an upbeat assessment of the positive impacts on economic efficiency through exposure and access to the foreign markets, as well as the breaking down of domestic provincial monopolies and protectionism. All of this will contribute to the development of 'comprehensive national power' and bringing Taiwan and Hong Kong closer to the embrace of the mainland. WTO entry can thus be presented as part of China's strategy of 'economic independence'. Unlike small states, such as Singapore, China's size means that depending on multinational firms and investment to develop its economy will incur unacceptably high costs. China will thus use the WTO to manage foreign investment and trade in a way that can cultivate the growth of national industries (*minzu qiye*). Foreign investment will be limited if it is detrimental to indigenous industries and multinational firms will be chosen as partners only if they facilitate the development of indigenous firms (577–80).

An even clearer indication of the strategy towards globalization developed under Jiang Zemin is the lengthy *China Investigation Report 2000–2001: Studies of Contradictions Among the People Under New Conditions* (CC 2001). Published by the Central Committee Organisation Department in May 2001, this document surveys the impact of the reform process on a range of economic, ethnic and religious issues across 11 provinces. Despite the fact that it was rapidly withdrawn from sale, it drew a lot of attention due to its discussion of the widespread pattern of collective protests and incidents sweeping the country, some of which involve tens of thousands of participants, as well as the rising tension between party officials and the masses as popular anger grows over inequality, corruption and aloofness. Moreover, it predicts that plans to speed up the opening of China's markets to foreign trade and investment will probably generate more social conflict, acknowledging that entry into the World Trade Organization may bring growing dangers and pressures, and it that in the ensuing period the number of group incidents might jump, severely harming social stability and even disturbing the smooth implementation of reform and opening up.

The department that produced this report is headed by Zeng Qinhong, an adviser to Jiang Zemin. There was speculation at the time that this report represented an attempt by Zeng to set a reform-oriented agenda for Party deliberations and the leadership changes expected in the next few years. The mystery surrounding the appearance of such a sombre analysis was only deepened by the way in which the report was rapidly withdrawn from sale by the Central Compilation and Translation Press office on the day of its release, after only a small number of copies had been purchased. The function of the document, however, can best be clarified by the way it insists that all of the problems spreading across Chinese society can be solved through the application of Jiang Zemin's ideology of the 'Three Represents'. The 61-page introduction is thus dedicated to a detailed explanation of the origins and meaning of the Three Represents, which is presented as the culmination of the Party's narrative of national salvation.

In this respect, the document can be seen as an attempt by Zeng Qinhong to establish his credentials as the guardian of the 'Three Represents', as Jiang Zemin's term as CCP General Secretary was drawing to an end with the approach of the Sixteenth Party Congress. Just as Jiang himself had to deal with the unresolved problems generated by the 'reform and opening' of the 1980s, his successors would have to deal with the same problems but magnified by the deepening of the reform process and entry into the WTO, in order to take advantage of the globalisation that they insist is structuring the world economy.

Like nationalism, then, the processes of globalisation can be used in Chinese political discourse to further a number of variant political strategies, ranging from He Qinglian's call for new social movements to balance the rise of the new social elite, to Zeng Qinhong's justification of the consolidation of its political status in Jiang Zemin's ideology of the Three Represents. In this respect, the techno-nationalism of the Three Represents offers the possibility for a new elite consensus for those who are prepared to accept it. That this consensus remains fragile even amongst China's up-and-coming elite is indicated by the way in which the staging of the country's first New Left drama, the story of Che Guevara, in Beijing in May 2000, proved to be a great hit with university students. Some travelled long distances to see it and were reduced to tears. They saw Guevara as representing a spiritual and cultural force and a new kind of value when faced by an increasingly unequal society. Its sights were clearly on globalisation and government policy when the play's characters sarcastically referred to the WTO as 'the locomotive of wealth', 'the immigration application form for the old world' (Xiao 2003: 414–15).

The new consensus of the Three Represents is, however, compatible with many of the views of a member of the rising nationalist intelligentsia like Wang Xiaodong. In the meantime, the 'liberal' Li Shenzhi died of pneumonia in April 2003, probably worsened by the way in which the central heating in Beijing is switched off on 15 March, even though the temperature often drops below freezing after this date. He Qinglian has gone into exile in the United States. Yet the optimism of those on the ascent is only possible when the fundamental problems in the three areas of policy-making marked by Deng Xiaoping as fundamental tasks for the CCP are glossed over after two decades of 'reform and opening', namely economic construction, national unification and opposing 'international hegemony'. How the discourse on nationalism and globalisation continues to link these three areas of policy-making will be explored in the following chapter.

4 What kind of a status quo power?

This work began by exploring how patriotism has been used since the late 1970s to link economic reform with national unification policy and foreign policy to form an ideological system for legitimating CCP rule. In the period immediately after Tiananmen and in the context of the end of the Cold War, the CCP leadership re-established these linkages in an international situation of 'economic globalisation and political multipolarity', arriving at the orthodoxy of Deng Xiaoping Theory and the Three Represents. Given the centrality of patriotism to the post-Tiananmen leadership's claim to legitimacy, this has considerably strengthened the nationalistic dynamics of the political dispensation inherited by the new leadership of President and CCP General Secretary Hu Jintao and Premier Wen Jiabao, installed at the Sixteenth Party Congress. This chapter will conclude by examining how the mission to achieve the tasks established by Deng Xiaoping in January 1980 continues to form links between domestic politics, national unification and foreign policy that constrain the ability of China's new leaders to contribute to the maintenance of a stable international status quo.

The value of unification

The way in which Deng Xiaoping Theory has continued to link the task of national unification with 'reform and opening' can be seen by the inclusion of the most overt declarations concerning CCP legitimacy in the third volume of Deng's *Selected Works*. These are Deng's warning to Margaret Thatcher that any Chinese leader who compromises under foreign pressure on the international stage will loose popular support and eventually be deposed (Deng 1993u: 330–3), and his view that any compromise on the issue of national unification will imply that China has not actually achieved independence (1993a4: 31). The texts in this volume also make frequent references to the linkage between the reform process and unity with Taiwan and Hong Kong, on the one hand, and the internal integration of the non-Han populations into the Chinese nation on the other. Deng thus appeals to 'all descendants of the Chinese nation' in the mainland, Taiwan, Hong Kong and Macao and among the overseas Chinese to 'struggle together, realising the unification of the motherland and national rejuvenation' (*minzu zhenxing*). He also stresses that attention is being paid to the 8 per cent of the population of the PRC that is not Han, so that China has the special characteristic of being free of ethnic friction (1993a2). Moreover, as he points out in a 1990 speech that proclaims the legitimacy of using the market under socialism, maintaining the 'people's democratic dictatorship' will prevent 'contradictions' between nationalities, regions, classes and central and local governments from leading to social polarisation (1993a3: 364).

Despite Deng's denial of the existence of a nationalities problem in China, however, 'reform and opening' has produced little evidence to support the belief that the United Front can successfully win over the hearts and minds of the diverse populations at which it is targeted. Under Hu Yaobang, the policy of cultural liberalisation for the non-Han populations in the PRC merely led to more open challenges to Chinese nationalism. The political repression that followed his downfall generated a series of anti-Chinese demonstrations in Lhasa, which culminated in March 1989 when between 75 and 750 Tibetans were killed in running battles with the police. This is the context within which Hu Jintao was appointed Party Secretary of the Tibet Autonomous Region. He faced the first test of his leadership mettle by imposing martial law in the Lhasa valley and initiating Beijing's reassertion of control over the monasteries and other religious institutions.

Since the Fourteenth Party Congress, the policy of accelerating economic development has not stopped unrest in the regions populated by non-Han ethnic groups. In May 1993, over a thousand people protested in Lhasa over rising food prices and the introduction of charges for medical prescriptions and school fees. The influx of entrepreneurs, technical experts and firms from the rest of China who were taking advantage of new infrastructure projects and a further opening up of the region gave these demonstrations an ethnic theme too. Yet when Premier Li Peng presided over the Third Tibet Work Forum in Beijing in July 1994, the solution was more of the same, with the target for economic growth set at 10 per cent per annum. Dissatisfaction was to be dealt with through an ideological policy that identified separatists as the main cause of instability, and a campaign to root out Tibetan nationalists (Shakya 1999: 438–46).

Often such disturbances have been caused by insensitivity towards the genuine nature of ethnic differences, as in case of the demonstrations triggered in Xinjiang in 1988 and 1989 after the publication of books that were seen as making racial slurs and blasphemous remarks against Kazaks and Uygurs. Such conflicts, however, create a context of intense dissatisfaction within which opponents of Chinese rule can gain support. In April 1990, tensions arose at Baren, some 50 kilometres to the southwest of Kashgar. During a prayer meeting, a group of mainly Uygur men began to criticise CCP policies towards ethnic minorities, which rapidly escalated into a mass demonstration with some members calling for a *jihad* to drive the Han out and establish an East Turkestan state (Dillon 2004: 60–3). By the time of the Fourteenth Party Congress, Uygur groups were resorting to acts of violence and sabotage, including a series of bomb attacks on buses and a cinema in Urumqi in February that year. In 1996, despite the seriousness of the Taiwan crisis at that time, the CCP identified the unrest in Xinjiang as the most serious threat to the stability and territorial integrity of China (Dillon 2004: 156). The launching of a repressive 'Strike Hard' campaign against 'violent and terrorist cases organised and manipulated by national separatist forces' in April that year merely generated more acts of defiance, culminating in the Yining Uprising of February 1997 (Dillon 2004: 84–109).

The high degree of concern among the leadership in Beijing over the failure of policy in Xinjiang is clear from the way in which only that region has two chapters devoted to it in the *China Investigation Report 2000–2001: Studies of Contradictions Among the People under New Conditions*, which are devoted to an analysis of the national and religious problems there. Given that the document was published in May 2001, this shows how the 'contradictions' in the region were clearly a matter for the highest degree of importance for the CCP leadership well before the terrorist attacks on the United States that occurred on 11 September that year. The limitations imposed on the Party for addressing such problems, however, are revealed by the way in which the solutions proposed for Xinjiang in this report have not moved beyond the faith that economic development, now legitimated by the ideology of the Three Represents, will resolve all issues of national identity. If anything, this shows how the CCP leadership can use such crises of internal unification to bolster the necessity of its own leadership rather than to address the *prima facie* complaints of the populations concerned. Religious belief is thus understood as the product of poverty and ignorance. The prescription for curing this delusion is more economic development and more interactions with the outside world, so that 'In the end, there will be more things of the mundane world in their brains, and "supernatural" and "heavenly" things will inevitably be diluted day-by-day' (CC 2001: 276).

The challenges to the CCP's version of patriotism posed by Han populations living in the territories of Hong Kong and Taiwan, beyond Beijing's control, presents a different kind of complexity. When massive crowds took to the streets in Hong Kong in the spring of 1989 out of sympathy for their compatriots who were demonstrating in Beijing, they donned the same white headbands that were being worn in Tiananmen Square and formed an umbrella organisation under the name 'Hong Kong Alliance in Support of the Patriotic Democratic Movement in China'. In schools, teachers had to start dealing with students who were radicalised by witnessing the repression in Beijing on television, and the authorities were faced with the challenge of developing a form of patriotism that would allow opposition groups to thrive within a democratic framework (Postiglione 1992: 32). For the CCP, though, this democratic patriotism presents a new challenge for the 'one country, two systems' formula. Whereas Deng Xiaoping had found it enough to stress that Hong Kong should be governed by local patriots, in January 1990 Jiang Zemin revealed his fear that this kind of democratic patriotism could become a serious challenge to the CCP's version, when he insisted that 'river water and well water should not mix' (*PD* 21–1–1990).

Since the 1997 transition of Hong Kong to PRC sovereignty, attempts by the government of the Hong Kong Special Administrative Region (HKSAR) to stifle the demands of those who want to move quickly towards universal suffrage for the former colony have merely antagonised the population. Since the arrival of the Hu-Wen leadership in Beijing, attempts to sidestep the HKSAR government and intimidate advocates of democratisation by portraying them as unpatriotic have been stepped up. On 1 July 2003, the sixth anniversary of Hong Kong's return to China, an estimated half-million marchers took part in a protest to defend civil liberties and demand democratic reforms, triggered by attempts to introduce new national security legislation. The inadequacy of the CCP's belief in economic determinism is revealed by the way in which it responded to the growing political discontent by signing a Closer Economic Partnership Agreement with the territory (CEPA), only to see pro-Beijing political parties lose substantial support in District Council elections that November. After Hu Jintao told Hong Kong Chief Executive Tung Chee-Hwa that Beijing would take a more direct interest in political developments in the territory when the two met in Beijing in December, mainland academics visiting the SAR began to stress that 'one country' is more important than 'two systems'.

Nationalism was also deployed by Beijing in a vicious campaign by the pro-Beijing press, spokespersons for the Chinese government and CCP supporters in Hong Kong, which singled out prominent pro-democracy campaigners for vilification as unpatriotic traitors and subversive elements (Human Rights Watch). When the *People's Daily* reprinted Deng Xiaoping's June 1984 speech on the future administration of Hong Kong, which states 'The criteria of a patriot are, respect for one's own nation, sincerely embrace the ancestral land's actions to return Hong Kong's sovereignty, do not damage the prosperity and stability of Hong Kong' (1993w: 61), the accompanying *People's Daily* editorial (20–2–04) left no doubt that patriots are those who support the central government. This is despite the fact that Deng's original text goes on to state that 'We do not demand that they [patriots] support China's socialist system, we just demand that they love the ancestral land, love Hong Kong'.

The United Front may be said to have worked insofar as a number of those taking part in the patriotism campaign were prominent members of the Hong Kong business community who also have seats as Hong Kong representatives to the National People's Congress in Beijing. Moreover, at a broader level, attempts to harness the themes of globalisation to nation-building through 'siliconisation' have created business alliances between the 'astronauts' who spend their lives flying between the economies of 'Greater China' and California. But the political potentials of what one commentator has called the 'silicon bridge' remain susceptible to the vagaries of the global ICT market and the scrutiny of local democratic forces over issues of financial probity (Sum 2003).

Internal political changes in Taiwan have created even more serious challenges for the CCP's version of patriotism. In the late 1980s, building blocks of democratisation were laid down with the establishment of the opposition Democrat Progressive Party (DPP) and the rise of the native Taiwanese elite to the top of the KMT under ROC President and KMT Chairman Lee Teng-hui. When Lee insisted in February 1988 that the CCP would have to give up its Four Cardinal Principles before unification could be considered, he broke with decades of KMT and CCP orthodoxy by bestowing a higher value on democracy than on the integrity of the Chinese nation (1988: 9). In March 1990, crowds of students donned white headbands and flocked to Taipei's Chiang Kaishek Memorial Plaza to oppose attempts by ageing National Assembly members who had been elected five decades earlier in the

Chinese mainland to expand their own powers and privileges; Lee sided with 'people power'. A new domestic consensus on constitutional reform emerged, challenging the principle that Taiwan's sovereignty is located in the Chinese nation. Although Lee did not challenge the position that Taiwan is a part of China at this time, a challenge to the legitimacy of the CCP was certainly implied when Taipei forestalled the possibility of unification until safeguards for human dignity, guaranteed fundamental human rights, and the practice of democracy and the rule of law could be established in the mainland (EY 1991).

The main features of Beijing's policy of 'peaceful unification' under 'one country, two systems', however, were established when Taiwan was still under the KMT dictatorship. Even Jiang Zemin's 'Eight Point' New Year speech of 30 January 1995 (*PD* 31–1–95), which was supposed to establish a new framework for Taiwan policy, was tightly constrained by the principles established in the 1980s. His call for talks to include a broader section of Taiwanese was made by Deng Xiaoping as early as 1984 (1993x: 86), the threat to use force against foreign intervention and secessionist forces remained in place, and the *volkisch* appeal to the population of Taiwan as 'all bone and flesh compatriots' was restated. This was a long way from Taipei's new position that shared culture might be taken as the foundation for developing exchanges, but unification could only be pursued in light of the reality of the political division between the two sides, which Lee Teng-hui restated in his own six-point reply to Jiang Zemin (*LHB* 9–4–95).

Moreover, such initiatives have become somewhat redundant since the DPP's Chen Shui-bian was elected President of the ROC in March 2000. The overall result of the United Front for Taiwan can be seen in the findings of opinion polls taken in Taiwan which show that fewer than 13 per cent of the island's population want either speedy unification with China or the maintenance of a status quo that leads to eventual unification. According to polls conducted by the Election Study Center at Taipei's National Chengchi University, the proportion of those identifying themselves as 'Chinese' fell from 26.2 per cent in 1992, to just 6.1 per cent by the end of 2004. While those who identify as 'Both Taiwanese and Chinese' stayed more or less constant at about 45 per cent in this period, the proportion of those who see themselves as just 'Taiwanese' rose from 17.3 per cent to 43.7 per cent.[1] Given that the Chengchi University survey discovered that a mere 2 per cent of respondents wanted unification with the mainland as soon as possible, in December 2004, it seems safe to say that the CCP's United

Front strategy has not achieved its aims of winning the hearts and minds of Taiwan's public after just over ten years of the practice of sovereignty through elections on the island.

Yet it is also problematic to propose that a strong sense of Taiwanese nationalism has taken root, with just 4.8 per cent wanting independence for Taiwan as soon as possible. Chen Shui-bian's victory in Taiwan's March 2000 presidential election was secured with only 39 per cent of the vote after a split in the KMT leadership, and only after he had campaigned on a platform that committed himself to the 'Four Nos' of not changing the national name of the Republic of China, not changing the constitution to include Lee Teng-hui's 'two-states theory', not holding a referendum on independence, and not declaring independence unless Taiwan is attacked by China. Such findings indicate that the 'Taiwanese consciousness' that has developed under democratisation is a highly complex phenomenon that is built on the minimum condition that sovereignty resides in the citizens of the island (*zhuquan zai min*), originally proposed by Lee Teng-hui in May 1994. With Taiwan remaining independent from the PRC in practice, Chen Shui-bian is thus able to claim that maintaining the 'status quo' in cross-Strait relations means preserving the island's political separation from the mainland. Meanwhile, the DPP's basic policy for countering the United Front is to preserve that independence by consolidating the island's democratic system and the loyalty of its citizens to Taiwan.

Rooted in the past and the factional politics of the CCP, Beijing's United Front strategy has proven unable to adapt to such changing realities and has resorted to vilifying Taiwan's elected leaders as 'lacking Chinese sentiments' (*zhongguo ren de ganqing*) (*WHB*; *PD* 16–6–94). Given the close linkage of national unification with CCP legitimacy, it has also been impossible for Beijing to respond positively to the various formulae proposed by Taipei for breaking the deadlock in cross-Strait relations. Even after Deng Xiaoping's Southern Tour had transformed the political climate in Beijing, Lee Teng-hui claims that divisions in Beijing still made it impossible for progress to be made on his demand for the signing of a non-aggression pact during secret talks between the two sides (Zou 2001: 198). Beijing has also rejected any proposals that would allow the island's democratisation to proceed and its international status to be raised while maintaining an ethnic conception of Chinese identity that can be used as the foundation for cooperation with the mainland and Hong Kong within a greater China, leading to possible political unification under democracy and the free market (MAC 1993: 14).

The most that can be said for the United Front policy in Taiwan is that lobbying the growing Taiwanese business community in the mainland could have exerted some constraints on the island's political leaders during the 1995–6 crisis (Hughes 1997a: 115–17). Yet this did not stop key figures in the island's business and academic elite moving to support Chen Shui-bian in Taiwan's 2000 presidential election. Consequent threats against Chen supporters such as Stan Shih, president of Acer Computers, and Xu Wenlong of Taiwan's Qimei Group, may have brought public apologies towards Beijing, but this appears to have done little to halt the development of 'Taiwanese consciousness' and the consolidation of democracy. For Taiwan's political elite, the combination of Beijing's insistence that negotiations can only take place if Taipei accepts the 'one China' principle and its opposition to allowing the island more space for international manoeuvre, has only made it difficult for any serious contender for power in Taiwan to advocate Chinese nationalism. Such was the experience of Chen Shui-bian's 'Blue' coalition opponents in the 2004 presidential election, KMT Chairman Lien Chan and James Soong of the People's First Party. The spectacle of Lien and Soong visiting the Chinese mainland in May 2005, after losing the election to Chen, is probably the biggest breakthrough for the United Front to date. But Lien has since retired from his post, and Soong's prospects for a political comeback are increasingly limited as a new generation of politicians comes on the scene in Taiwan.

The pressure exerted on Taiwan by Beijing, on the other hand, has been counter-productive for the United Front. When Nauru broke diplomatic relations with Taipei and recognised Beijing on the day that Chen Shui-bian became Chairman of the DPP in July 2002, for example, he responded the following month, telling independence activists in Tokyo on 3 August that 'there is one country on each side of the Strait' (*yi bian yi guo*). He then went on to explain the need for Taiwan to implement legislation to allow the holding of referendums. Hampered by a sluggish economy and deadlock in cross-Strait relations, the DPP was able to divert attention from its domestic record by focusing public attention on the opposition's attitude towards Taiwan's identity and status. In the course of 2003, the DPP was greatly aided by the spread of the SARS outbreak to the island from mainland China, after which the Beijing continued to block Taiwan from becoming an observer at World Health Assembly (WHA). The day after people in Taiwan had been particularly outraged by witnessing on television China's UN representative in Geneva telling Taiwanese journalists to 'shut up' and asking 'who cares about you?', Chen Shui-bian told a DPP central committee meeting that he would consult social groups over whether to hold a plebiscite on the issue of World Health Organization (WHO) entry.

The unfolding of the referendum issue in Taiwan in the run-up to the island's presidential election may have cost Taipei some support in Washington. Yet it forced Chen's opponents in the presidential election to indicate their commitment to democracy and the location of sovereignty in the citizens of Taiwan by accepting the legitimacy of holding referenda. While the Blue majority in the Legislative Yuan managed to water down the contents of the referendum legislation, and the referendum questions and outcomes could not be interpreted as a vote for independence, the issue had a powerful impact on the election campaign. Not only did the Blues adopt the rhetoric of Taiwanese nationalism to prove their loyalty to the island, but both Lien Chan and the KMT speaker in the Legislative Yuan (parliament), Wang Jyng Ping, made statements indicating that the KMT did not rule out independence as an option for Taiwan.

Given the CCP's equation of patriotism with its own leadership, and the foundation of the United Front on historical-materialist ideas about the nature of identity that go back to the Marxism-Leninism of the 1920s, Beijing has found it difficult to respond to the challenges to its version of patriotism posed by the ethnic aspirations of non-Han citizens of the PRC and by the democratic aspirations of the people of Hong Kong and Taiwan. Yet so long as the legitimacy of 'reform and opening', and by extension the CCP itself, is closely linked to the task of unifying the motherland, methods of repression and intimidation will remain a characteristic of PRC politics. Moreover, this preoccupation with attempting to achieve national unification under CCP leadership inevitably spills over into foreign affairs, where it is linked with the mission of opposing 'international hegemony' and undermines Beijing's attempts to present the PRC as engaged on a 'peaceful rise' to great power status.

Multipolarity, multilateralism and shaping norms

At the centre of Beijing's initiatives to contain challenges to the fulfilment of the CCP's mission of national unification is an attempt to prevent the emergence of international norms that threaten to erode the state-centric version of international relations that is enshrined in the Five Principles of Peaceful Coexistence. In this sense, the advocacy of multipolarity in PRC diplomacy can be understood as a form of continuity with Cold War attempts to align with the developing states of the South and use the United Nations as a mechanism to balance the hegemony of the superpowers. Given the unrest in Xinjiang, and the fact that many of China's intellectuals vigorously dismiss the views of Samuel Huntington's thesis on the 'Clash of Civilisations' (Hughes 1997a: 109–117), it is rather ironic that Deng Xiaoping can claim that China will not stand alone in shaping the post-Cold War order because the Islamic and African countries will also be unable to copy the Western model of democracy (1993a5: 359–61). However, the fact that most Asian states did not support the sanctions imposed on China in 1989 and developed a common position on the principle that human rights concerns should be guided by the principles of non-interference in the internal affairs of states at the 1993 UN World Conference on Human Rights (United Nations 1993), Beijing has been given grounds for optimism that multilateralism can be used to further its agenda of shaping international norms.

This opposition to what Deng Xiaoping Theory condemns as the tendency to put 'individual rights above state rights' has become increasingly important as populations alienated by CCP nationalism appeal to a liberal conception of globalisation that privileges respect for democracy and human rights over principles of non-intervention. Repression in Tibet and Xinjiang has long drawn the attention of international NGOs. The Dalai Lama has considerable charisma in the international community, and in the late 1980s was already lobbying the United States Congress and the European Parliament over human rights abuses. After the events of 1989 in Beijing, appeals made in Hong Kong for international attention to be paid to the democratisation of the territory's political system fell on sympathetic ears around the world, including those of the former British Conservative Party Chairman Chris Patten, after he was appointed governor in 1992. In 1991, Lee Teng-hui could deploy globalisation discourse and appeal to the states of the Asia-Pacific region to move towards an economic integration that would 'transcend political borders and accelerate the interaction and development of regional economy and trade', strengthening respect for democracy and human rights, the use of diplomacy to resolve disputes, the promotion of a market economy, a collective security system, and promoting a consensus that problems could be jointly tackled in the 'global village' (1991: 122–3).

It is because such appeals pose a direct challenge to the linkage between unification and CCP legitimacy that confirming principles of non-intervention and respect for territorial integrity is a priority in Beijing's diplomatic initiatives. India's non-participation in the post-Tiananmen sanctions was particularly welcome in this respect, and in December 1991, shortly after President George Bush had a meeting with the Dalai Lama, Premier Li Peng visited New Delhi to continue the business of rapprochement begun in the 1980s. In 1992, Boris Yeltsin's agreement that Moscow would only develop unofficial relations with Taiwan was a crucial step in the development of the 'strategic partnership' with Russia. Since then, Chinese analysts have been quick to draw attention to frictions between Russia and the US over issues such the Chechnya crisis, Russian attempts to establish a sphere of interest in the CIS, and the eastward expansion of NATO (*BR* 38(14–15) 1995: 22–4).

Just as with multipolarity, Beijing's increasing practice of multilateralism can also be seen as growing directly out of concerns over the domestic problems faced by the CCP's unification policy. By the time of the Fourteenth Party Congress Jiang Zemin could already claim that China had become an observer member of the Non-Aligned Movement and intended to strengthen its ties with some 77 international groupings with which it already had relationships. By the time of his report to the Fifteenth Party Congress, this endorsement of multilateralism had become much more explicit, as Jiang stated that one of the main aims of foreign policy is 'To actively participate in multilateral diplomatic activities, fully wielding our country's function in the United Nations and other international organisations'. As Yan Xuetong, one of China's most influential international relations academics, explains in an article on 'The Possible Choices for China's Rise', this use of multilateralism is a much more effective way to prevent the emergence of international norms detrimental to China's national interests than resorting to a defiant nationalism that can only antagonise the far more powerful United States and allow Washington to portray China as a threat. Yan could thus hope that it was possible for nationalism to be deployed in a constructive manner by arguing that the creation of a better future for the world is a burden that has to be shouldered by a great nation (*weida minzu*) (Yan 1995).

That such attempts to moderate the domestic debate on nationalism should not be confused with a departure from the CCP's core task of achieving national unification, however, has become increasingly clear as China's international environment has been transformed by the crises that have occurred since 1995 in the Taiwan Strait. After the failure of Beijing's bid for the 2000 Olympic Games and its hopes to become a founding member of the WTO, and with pressures from the West mounting over human rights issues, the granting of Lee Teng-hui's visa to visit the United States before he stood as a candidate in Taiwan's first presidential election was seen as one more link in a grand US strategy of containment. The naval stand-off in the run-up to the election and the sanctions taken by Beijing against Washington all served to reinforce the linkage between nationalism and foreign policy that is so clearly established in Deng Xiaoping Theory. Beijing's most dramatic response was the holding of a series of military exercises which lasted up until Taiwan's March 1996 presidential election, and which included the firing of live missiles at targets near the coast of the island. From a diplomatic perspective, such measures were used to show Washington that a loss of cooperation with Beijing due to the Taiwan issue would have serious consequences. But they also had to send a message to the Chinese population that the CCP leadership was able to 'say no' when an issue it had defined as a core national interest was at stake.

As has been argued in Chapter 3, even when Beijing and Washington attempted to mend their relationship, this backfired on the relationship as the domestic debate on defying the United States grew in intensity. The 1999 Belgrade crisis posed a further challenge to liberal attempts to prevent the rise of the anti-American nationalism found in books like *China Can Say No* and the works of authors like Wang Xiaodong, let alone the spreading of nationalism in Chinese cyberspace. Within this domestic political context, originally moderate views on multi-lateralism were recast with a new emphasis on the pursuit of national-ist objectives. When Yan Xuetong republished his 1995 article in a collection of his essays in 2000, the title of the volume was *American Hegemony and China's Security*, and nearly one-third of its content is devoted to exploring the nature of the Taiwan problem and methods for bringing it back to the embrace of the motherland. In the process, Yan strongly argues in favour of maintaining the PRC's military threat and blames the deadlock in cross-Strait relations entirely on Lee Teng-hui's lack of 'Chinese feelings' due to his upbringing under the Japanese occupation of Taiwan (Yan 2000: 125–90). In the wake of the Belgrade crisis, even an originally cautious commentator like Yan Xuetong, who wants to promote Deng Xiaoping's line that foreign policy should be put to the service of economic construction and that China should not lead the opposition against United States hegemony, is careful to explain that moral protests might be appropriate for opposing the hegemony of the United States over an issue like the independence of Kosovo, but when it comes to 'crucial issues of inter-est such as upholding our country's unity, our foreign policy cannot be soft' (Yan 1999: 10).

Such a position is very much in accord with the vision of the international system presented in Jiang Zemin's report to the Fifteenth Party Congress, where it is portrayed as being destabilised by the legacy of Cold War thinking, hegemony and great power politics, the expansion of military blocs and alliances and an unequal economic system, the use of 'human rights' to interfere in the domestic affairs of states and the destabilisation of regional politics due to issues of national (*minzu*), religious and territorial factors. Scholars writing in China's most influential international relations journals can, however, continue to articulate the leadership's view that it is folly to confront the United States when the promotion of multipolarity can be left to more powerful states such as Russia, Japan, France and Germany. In the meantime, Deng's advice of 'biding time' should be adhered to, allowing China to develop its economic and technological power, making efforts to understand the nature of modern warfare and preparing as much as possible to ensure that the gap between US and Chinese conventional weapons does not get larger (Chu and Wang 1999).

It is important to take into account this domestic discourse on foreign policy when explaining Johnston's observation that the use of multipolarity began to decline in academic texts at this time, and was replaced by alternative concepts such as globalisation (Johnston 2003: 35). Rather than this indicating any shift in Beijing's strategic outlook and national priorities, it can be taken as symptomatic of the way that multipolarity was revealed to be an essentially vacuous concept when faced by the preponderance of United States power throughout the world. In fact, nowhere do the many texts in the third volume of Deng Xiaoping's selected works that discuss foreign policy actually say how China can influence the trend towards multipolarity. Neither is there any explanation of how change occurs in the international system. There is no explanation of what a pole is or how many there should be, other than a statement that they should at least include the United States, the Soviet Union and China. That around two-thirds of the March 1990 text in which Deng first presents multipolarity is actually concerned with advocating speeding up economic reforms is indicative of the fact that this discourse is orientated towards domestic politics rather than foreign policy (1993s).

The weakness of multipolarity as a strategy for balancing American power was certainly clear to a commentator like Yan Xuetong by 1999. Given that even the developing states on the UN Security Council had to vote with the United States in support of the intervention in Kosovo, he could argue that the states of the South were no longer able to resist the imposition of the new doctrine of using humanitarian intervention to promote democracy and human rights. Moreover, this new approach to international relations was already being built into the work of international organisations, with the

WTO becoming a kind of economic UN as it strengthened the rules widening the scope of free trade and capital flows, while the G8 seemed to have become a kind of second UN Security Council (Yan 2000: 193–203). It is when he is faced by this prospect of a failed multipolarity that Yan argues the necessity for Beijing to continue developing its multilateral activities. Only in this way will it be possible for the PRC to reduce frictions with other states, raise its status in the international mainstream, and win support for the international norms it advocates (Yan 2000: 7–11).

The rise of multilateralism should not, therefore, be confused with a change of the fundamental values that shape the CCP's foreign policy. Instead, it is an alternative way to shape international norms in ways that will facilitate China's unification and prevent the application of the strengthening post-Cold War doctrine of humanitarian intervention to populations that are claimed to be part of the Chinese nation. Academic commentators who propose a constrained foreign policy based on multilateralism are thus fixated by the possible threat that the doctrine of 'putting human rights above state rights' could pose to China's unity by encouraging independence movements in Tibet and Xinjiang. In this respect, even the 'two states theory' advocated by Lee Teng-hui in 1999 is seen as an attempt to use the Kosovo effect to achieve Taiwanese independence. All commentators who warn against directly opposing the United States thus add the rider that this only holds 'Unless there occurs a large scale invasion of Chinese territory or the separation of Taiwan' (Chu and Wang 1999: 6).

Rethinking security under globalisation

It may be right to say that the kind of foreign policy articulated for the CCP by academics like Yan Xuetong is not a challenge to the international status quo, insofar as it espouses the conservative state-centric norms of the Five Principles of Peaceful Coexistence (Johnston 2003: 33). Yet the strategic goal of Beijing's multipolarity and multi-lateralism remains a recipe for instability insofar as it strengthens rather than weakens the vital link between the domestic politics of CCP legitimacy and foreign policy. This not only has obvious implications for the fate of non-Han citizens of the PRC and for the security of Taiwan, it also it leads to friction with the United States and other liberal democracies over the development of appropriate norms for ensuring international stability in a changing world.

If Washington can be accused of hanging on to a 'Cold War mentality' in this respect, then Beijing has barely moved from the state-centric realpolitik of nineteenth-century Europe when faced by the rethinking of international security that is taking place with the rise of non-traditional security threats at the start of the new millennium. Key diplomatic initiatives, such as the strengthening of the 'strategic partnership' with Russia and the establishment of a multilateral regional security architecture in Central Asia, have all been premised on a shared opposition to the doctrine of humanitarian intervention and a continuing attachment to the sanctity of state sovereignty in the face of secessionist movements. In this respect, China's participation in the campaign against international terrorism was a force driving its multilateralism well before the events of 11 September 2001 in the United States. In June 2000, when Jiang Zemin heralded the decision to transform the Shanghai Five into the 'Shanghai Cooperation Organization' (SCO), with the additional member of Uzbekistan the following year, he thus called for its members to not only join together in striking against nationalist splittism, international terrorism and religious extremism, but also to oppose international hegemony and great power politics and to promote multipolarity (*PD* 6–7–2000).

Well before the terrorist attacks against the United States on 11 September 2001, Chinese policy was thus to use multilateralism as a defence against both the traditional threat posed by the hegemonic power of the United States and to criticise versions of the new discourse on non-traditional security threats that could supersede state sovereignty. The United States was thus accused of double standards because it had a record of supporting Osama Bin Laden and secessionist movements not only in places like Kosovo and Kashmir, but also in China's own regions of Tibet and Xinjiang. Moreover, it could be claimed that the forces of secession, terrorism and religious extremism had all been exacerbated in developing states because globalisation had worsened the poverty gap and increased frictions between cultures as it was still dominated by an old economic and political system that only benefited the developed states (He and Jiang 2000).

This strategy of using multilateralism to ensure that the rise of non-traditional security threats does not erode the sanctity of state sovereignty can be seen in the articulation of what Beijing calls its 'New Security Concept'. Based on the four principles of 'mutual trust, mutual benefit, equality and cooperation', this was presented to the ASEAN Regional Forum (ARF) Foreign Minister's conference at Bandar Seri Bagawan on 31 July 2002. Chinese commentators trace the origins of its key elements back to the report delivered by China to the 1996 ARF Inter-Sessional Support Group on Confidence-Building Measures in Tokyo, which accepts that engaging with multilateral security organisations, formal dialogues and track two dialogues are all ways to protect national security (Lu 2003: 56).

Although the New Security Concept remains nebulous, it is not hard to see that it is to preserve the state-centric understanding of multilateralism characterised by the Five Principles of Peaceful Coexistence. Drifte, for example, summarises the main themes of the 1996 document as being resistance against the external imposition of values and ideologies, the splitting of China, indiscriminate sanctions against China on international issues, conflicts and wars in some regional countries, encroachments on China's sovereignty, and defence of maritime rights and interests (Drifte 2003: 36). Such an interpretation is in line with the views of Chinese commentators, who stress that the principle of 'equality' in the New Security Concept amounts to ruling out the use of non-traditional security threats by 'powerful states' as an excuse to interfere in the domestic affairs of weaker states. Moreover, they point out that there is little room in the formula for the role of non-state actors. The concept is also said to indicate a fundamental difference between the ways in which the developed and the developing states view the new security agenda. While the former more readily emphasise the impact of threats such as environmental problems on non-state referent objects, such as human health and welfare and the global ecology, the latter are more concerned about how such threats pose a challenge to their own survival as states (Lu 2003: 57).

It is, of course, no coincidence that this emphasis on state sovereignty in the New Security Concept is fully in harmony with the Association of Southeast Asian Nations' (ASEAN) principles, as enshrined in the Treaty of Amity and Cooperation to which China has now signed up. Both China and the ASEAN states share the view that there need be no direct clash between multilateralism, maintaining statehood, and dealing with transnational threats such as terrorism. The same is true of the members of the SCO, who have defended their national interests by signing agreements on reducing the military presence in the border areas, and combating 'terrorism, splittism and extremism'. The possibility that such initiatives might antagonise the United States is minimised by presenting them as part of the struggle against terrorism with a global reach.

One of the main benefits for China in promoting its state-centric New Security Concept is that it has been able to reap substantial gains in the trade-off between a foreign policy that has to concede the realities of United States predominance, on the one hand, and the need to promote nationalistic goals of unification in domestic politics, on the other. Visible examples of this have been the listing of the East Turkestan

Independence Movement (ETIM) by the United States as a terrorist organisation in August 2002, and the refusal of the United States to sponsor a resolution in the United Nations criticising China's human rights record in April 2003. The 9/11 incident has given considerable credibility to the opposition in Deng Xiaoping Theory to the principle of putting 'individual rights above state rights'. Human rights were not visible on the agenda when APEC heads of state met in Shanghai in October 2001 and issued a Declaration on Counter Terrorism that called for cooperation in protecting critical sectors of society, electronic records systems for tracking the movement of people, and economic and technical cooperation to enhance counter-terrorism. In June the following year, the SCO summit in Petersburg produced an 'Agreement on a Regional Anti-Terrorist Regime', and China and ASEAN signed a 'Joint Declaration on Cooperation in Non-Traditional Security Areas'. This complex integration of different themes is illustrated by the speech on 'The Global Challenge of International Terrorism' given to the Munich Conference on Security Policy in February 2003 by the Deputy Chief of the General Staff of the PLA, Xiong Guangkai, which explains China's counter-terrorism policy in terms of the New Security Concept. The premise he establishes for success in this struggle is that the international community has deepened its understanding of Moscow's actions against the Chechens and has listed the ETIM as an international terrorist group. 'As a Chinese folk-saying goes, terrorists are just like "rats running in the street, being chased and beaten wherever they appear"', explains Xiong (2003).

Most important of all for the pursuit of the major tasks set for the CCP under 'reform and opening' is the way in which Washington's changed foreign policy priorities have allowed the Bush administration to move away from President Clinton's strategic ambiguity over Taiwan and towards a public stance of opposing Taiwanese independence. It should be said that there is no evidence to prove a direct linkage between Washington's changing policy and the War on Terror, and that domestic developments in Taiwan such as Chen Shui-bian's decision to hold the 'defensive referendum' in tandem with the island's 2004 presidential election, have been at least as important in this process. Yet a seasoned commentator on international affairs like Assistant Foreign Minister Shen Guofang, is still able to argue that the 9/11 incident created the conditions for President Bush to confirm adherence to the 'one China' policy and state his opposition to Taiwanese independence because Washington had to drop its view of China as a 'strategic competitor' and to positively appraise Sino-US cooperation in the War on Terror. From Beijing's perspective, then, the truth of Jiang Zemin's statement to the Sixteenth Party Congress that 'the development of the world towards multipolarity and economic globalization provides good conditions for world peace and development' has been substantiated (Shen 2003: 40–1).

Taiwan: the limits of China's 'peaceful rise'

Yet despite the support that Beijing has accrued from the developing states and Russia for its opposition to emerging doctrines of humanitarian intervention, the very success of China's economic construction presents a new kind of problem that the established discourse is not well equipped to deal with. This is the problem of how a rising power impacts on the structure of the international system. In this respect, the late 1990s was a psychological turning point. Not only did China face a series of international crises from the 1995–6 Taiwan Strait tension to the 1999 Belgrade Incident, economic statistics also began to transform the vision of China as a developing economy. When the World Bank announced that in 1996 Chinese per capita GNP had reached $3,330, based on the purchasing power parity (PPP) method of calculation (World Bank 1998), this may have been low by the standards of the industrialised economies (USA US$28,020; Japan US$23,420), but multiplied by a population of 1.2 billion, it presented the world with a significant and growing market. It also presented China's leaders with an unprecedented reserve of economic power to use in the development of Beijing's diplomacy.

As discussed in Chapter 3, as early as 1994 an author like Wang Shan was already aware that the spectacle of a rising China would raise fears in the West based on analogies with the rise of Wilhelmine Germany. In 1995, Yan Xuetong could point to the need for China to begin to play a more positive role in creating a better future for the world, commensurate with the burden shouldered by a great nation (*weida minzu*) (Yan 1995). The expectations for China held by many in the international community were summed up by United States President Bill Clinton in June 1998, when he marked his visit to China by publishing an article in *Newsweek* in which he explained how a cooperative relationship was necessary for stability in Asia. He applauded Beijing's support for Washington's condemnation of the nuclear tests that had recently been carried out by India and Pakistan. He also welcomed China's support for the peace talks on the Korean Peninsula and its support for efforts to freeze North Korea's nuclear programme. He was also grateful for the way in which China had acted as a firebreak in the Asian financial crisis by not devaluing the

Renminbi Yuan. Finally, he was positive about China contributing to a reduction in tensions by pursuing negotiations with Taiwan (Clinton 1998). As has been argued above, however, since the foreign-policy crises of 1995–9 the emergence of China as a major economic power has also been accompanied by a hardening of a defensive doctrine of non-intervention that is more characteristic of a developing state than an emerging great power.

A more immediate problem for Beijing, however, is the need to allay the concerns of neighbouring states over the growth in China's economic and military power. The ASEAN states, for example, have expressed their concern over the use of force to assert the PRC's claims to islands in the South China Sea. The setback to the economies of Southeast Asia caused by the Asian Financial Crisis, coupled with concerns over the impact of China's WTO membership on regional trade balances, has made it even more important to allay suspicions about China's economic intentions. If China projects its economic power too far and too fast, it will do little to allay the fears that it acknowledges exist in the capitals of the region, where the US presence is still valued as a force for external security (Haacke 2002: 36). Moreover, if Beijing sees its policy in Southeast Asia in terms of promoting multipolarity, this will set alarm bells ringing in Washington, where its policy in Southeast Asia has already been described as 'challenging the status quo aggressively' by United States Assistant Secretary of State James Kelly (House Committee on International Relations 2004). No doubt this is why Chinese texts do not refer to ASEAN as a 'pole' of global power, even though the EU qualifies as such.

China faces a similar problem of perception in South Asia. In May 1998, Indian Defence Minister George Fernandes accused China of being his country's greatest security threat. A week later, India carried out five nuclear tests. For all of China's talk of the Five Principles of Peaceful Coexistence, from the perspective of New Delhi, the announcement by Jiang Zemin and Bill Clinton in June 1998 that they would work together to prevent a nuclear arms race in South Asia was tantamount to China joining the US to perpetuate 'the hegemonistic mentality of a bygone era' (*FT* 29–6–98: 4). As a retired cabinet secretary of the government of India describes, states like India are concerned that that when China chooses to enforce its 'historic claims to sovereignty' over a certain territory, it views this as a justified action in self-defence undertaken in its own territory, which was unjustifiably under the control of others. Sometimes this has led Beijing to resort to actions hostile to the interests of its neighbours, such as the provision of clandestine assistance to Pakistan in the fields of nuclear and missile technologies. While such actions may be seen by Beijing as justified by its national interests, they make the countries of the region uneasy, not only over China's growing economic strength and military capability, but also over the increasing use of nationalism as the cement that will prevent the country from suffering the fate of the Soviet Union (Raman 2003).

It is to pre-empt the growth of such fears that Jiang Zemin included a policy of 'good neighbourliness' in his report to the Fifteenth Party Congress, explaining that disputes with neighbouring states should be handled through negotiations and in a way that enhances peace and stability. Such a moderate policy involves a trade-off between the priorities of domestic nationalism and the requirements of foreign policy, especially over the numerous territorial disputes China has with its neighbours, which Jiang explained could be temporarily shelved (*zhanshi ge zhi*). In making this move, Jiang could rely on the way in which a strategic flexibility over the handling of territorial disputes is built into Deng Xiaoping Theory. The key text for this is a talk given by Deng in 1982 to a delegation of Indian social scientists, in which he states that it is possible to resolve border disputes when both contending sides make concessions (1993a6: 19). Of even more significance is Deng's February 1984 talk with a delegation from Georgetown University, in which he states that the formula of 'one country, two systems', first developed to bring about unification with Hong Kong and Taiwan, might also be useful for resolving disputes in other parts of the world. This is because it allows questions of sovereignty to be 'shelved' (*ge zhi*) while disputed territories are jointly developed. As Deng explains, 'I also envisage that some international territorial conflicts need not first discuss sovereignty, can first begin joint development. This kind of problem must start from respecting reality, to find a new road for resolution' (1993a7: 49).

Yet, so long as the pursuit of national unification remains central to the ideology of Deng Xiaoping Theory, China's leaders will continue to be constrained by nationalist discourse and flexibility over territorial disputes will be seen by others as part of a grander nationalist-inspired strategy rather than a true ability to compromise on fundamental principles. The South China Sea disputes thus remain unresolved, while ASEAN's acceptance that Taiwan is a part of China is the fundamental principle on which the relationship with ASEAN has been established. Even regional economic integration adds a new complexity to old nationalistic problems. Maintaining a hands-off policy towards the ethnic Chinese populations of Southeast Asia, for example, is already becoming more complex as their economic role offers both a tempting resource for expanding China's influence in the region under multi-lateralism, which could resurrect questions over their loyalty and protection both inside China itself and in their countries of residence (Deng, S. 2003). Outward migration also fuels often irrational fears of a new type of colonial expansion into the Russian Far East and the states of Central Asia, where the presence of a growing ethnic Chinese population may also demand protection from the PRC in times of domestic upheaval.

The diversion of Washington's attention after 9/11 may have allowed Beijing to ease public discontent over its foreign policy and gain concessions on issues such as Xinjiang and Taiwan. China's post-Jiang Zemin leadership of President and CCP general secretary Hu Jintao and Premier Wen Jiabao, however, have inherited an ideological formula in which the CCP's nationalistic goals still have to be reconciled with international concerns over the long-term implications of their country's growing economic and military power. The most prominent attempt to deal with this issue to date has been the promotion of a new discourse on China's 'peaceful rise' (*heping jueqi*). Although it had already been used in academic circles for some years, this term began to be promoted at a high level in November 2003, when it was presented by the veteran Party theorist Zheng Bijian in a speech on 'A New Path for China's Peaceful Rise and the Future of Asia', presented to the Bo'ao Forum on China's Hainan Island, an Asian equivalent of the World Economic Forum that was established under the auspices of Jiang Zemin.

By the time Zheng had organised a follow-up conference on the concept in April the following year, however, it appears to have run into some opposition from elements of the Party leadership, which became evident in the way that leading figures did not take it up. That the new leadership was having difficulty surmounting this opposition became clear when Hu Jintao himself failed to use the term 'peaceful rise' in his own address to the Bo'ao Forum, speaking instead about 'peace and stability', 'peace and security' and 'peaceful coexistence'. This erasure of 'peaceful rise' was made even more clear when the key Jiang Zemin loyalist on the Standing Committee of the Politburo, Zeng Qinhong, did not use it in a speech he made to the UN Economic and Social Commission for Asia and the Pacific two days later. Zeng preferred to stay with the phrase 'peace and development', drawn from the orthodox canon of Deng Xiaoping Theory.

Robert Suettinger (2004) has proposed that the propagation of 'peaceful rise' discourse is handicapped by three factors: the need to retain the option of using force to resolve the Taiwan issue, the incompleteness of the theory, and factional struggles at the top of the Party. The second of these reasons is not particularly strong, however, because the theory has been elaborated at length by academics and think tanks. It is undoubtedly true, though, that the need to maintain a credible military threat towards Taiwan is a major problem for 'peaceful rise'. That this links the concept with an issue so central to nationalist discourse, moreover, must make its proponents open to attack within the factional politics of the party elite.

The way in which this complex linkage of nationalism and foreign policy continues to constrain the Hu-Wen leadership can be seen in the efforts made by protagonists of 'peaceful rise' to reinforce their patriotic credentials. When Zheng Bijian addressed the Bo'ao Forum himself, he did not share the defiance of the orthodox line that a figure like Li Shenzhi had shown in his condemnation of the previous leadership's deployment of nationalism. Instead, he went to pains to stress that 'peaceful rise' was merely a continuation of the path of the previous 25 years, creating a link between Hu Jintao, Jiang Zemin and Deng Xiaoping. In an interview the following June, Zheng went to even greater lengths to stress continuity with the past, concluding his explanation of the theory with a call to 'Hold high the great banner of Deng Xiaoping Theory and the important thinking of the Three Represents' (Suettinger 2004: 5–6).

More recently, academic advocates of 'peaceful rise' theory have gone to some lengths to demonstrate its compatibility with Jiang Zemin's theory of the Three Represents. In the process they cite what appear to be differing positions amongst the pronouncements of leading figures as evidence of continuity. A good example of how this works can be seen in the book-length explanation and analysis of 'peaceful rise' produced by Jiang Xiyuan and Colonel Xia Liping of the Shanghai Institute of International Studies (Jiang and Xia 2004). It is worth looking in some detail at the argument developed by Jiang and Xia, because the Shanghai Institute was originally established by Zhou Enlai to provide an input into the foreign policy process from outside Beijing. That their views might be seen as an attempt to test the limits of ideological orthodoxy is shown in numerous places. They propose, for example, that American hegemony can be used for positive purposes, such as fighting terrorism, controlling the spread of WMD and providing aid to developing countries. They also urge China to shape international organisations and norms, not only through multilateral governmental organisations but also by working with NGOs and multinational corporations (16–25).

What is most interesting about this work for nationalist discourse, however, is how it deals the Taiwan issue. Jiang and Xia are explicitly concerned about the way in which the various policy areas of domestic development and foreign policy have been linked with the cause of national unification by making the Taiwan issue the criterion of whether China has become a great power. It is to break these links that the authors develop an alternative historical argument about the rise of great powers by pointing out that nineteenth-century Britain, and post-war Japan, Germany, Russia and South Korea were all able to increase their international standing while not being completely united internally. Conversely, the Qing dynasty collapsed even though it had been in control of Taiwan for more than 200 years. China's recent rapid development, they point out, has taken place while it is not united with Taiwan. In this way, Jiang and Xia can conclude that 'National unification does not necessarily have to take place before China's peaceful rise'. On the contrary, if unification is attempted by force, a huge economic and political burden will be imposed while China does not have the capability to confront the United States. Moreover, the ability of domestic opponents of the extreme right-wing advocates of the 'China threat' theory in Japan and the United States will be weakened (342–4).

This attempt to delink foreign policy from unification policy and the domestic politics of nationalism should be seen as a strategic manoeuvre, then, rather than a departure from the principles of CCP ideology. The authors stay well within the principles of Deng Xiaoping Theory when they argue that the government should tell the people that economic and technological development is more important than unification in achieving the status of a great power and that unification will necessarily be achieved in the course of development. Their boldest departure from established thinking can be seen in their prescriptions for a foreign policy that will maximise the possibility of achieving unification. This involves recognising the contribution of the US–Japan alliance to stability in Northeast Asia, and even trying to become an observer of what would amount to a trilateral security architecture with those two powers. With China being seen as a force for stability, other states would then join the cause of eradicating the Taiwan independence movement and 'urge America to control independence' (*cu mei zhi du*). With the United States needing China's support in the Middle East, North Korea and with the war on terror, both parties in Congress realising the dangers of encouraging Taiwanese independence, and Chen Shui-bian ignoring Washington's opposition to his 'defensive referendum', the pragmatism of the American people would be able to accept any kind of unification of China in the end. As Japan and the Southeast Asian states become increasingly dependent on the Chinese economy, moreover, they will follow suit. The European Union, too, can be won over to China's side, as evidenced by French President Jacques Chirac's condemnation of the referendum in Taiwan in a meeting with Wen Jiabao in February 2004, its criticism of American arms sales to Taiwan and its belief that it was in a better position than the United States to play a role in facilitating a settlement between the two sides of the Strait (344–54).

While this grand strategy fits well with the emerging ideological orthodoxy behind Beijing's diplomacy, however, the authors are at their most daring when they grapple with the complex implications of the events unfolding inside Taiwan itself. They are certainly aware that public opinion polls in Taiwan show that an increasing number of the islanders identify as Taiwanese and do not favour unification with China. The book was also written in time to know that Chen Shui-bian won the 2004 presidential election. Despite the controversial nature of that victory, involving the assasination attempt on Chen's life the day before polling, the authors concede that his ability to win with an increase of 11 per cent on his previous performance marks a consolida-tion of the DPP powerbase and has upset Washington's calculations (364). Despite such setbacks, however, Jiang and Xia are able to take comfort from the findings of foreign experts, who agree that opinion polls on the island indicate that the Taiwanese are not really searching for independence but for a high degree of autonomy, security, respect and prosperity. What is needed, therefore, is the continuation of a soft policy towards the island, appealing to the moderate Chinese tradition of the Confucian 'royal way' (*wang dao*) of leading by example, which had unified China in the past, rather than the Legalist heritage of 'hegemony' (*ba dao*).

What is most remarkable of all about the recommendations of Jiang and Xia for Taiwan, though, is what they have to say about 'emancipa-tion of thought' on several of the key issues that have proved stum-bling blocks for any progress. This includes accepting that attempts to obfuscate the issue of the legitimate continuity of the Republic of China have so far failed to achieve anything, and that it is time to accept that 'two Chinas is better than "one China, one Taiwan"', so long as toleration of the ROC does not lead to Taiwanese independ-ence. Similarly, the authors are able to say that the dramatic changes to China's domestic system since the formula of 'one country, two systems' was produced in the late 1970s and early 1980s means that Beijing's position that anything can be discussed so long as the 'one China' principle is accepted should not mean that talks have to be limited to Deng Xiaoping's formula (355–60).

While such open flexibility on the Taiwan issue is remarkably radical within the context of PRC political discourse, it also reveals the limitations of 'peaceful rise' theory when it comes to reassuring the world about the implications of China's growing economic and military power. The fact that well-informed authors such as Jiang and Xia downplay the military option is due partly to their realisation that the PLA does not have the ability to solve the problem by force because it cannot gain control of the air or seas around Taiwan, not to any reappraisal of the PRC's claim to the island. The rational policy is, therefore, to wait while China becomes the workshop of the world and use the deepening links between the Chinese economy and Western multinationals and political circles throughout the world to oppose Taiwanese independence (363–4).

Whether such tendencies can be effectively cultivated and sustained by Beijing remains something of a moot question, given that the eventual goal of this policy is still rooted firmly in the CCP's quest for unification that drives domestic nationalism and also the fears of China's neighbours. If the PRC really does want to make its peaceful rise analogous with the rise of post-war Germany and Japan, as Jiang and Xia suggest, then this would entail giving up its nuclear arsenal, renouncing the use of force as a tool of foreign policy, and allowing massive numbers of foreign troops to be based on Chinese soil. If this is the inevitable logic of following through the idea of China's 'peaceful rise', it should not be surprising that the theory has had a short life amongst China's political elite.

Japan: popular nationalism and the limits of elite discourse

While new possibilities for academic discourse may have been opened up by 'peaceful rise' theory, nowhere are the continuing constraints of CCP ideology on foreign policy more evident than in outbursts of popular nationalism towards Japan. Given that the birth of popular nationalism as a protest against the government took place with the May Fourth Movement, when students demonstrated in Peking against the transfer of German concessions to Japan at the 1919 Paris Peace Conference, the handling of relations with Japan has long had a potent symbolic significance in the politics of legitimacy in China. Under Mao Zedong, the CCP strived to maintain good relations with Japan by distinguishing the majority of its people from the militarists who had been responsible for past aggressions in Asia. Under 'reform and opening', however, the linkage of policy towards Japan with leadership legitimacy ran through the demonstrations of the 1980s and the downfall of Hu Yaobang. Since Tiananmen, memories of Japan's past aggression have been systematically used as part of the patriotic education campaign. At the same time, demonstrations in Taiwan and Hong Kong and amongst the Chinese overseas over the disputed Diaoyu Senkaku archipelago in the East China Sea have fed through into domestic politics to pose yet another challenge to the patriotic rhetoric of the CCP. The complex linkages and dilemmas posed by this issue are represented most acutely by the way in which even Hong Kong's Democrats became a spearhead of the worldwide campaign to reclaim the Diaoyu archipelago for the Chinese nation, which was revived after a group of Japanese rightwing extremists erected a lighthouse on the islands in 1996. In September that year, ethnic Chinese journalists and news editors around the world organised a petition demanding that Beijing should mobilise its military to deal with the issue (*MB* 7–9–96).

According to Deng Xiaoping Theory, however, it is essential that a workable relationship with Japan is maintained as part of the strategy of creating the right conditions for economic construction to proceed. Given that the two economies have now become highly integrated through the flow of Japanese FDI into China and the way in which they are bound together in the global production chain (Hideo 2004), the future of this economic relationship is thus something of a barometer for measuring how China's leaders can achieve an optimum balance between economic globalisation and the cultivation of domestic nationalism. As an indication of the difficulties this presents for CCP legitimacy, it is interesting to note that the texts included in Deng Xiaoping Theory to establish the principle of 'shelving' sovereignty do not include Deng's earliest statement on this issue. This is when Deng told a Japanese reporter in November 1978 that discussion of the disputed Diaoyu/Senkaku islands could be shelved for around ten years, leaving it for the next generation to solve (Suganama 2000: 138).

As mentioned in Chapter 3, it was also in 1996 that Jiang Zemin's handling of the relationship with Japan began to be an object of domestic criticism due to his failure to take any action against the signing of the Joint US–Japan Security Declaration in April that year. In Beijing, this was seen as an expansion of the scope of Japan's security commitments to include the Taiwan Strait. Jiang's attempt to put relations with Tokyo on a better footing with his visit to Japan in

November 1998, also proved to be something of a disaster. This already difficult relationship became even more sensitive for Jiang when the populist Junichiro Koizumi became Japan's Prime Minister in April 2001 and resumed the practice of doing obeisance at the Yasukuni Shrine to the war dead in Tokyo that August. The following month, the relationship became a major issue in China's domestic politics after members of an already unsettled public found an object on which to focus their anger when a Chinese fashion magazine featured a photograph of the popular film star Zhao Wei wearing a dress decorated with an imperial Japanese flag. In the wave of popular indignation that this generated in the printed press and on the Internet, Zhao was condemned as a traitor and bombarded with obscene insults. The episode reached an ugly climax in December, when an angry young man smeared faeces over Zhao on stage during a New Year's event.

Among the academics and writers attached to the official media who tried to bring some sense of moderation to this rising tide of anti-Japanese sentiment was the *People's Daily* journalist Ma Licheng, whose attempts to oppose the rise of popular nationalism after 1996 as a co-author of *Crossed Swords* and *Outcry* were discussed in Chapter 3. In the late 2002 issue of *Strategy and Management*, Ma published an article which described his feelings about the treatment of Zhao Wei and the general rise in anti-Japanese sentiment following his own trip to Japan in January, under the title 'New Thinking on Sino-Japanese Relations' (Ma 2002). Continuing his earlier criticism of works like *China Can Say No* and *Behind the Demonization of China* for their self-aggrandisement of China, and extending this to the isolationism of more recent nationalist outbursts such as Wang Xiaodong's *China's Road Under the Shadow of Globalization*, Ma even went so far as to suggest that the anti-Japanese outbursts were a characteritistic of fascism, as defined by the Frankfurt School of Marxism.

As with his earlier works, Ma's new article associated his response to popular nationalism closely with that of the leadership and the Party line, restating the need for a peaceful international environment to solve China's domestic problems, and citing a February 2002 statement by Jiang Zemin that emphasised the need for friendship between China and Japan. He also deployed many of the themes associated with the discussion of 'China's peaceful rise' by restating the necessity of adhering to the 'good neighbour' regional policy and approving of the way in which multilateralism had been used to counter talk of the China threat in the United States and Japan. Citing opinion polls that show how anti-Japanese activities are feeding a bad impression of China in Japan, he gave a fairly positive assessment of that country, sympathising with the anxieties of the Japanese about being overtaken by China economically and refuting those in China who argue that the Japanese are still militaristic.

What is most controversial about Ma's article for Chinese politics, however, is the way in which he draws out certain recommendations for improving relations with Japan, which follow on from the premises of the Party orthodoxy on foreign policy. Calling for China to adopt the magnanimous attitude of the victor in the war, he argues that after sixty years it is time to accept that the Japanese have already apologised sufficiently for the past wrong doings of their country. Moreover, the Chinese should recognise and properly value the economic aid that Japan had given to China since 1979 in the form of soft loans. Taking the orthodox line to its logical conclusions in this way was what aroused criticism, not only from academic publications, but more importantly on Internet forums, where Ma was denounced as a 'traitor' and received threats to his property and even his life. In the summer of 2003, Ma took early retirement from the *People's Daily* and took a post working for Phoenix TV in Hong Kong.

An alternative strategy for defending the attempt to build good relations with Japan was deployed by Shi Yinhong, a Professor of International Relations at Beijing's Renmin University, who published an article in *Strategy and Management* (Shi 2003) that is sympathetic with Ma Licheng's concerns and promotes a 'diplomatic revolution' in Sino-Japanese relations. Yet Shi's argument is presented as a matter of geopolitical necessity for China, allowing the country to concentrate its energies on dealing with anti-Chinese forces in the United States and on opposing pro-independence forces in Taiwan. It is, therefore, in China's national interests not to harp on the question of Japan's view of history. Instead, economic relations with Japan should be strengthened to take the place of those with the United States and the European Union. Japan should also be formally thanked at the highest level for the ODA it has provided to China over the years. Instead of exaggerating claims about the rise of Japanese militarism, China would serve its own national interests much better by welcoming Japan's participation in regional and international politics as a 'great power', and supporting Japanese efforts to become a permanent member of the UN Security Council.

Shi Yinhong's article was followed in *Strategy and Management* by the most direct and detailed defence of the Party line, when Professor Feng Zhaokui of the Japan Research Institute at the Chinese Academy of Social Sciences published an article under the title 'On the New Thinking Towards Japan' (Feng 2003). As Feng explains, the spirit of the 'new thinking' on Japan policy can be drawn from the section of Jiang Zemin's address to the Sixteenth Party Congress that covers the international situation. It is there that Jiang observes 'A new world war will not happen in the foreseeble future. It is realistic to bring about a fairly long period of peace in the world and a favourable climate in areas around China.' Accepting this premise allows Feng to restate the emerging orthodoxy of strengthening good neighbourly relations so that the nation's efforts can be focused on economic development. He is thus able to deploy most of the foreign-policy themes that are found in Deng Xiaoping Theory and the Three Represents, such as the need to put a premium on good economic relations in an age of globalisation, the need to ensure an 'Asian revival', and the need to cooperate on combating non-traditional security threats such as terrorism and epidemics.

Addressing more traditional geopolitical concerns, Feng has a somewhat different emphasis from Shi Yinhong, insofar as he dismisses the possibility of supplanting the United States–Japan alliance, although he does agree that the better relations are between China and Japan, the weaker the United States–Japan alliance will be. The rise of Japan to great power status, moreover, can be accepted as being in accordance with the beneficial trend towards multipolarity, which will also weaken the unilateralism of the United States. While Feng avoids provoking the same kind of controversy as Ma Licheng has stimulated on the history issue by arguing that a country's textbooks must be its own domestic affair, he does agree that solving this issue should not be made a precondition for good relations because freezing high-level contacts will only encourage right-wing forces in Japan to distort history. What is most interesting for the relationship between domestic politics and foreign policy, though, is the way in which Feng cites Deng Xiaoping to insist that it is important to always start from thinking about the national interest when developing relations between states, and not to fret over historical resentments or differences between social systems and ideologies (Feng 2003: 2).

Such attempts to find a rational argument to counter the growing tide of anti-Japanese sentiments show just how difficult this task of keeping foreign policy separate from domestic politics has become for the new leadership of Hu Jintao and Wen Jiabao. From the summer of 2003 onwards, popular anti-Japanese activities multiplied. June saw the burning of a Japanese flag near the contested Diaoyu/Senkaku islands by the first group of Mainland Chinese activists to have reached the area. This was followed by the organisation of an Internet-based petition to demand that the contract to build a Beijing-Shanghai high-speed rail link should not go to a Japanese firm. The issue of chemical weapons left in China by Japan after World War II came to a new head after one person was killed and dozens were injured by the explosion of wartime gas munitions in the northeast. The exposure of an orgy involving hundreds of Japanese businessmen and Chinese prostitutes in the southeastern city of Zhuhai caused widespread disgust and outrage, and a drag show put on by Japanese students at the Northwestern University in Xian triggered student demonstrations because it was considered to be disrespectful. The following year, Chinese fans hurled insults and missiles at the Japanese soccer team as it toured the country for the Asian Cup tournament in August.

In April 2005, outbursts of anti-Japanese sentiment seemed to be developing into a nationwide movement coordinated over the Internet. These linked together issues such as the approval of new school text-books by Tokyo's Ministry of Education that glossed over Japan's wartime atrocities and Japan's bid to become a Permanent Member of the UN Security Council, following the release of UN Secretary General Koffi Annan's recommendations for reform of the organisa-tion. Large-scale demonstrations began to occur in cities across China, coming to a head on 16 April, when attacks took place against Japanese consulates, restaurants, shops and even passersby who hap-pened to be driving the wrong kind of car on the wrong day. The events were particularly large and violent in that most cosmopolitan of China's cities, Shanghai, Deng Xiaoping's showpiece for the global era.

Chinese nationalism in the global era

At a time when China is becoming better known around the world for the way in which its corporations are acquiring assets in Western multinational firms from electronics through automobiles, energy and banks, many foreign observers have been surprised and puzzled by this tide of anti-Japanese sentiment. Reports in the Western media seem to present two Chinas: one nationalistic and the other linked firmly in the discourse of globalisation. Phenomena such as anti-Japanese demon-strations, however, show how these two aspects of China have been a mutually interdependent characteristic of politics under 'reform and opening' at least since the anti-Japanese demonstrations of the early 1980s. If anything, such outbursts are becoming more frequent as China is increasingly exposed to the international economy and foreign cultures. Moreover, because China's present leaders have inherited their post-Mao predecessors' location of patriotism, national unification and opposition to 'international hegemony' at the centre of the CCP's claim to legitimacy, it is increasingly difficult to keep foreign policy separate from domestic politics.

The resulting balancing act can be seen in the response of the government to the anti-Japanese demonstrations of early 2005. On the one hand, China's leaders had to live up to their patriotic rhetoric by making shows of defiance. The Foreign Ministry reiterated China's claim to the Diaoyu/Senkaku archipelago, the Zhuhai orgy was condemned, and the Chinese participants were given harsh penal sentences. Japan's Minister of Transportation was snubbed when she visited Beijing to discuss the high-speed rail contract. When Japanese Foreign Minister Nobutaka Machimura visited Beijing in the expectation of receiving an apology for the 16 April demonstrations from his Chinese counterpart, Li Zhaoxing, he was informed instead that Japan had hurt the feelings of the Chinese on a series of issues, including relations with Taiwan and the dispute over history.

While these gestures were being made towards Japan, however, repressive measures were also taken to prevent any recurrence of the demonstrations as the anniversary of the May Fourth Movement approached. Some 42 people were arrested in Shanghai for taking part in the demonstrations of 16 April. As the city's new citizens of the global information revolution found out when they checked their mobile phones for text messages, further demonstrations had been forbidden. The anniversary of the patriotic May Fourth Movement that year was to involve little more than the usual ritualistic campus shows and children's parades. As was explained by Shanghai's *Liberation Daily*, the organ that Deng Xiaoping had used to launch his ideological counter-attack in 1991, patriotic ardour might be understandable and valuable, but it should not be expressed by illegal means that can be exploited by 'criminal elements and organisations' with ulterior motives for committing illegal acts (*JFRB* 26–04–05). Meanwhile, two days after Li Zhaoxing had refused to apologise to Japan's Foreign Minister, he delivered a familiar message when he told a meeting of 3,500 cadres, government officials and soldiers in Beijing: 'Turn your patriotic fervour toward concrete actions in your work and diligent studies, so as to contribute to the rejuvenation of the Chinese nation' (Reuters 19–4–05).

It is not necessary to propose that the CCP leadership takes specific actions to encourage activities like the anti-Japanese demonstrations, to explain why they should have occurred. More significant is the observation that making nationalism so central to the claim to CCP legitimacy means that any actions taken by China's leaders on sensitive issues such as Japan, Taiwan and the United States, will have very broad implications for domestic politics. The resulting expressions of public anger are not only detrimental to the presentation of China as a peacefully rising power, they also pose a risk to the party's core task of economic development. As a survey of Japanese businesses in China carried out by the Japan External Trade Organization (JETRO) in June 2005 found out, some 10 per cent of those polled had suffered a negative impact on production and sales activities, and 37 per cent were concerned about future impacts. 'Cold water' had been thrown on the willingness of Japanese firms to expand their operations in China, and a majority felt that the risk of operating in China had increased (JETRO 2005).

Yet the fact that nationalistic themes are inculcated in Chinese children as they are taught subjects across the curriculum makes it unsurprising that young people should find it natural to condemn those who appear to be working for better relations with the 'enemy', whether it be a leader like Premier Zhu Rongji in 1999 or an academic like Ma Licheng in 2003. The resulting tensions between domestic politics and foreign policy only fuel the already intense discussions of the implications of China's rising power amongst academics and policy-makers around the world. As the above analysis shows, nowhere is this debate more intense than in China itself, where commentators are aware that previous rising powers have challenged the status quo through warfare, most notoriously in the cases of the modernising states of pre-war Japan and Germany.

Among American neo-realists, John Mearsheimer's general account of the 'tragedy of the great powers' presents probably the clearest and most consistent argument that the structure of international politics makes conflict between a rising China and the existing hegemon of the United States inevitable (Mearsheimer 2001). Former National Security Secretary of State for the George W. Bush administration, Condoleeza Rice, perhaps also reflected this way of thinking when, shortly before she became National Security Advisor in the first Bush administration, argued that China 'is not a status quo power' (Rice 2000: 56).

An alternative view has been proposed by Alastair Iain Johnston (2003), based on extensive research into primary Chinese international relations texts. According to this argument, the way in which Beijing has come round to exerting its influence through shaping international regimes and engaging in multilateralism indicates that China has found a way to pursue the national interest without challenging the status quo, however it is defined. In this respect, China is no exception among states when it protects its national interests through activities such as 'internal balancing' through military procurement.

To date, there is evidence to support the views of both Mearsheimer and Johnston. From a structuralist perspective, the economic development of a country the size of China must in itself represent a change in the international distribution of power, *per se*. Moreover, the political frictions between China and Japan, Taiwan and the United States show the limitations of any theory based on the premises of liberal interdependence, that economic integration will enhance regional stability. Yet, Johnston is also right to draw attention to Beijing's strenuous efforts to reassure its neighbours about its intentions and to work through multilateral avenues and international regimes. If China were like any other state, then there would be no strong reason to expect that it will not be possible to manage its rise peacefully.

Yet, if constructivist theorists are correct to point out that 'international anarchy is what states make of it' (Wendt 1999: 297–312), then the question about China's rise should be framed as 'What *kind* of a status quo can be created by the values promoted by China's leaders?' In this respect, the values that determine the 'culture of anarchy' for China's leaders have been unusually clear, at least since January 1980, as the analysis throughout this work has demonstrated. When Jiang Zemin gave a speech on 1 July 2001 to mark the 80th anniversary of the founding of the CCP, he was in no doubt about the legacy he was leaving for the successor generation, as he stated:

> The status of Taiwan shall in no way be allowed to change. The Chinese communists are rock firm in their resolve to safeguard state sovereignty and territorial integrity. While we do have the greatest sincerity to work for a peaceful unification, we cannot and will not undertake to renounce the use of force. We are fully capable of checking any attempt to split China by seeking Taiwan's 'independence'.
>
> (Jiang 2001)

This came at the end of a lengthy restatement of the narrative of the CCP's climb to power and salvation of the nation, followed by an explication of the new ideology of the Three Represents.

Given the nature of the values that are so dear to China's leaders, it would be a fundamental error to see the issue of Taiwan as the exception to the rule in China's international behaviour. As has been demonstrated above, Taiwan is in fact probably the most important of the rules that determine China's international behaviour, and it is rooted firmly in domestic politics. Other similar rules are the opposition to humanitarian intervention and a rigid adherence to the doctrine of the inviolability of state sovereignty. The territorial disputes with ASEAN and India have thus been 'shelved' rather than resolved. The way in which a future generation will address these issues, when Beijing has more relative power at its disposal, is impossible to predict. However, the rise of China's technocratic elite does not give reason to support the view that exposure to the West will lead to moderation in world view. On the contrary, it is a phenomenon of the new nationalism that many of its leading advocates have been exposed to the West and Japan. Wang Xiaodong spent three years as a student in Tokyo in the early 1980s, and all of the authors of *Behind the Demonization of China* had studied or worked in the United States.

When the unchanging core values of the CCP are taken into account, the significance of the way in which references to globalization in Chinese academic journals have surpassed those to multipolarity (Johnston 34–5) lies not in a declining interest in nationalism. This would indeed be a perverse conclusion to draw, given that the interest in globalization takes the lead over multipolarity in the crisis year of 1999, when popular nationalist activism reaches its highest peak. When the vacuousness of multipolarity as a guide to foreign policy making is taken into account, the prominence of globalization is better explained as no more than the most recent stage in a longer process of appropriating various foreign policy themes to strengthen the nationalist credentials that have been established to assess the legitimacy of the CCP leadership. If this pattern continues, then Beijing's apologists for a faster move towards entry into the world trade system can be expected to resort to more nationalistic rhetoric as contradictions increase amongst China's peoples.

When a Chinese expert on international relations theory like Yan Xuetong was writing in 1995 about the need for China to have a positive input into the shaping of international norms, it is unlikely that he was thinking about support for violently repressive regimes such that of Islom Karimov in Uzbekistan or Robert Mugabe in Zimbabwe, or opposition to UN intervention in Sudan to prevent the genocide in Darfur, that have characterised foreign policy under Hu Jintao (Alden 2005: 155). However, as has been shown above, since China's international crises of 1995–99, opposition to humanitarian intervention has hardened. Since the 9/11 Incident in the United States, this has fallen on increasingly receptive ears around the world. It creates a good situation in which Beijing can court regimes that the

Western powers wish to transform, often gaining significant economic resources in the process.

Whether or not some of the more radical implications of 'peaceful rise' theory will be able to make it onto the foreign policy agenda of the Hu-Wen leadership will depend in part on the delicate balance that has to be reached in factional politics at the top of the CCP. Equally important, though, is the way in which building a consensus among the elite is still influenced by the growth of popular nationalism through the new media in an increasingly pluralistic society, given that the objectives of opposing 'international hegemony' and achieving national unification remain at the core of the CCP's claim to legitimacy. The constraints imposed by the resulting dynamics of elite-popular discourse on any attempt to delink foreign policy from domestic politics have been illustrated quite clearly at the elite level by the erasure of the discourse of 'peaceful rise' and at the popular level by the fate of the 'new thinking' on Japan.

The leadership of Hu Jintao shows no sign of being able to break this cycle. Hu is not seen as a figure with the ability to take any radical new departures that would entail a challenge to the fundamental values established so clearly in Deng Xiaoping Theory. Instead, the military build-up opposite Taiwan has continued, with the latest estimate by the US Department of Defense claiming that some that between 650 and 730 short-range missiles are now located opposite the island, a number that is increasing at the rate of 100 per year (Department of Defense: 4). It has been argued by some (Wang 2005) that democracy would only make nationalism stronger by allowing the population to demand stronger actions from the government. That will remain a moot question so long as democratisation remains a very distant prospect for China. What can be said at present, though, is that the current one-party system cannot exist without using nationalism as a reason to prevent the emergence of multi-party democracy. The claim that only the CCP can deliver the nation from humiliation by achieving certain goals in economic, unification and foreign policy, is what determines the 'culture of international anarchy' for China in the global era.

Notes

Introduction

1 The CNKI is itself a remarkable achievement of the information revolution, being a database run from Tsinghua University in Beijing that includes the full text of articles of most journals published in the PRC from 1992 to 2003. It can be accessed at: http://www.global.cnki.net/academic.htm.

2 This list is compiled from the works of Zheng, Zhao (1997) and Fewsmith.

1 The globalisation of nationalism under 'reform and opening'

1 This is a modification of the official English version, which reads 'issues of global strategic significance'. This does not have the same implication as the original '*dai quanqiu xing de zhanlue wenti*', rendered here as 'strategic problems with a global nature'.

2 '86' meaning '1986', and '3' being March, the third month of the year.

2 After 1989: nationalism and the new global elite

1 The author would like to express his gratitude to Father Dominique Tyl of the Socio-Cultural Research Center, Furen Catholic University, Taiwan, for allowing access to his collection of the PRC teaching materials used in this section. The texts referred to are collected together in the bibliography of this volume for ease of reference.

3 Globalisation and its discontents

1 The wording '*wu xin jiaoyu*', literally 'Five Hearts Education', appears to be a play on the wording of the Confucian doctrine of the 'Five Relationships' (*wu lun*) between 'sovereign and subjects, father and sons, husband and wife, among brothers and among friends'. Xiao does not say what are the other two 'loves' in the formula adopted by the Heilongjiang school.

2 This is the date of the preface written by the authors.

4 What kind of a status quo power?

1 See chart available at Election Study Center, National Chengchi University, Taipei, Taiwan. Online. URL at: http://www2.nccu.edu.tw/~s00/eng/data/data03–3.htm (accessed 11 May 2005).

Bibliography

Alden, C. (2005) 'China in Africa', *Survival* (47:3): 147–63.

Anon. (ed.) (1988) *Fang Lizhi Liu Bingyan Wang Ruowang yanlun gaobian* [Scripts of Speeches and Texts by Fang Lizhi, Liu Binyan, Wang Ruowang'], Hong Kong: Shuguang tushu.

Anon. (1995) 'Yingxiang wo guo guojia anquan de ruogan yinsu', [Various Factors Influencing the Country's National Security] (aka *The Ten Thousand Word Letter*) reprinted in Shi (1997): 25–48.

Anon. (1996) 'Weilai yi, ershi nian woguo guojia anquan de nei wai xingshi zhuyao weixie de chubu tantao', [Preliminary Investigations into the Internal and External Situation and Main Threats Affecting Our Country's Security over the Next 10–20 Years], reprinted in Shi (1997): 133–45.

ASEAN (2003) 'Joint Declaration of the Heads of State/Government of the Association of Southeast Asian Nations and the People's Republic of China', 8 October, Bali, online, available: <*http://www.aseansec.org/15265.htm*> (accessed 30 June 2004).

ASEAN (2004) *ASEAN China Foreign Ministers' Informal Meeting Joint Press Release*, 21 June, Qingdao, China, online, available: <*http://www.aseansec.org/16167.htm*> (accessed 30 June 2004).

Barme, J. (1999) *In the Red: On Contemporary Chinese Culture*, New York: Columbia University Press.

Breslin, S. (2000) 'The Virtual Market', *China Review*, Autumn/Winter: 22–4.

Chu Kemin, Zhang Tao, Zhang Ximing and Weng Jieming (eds) (1996) *Yu zongshuji tan xin* [Heart to Heart Talks with the General Secretary], Hong Kong: Mingbao chubanshe.

Chu Shulong and Wang Zaibang (1999) 'Guanyu guoji xingshi he wo dui wai zhanlue ruogan da wenti si kao', [Thoughts on Some Big Problems in the International Situation and Our Country's Foreign Strategy], *Xiandai guoji guanxi* (8): 2–6.

Clark, I. (2001) 'Globalization and the Post-Cold War Order', in John Baylis and Steve Smith (ed.), *The Globalization of World Politics* (second edition), Oxford: Oxford University Press: 634–47.

Clinton, Bill (1998) 'Why I'm Going to Beijing', *Newsweek*, 29 June: 16B.

Coalition of Students (1989) ' "Let Our Cries Awaken Our Young Republic!", Proclamation of the Coalition of Students' Self-Governing Councils of Beijing Higher Educational Institutes', translated in *Chinese Sociology and Anthropology*, (Vol. 23, No. 1, 1990): 16 (translator not named).

Cui, X. (1996) 'Lingtu zhengduan de zhanlue sixiang yu shijian', [Thought and Practice on Territorial Disputes], in Gong Li (ed.) *Deng Xiaoping de waijiao sixiang yu shijian*, [*Deng Xiaoping's Foreign Policy Thinking and Practice*], Heilongjiang jiaoyu chubanshe: 250–65.

Dai, Xiudian (2003) 'ICTs in China's Development Strategy', in Hughes and Wacker (eds): 8–29.

Deng, Shichao (2003) 'Zhongguo-dongmeng ziyou maoyi qu dui dongnanya huaren zhengzhi de yingxiang shixi', [Preliminary Analysis of the Impact of the China-ASEAN Free Trade Area on the Overseas Chinese in Southeast Asia], *Dongya yanjiu* (*Southeast Asian Studies*), (3): 63–8.

Deng, Xiaoping (1984a) 'On the Reform of the System of Party and State Leadership', *Selected Works of Deng Xiaoping (1975–1982)*, Beijing: Foreign Languages Press: 302–25.

—— (1984b) 'Emancipate the Mind, Seek Truth from Facts and Unite as One in Looking to the Future', *Selected Works (1975–1982)*: 151–65.

—— (1984c) 'Mao Zedong Thought Must be Correctly Understood as an Integral Whole', *Selected Works (1975–1982)*: 55–60.

—— (1984d) 'Speech at the National Conference on Education', *Selected Works (1975–1982)*: 119–26.

—— (1984e) 'Speech at the Opening Ceremony of the National Conference on Science', *Selected Works (1975–1982)*: 101–16.

—— (1984f) 'Uphold the Four Cardinal Principles', *Selected Works (1975–1982)*: 166–91.

—— (1984g) 'The Present Situation and the Tasks Before Us', *Selected Works (1975–1982)*: 224–58.

—— (1984g1) 'Muqian de xingshi he renwu', [The Present Situation and the Tasks Before Us], *Deng Xiaoping wenxuan (1975–1982)*: 203–37.

—— (1984h) 'Remarks on Successive Drafts of the 'Resolution on Certain Questions in the History of Our Party since the Founding of the People's Republic of China', *Selected Works (1975–1982)*: 276–96.

—— (1984i) 'Speech at a Plenary Meeting of the Military Commission of the CPC', *Selected Works (1975–1982)*: 87–100.

—— (1984j) 'Hold High the Banner of Mao Zedong Thought and Adhere to the Principle of Seeking Truth from Facts', *Selected Works (1975–1982)*: 141–4.

—— (1984k) 'Implement the Policy of Readjustment, Ensure Stability and Unity', *Selected Works (1975–1982)*: 335–55.

—— (1984l) 'Speech at the Opening Ceremony of the National Conference on Science', *Selected Works (1975–1982)*: 101–16.

—— (1984m) 'Concerning Problems on the Ideological Front', *Selected Works (1975–1982)*: 369–70.

—— (1985) *Build Socialism with Chinese Characteristics*, Beijing: Foreign Languages Press.

—— (1993a) 'Heping he fazhan shi dangdai shijie de liang da wenti', [Peace and Development Are the Two Outstanding Issues in the World Today], *Deng Xiaoping wenxuan (Selected Works of Deng Xiaoping)*, Vol. 3, Beijing: Renmin chubanshe: 104–6. English version available online: *http://english.peopledaily.com.cn/dengxp/vol3/text/c1330.html* (accessed 6 June 2005).

—— (1993a1) 'Gao zichanjieji ziyouhua jiushi zou zichan jieji zhuyi daolu', [Advocating Bourgeois Liberalisation is Taking the Road of Capitalism], *Deng Xiaoping wenxuan*, Vol. 3: 123–5.

—— (1993a2) 'Gongtong nuli, shixian zuguo tongyi', *Deng Xiaoping wenxuan*, Vol. 3: 362.

—— (1993a3) 'Shan yu liyong shiji jiejue fazhan wenti', *Deng Xiaoping wenxuan*, Vol. 3: 363–5.

—— (1993a4) 'Zhongguo dalu he Taiwan heping tongyi de shexiang', [A Proposal for the Unification of Mainland China and Taiwan], *SW3*: 31.

—— (1993a5) 'Zhongguo yongyuan bu yunxu bie guo ganshe nei zheng', [China Will Never Agree to Other Countries Interfering in Internal Politics], *Deng Xiaoping wenxuan*, Vol. 3: 359–61.

—— (1993a6) 'Zengjin Zhong Yin youyi, jiaqiang nan nan hezuo', [Enhancing Sino-Indian Friendship–Strengthening South-South Co-operation], *Deng Xiaoping wenxuan*, Vol. 3: 19–20.

—— (1993a7) 'Wending shijie jushi de xin banfa', [A New Method for Stabilising the World Situation], *SW3*: 49–50.

—— (1993b) 'Heping gong chu yuanze chuyu qiangda shengming li', *Deng Xiaoping wenxuan*, Vol. 3: 96–7.

—— (1993c) 'Zhongguo gongchangdang di shi er ci quanguo daibiao dahui kaimu ci', [Opening Speech at the Twelfth National Congress of the CPC], *Deng Xiaoping wenxuan*, Vol. 3: 1–4.

—— (1993d) 'Wo guo fangzhen de liangge jiben dian', [The Two Basic Elements in China's Policy], *Deng Xiaoping wenxuan*, Vol. 3: 248–50.

—— (1993e) 'Ban hao jingji techu, zengjia dui wai kaifang chengshi', *Deng Xiaoping wenxuan*, Vol. 3: 51–2.

—— (1993f) 'Wei jingshan xuexiao ti ci', *Deng Xiaoping wenxuan*, Vol. 3: 35.

—— (1993f1) 'Dang zai zuzhi zhanxian he sixiang zhanxian shang de poqie renwu', *Deng Xiaoping wenxuan*, Vol. 3: 36–48.

—— (1993g) 'Jianshe you zhongguo te se de shehui zhuyi', *Deng Xiaoping wenxuan*, Vol. 3: 62–6.

—— (1993h) 'Zai dang de shier qie liu zhong quan hui shang de jiang hua', [Speech at the Sixth Plenum of the Twelfth Party Congress], *Deng Xiaoping wenxuan*, Vol. 3: 181–2.

—— (1993i) 'Yong zhongguo lishi jiaoyu qingnian', [Use Chinese History to Teach the Young], *Deng Xiaoping wenxuan*, Vol. 3: 204–6.

—— (1993j) 'Yiqie cong shehui zhuyi chuji jieduan de shiji chufa', [Everything

Starts Out from the Primary Stage of Socialism], *Deng Xiaoping wenxuan*, Vol. 3: 251–2.

—— (1993k) 'Jihua he shichang dou shi fazhan shengchanli de fangfa', [Planning and the Market Are Both Methods for Developing Production], *Deng Xiaoping wenxuan*, Vol. 3: 203.

—— (1993l) 'Huijian xianggang tebie xingzhengqu jibenfa qicao weiyuanhui yuan de jianghua', *Deng Xiaoping wenxuan*, Vol. 3: 215–22.

—— (1993m) 'Zai junwei kuoda huiyi shang de jianghua', *Deng Xiaoping wenxuan*, Vol. 3: 126–9.

—— (1993n) 'Yao xishou guoji de jingyan', *Deng Xiaoping wenxuan*, Vol. 3: 266–7.

—— (1993n1) 'Zai jiejian shodu jieyan buduijun yishang ganbu de jianghua', *Deng Xiaoping wenxuan*, Vol. 3: 302–8.

—— (1993o) 'Zai wuchang, shenzhen, zhuhai, shanghai deng di de tanhua yaodian', [Excerpts from Talks Given in Wuchang, Shenzhen, Zhuhai and Shanghai], *Deng Xiaoping wenxuan*, Vol. 3: 370–83.

—— (1993p) 'Gao zichan jieji ziyouhua jiushi zou ziben zhuyi daolu', [Practising Bourgeois Liberalisation is Taking the Capitalist Road], *Deng Xiaoping wenxuan*, Vol. 3: 123–5.

—— (1993q) 'Shehuizhuyi de Zhongguo shei ye dongyao bu liao', [Nobody Can Shake Socialist China], *Deng Xiaoping wenxuan*, Vol. 3: 328–9.

—— (1993r) 'Jianchi shehui zhuyi, fangzhi heping yanbian', [Uphold Socialism, Prevent Peaceful Evolution], *Deng Xiaoping wenxuan*, Vol. 3: 344–6.

—— (1993s) 'Guoji xingshi he jingji wenti', [The International Situation and Economic Problems], *Deng Xiaoping wenxuan*, Vol. 3: 353–6.

—— (1993t) 'Women you xinxin ba zhongguo de shiqing zuo de geng hao', [We Have Confidence in Handling China's Affairs Even Better], *Deng Xiaoping wenxuan*, Vol. 3: 324–7.

—— (1993u) 'Jieshu yanjun de Zhong Mei guanxi yao you Meiguo caizhu zhudong', [Ending Strained Sino-US Relations Must Come from US Actions], *Deng Xiaoping wenxuan*, Vol. 3: 330–3.

—— (1993v) 'Gaige kaifang zhengce winding, zhongguo da you xiwang', [The Policy of Reform and Opening Is Stable, China Has Great Hope], *Deng Xiaoping wenxuan*, Vol. 3: 315–21.

—— (1993w) 'Yi ge guojia, liang zhong zhidu', [One Country, Two Systems], *Deng Xiaoping wenxuan*, Vol. 3: 58–61.

—— (1993x) 'Zai zhongyang guwen weiyuanhui di san ci quanti huiyi shang de jianghua', *Deng Xiaoping wenxuan*, Vol. 3: 83–93.

—— (1993y) 'Baochi xianggang de fanrong he wending', *Deng Xiaoping wenxuan*, Vol. 3: 72–6.

—— (1993z) 'Women dui Xianggang de jiben lichang', *Deng Xiaoping wenxuan*, Vol. 3: 12–15.

Department of Defense (DoD United States) (2005) *The Military Power of the People's Republic of China 2005*, online, available: <http://

www.defenselink.mil/news/Jul2005/d20050719china.pdf> (accessed 8 August 2005).

Dillon, M. (2004) *Xinjiang – China's Muslim Far Northeast*, London and New York: Routledge Curzon.

Ding, Weizhi and Chen Song (1995) *Zhong xi ti yong zhi jian*, [*Between China and the West, Essence and Function*], Beijing: Zhongguo shehui kexue chubanshe.

Drifte, R. (2003) *Japan's Security Relations with China since 1989*, London and New York: Routledge.

Fan, Liqin (1996) 'Gaige kaifang, bu rong dongyao: ping Deng Liqun de "wan yan shu"', [Reform and Opening Cannot Be Permitted to be Shaken: A Critique of Deng Liqun's 'Ten Thousand Word Letter'], in Shi (1997): 49–122.

Fang, Lizhi (1985) 'Fang Lizhi zai Zhejiang daxue de jianghua gaoyao', [Script of Fang Lizhi's Speech at Zhejiang University], in Anon. (ed.) (1988) *Fang Lizhi Liu Bingyan Wang Ruowang yanlun gaobian*, [Scripts of Speeches and Texts by Fang Lizhi, Liu Binyan, Wang Ruowang], Hong Kong: Shuguang tushu: 5–14.

—— (1986) 'Zhishi fenzi yu Zhongguo shehui – Fang Lizhi zai Shanghai jiaotong daxue de jianghua gaoyao', [Intellectuals and Chinese Society – Script of Fang Lizhi's Talk at Shanghai's Jiaotong University], in Anon. (ed.) (1988) *Fang Lizhi Liu Bingyan Wang Ruowang yanlun gaobian*' [Scripts of Speeches and Texts by Fang Lizhi, Liu Binyan, Wang Ruowang], Hong Kong: Shuguang tushu: 25–9.

Fang, Ning, Wang, Xiaodong and Song, Qiang (1999) *Quanqiuhua yinying xia de Zhongguo zhi lu*, [*China's Road under the Shadow of Globalization*], Beijing: Zhongguo shehui kexue chubanshe.

Feng, Z. (2003) 'Lun dui Ri guanxi xin siwei', [On the New Thinking Towards Japan], *ZLGL* (4): 1–16.

Fewsmith, J. (2001) *China since Tiananmen: The Politics of Transition*, Cambridge: Cambridge University Press.

Gan, Yang (2003) 'Zhongguo ziyou pai de youlai', [The Origins of China's Left Wing], in Gong Yang (ed.): 110–20.

Gao, Xin and He, Pin (1996) *Zhu Rongji Zhuan*, [*Biography of Zhu Rongji*], Taipei: Xin xinwen.

Giddens, A. (1990) *The Consequences of Modernity*, Cambridge: Polity Press.

Goldman, M. (1994) *Sowing the Seeds of Democracy in China: Political Reform in the Deng Xiaoping Era*, London: Harvard University Press.

Gong, Li (1996) 'Bashi niandai zhongguo tiaozheng dui wai fangzhen de youlai', [Origins of the Adjustment of China's Foreign Policy in the 1980s], in Gong Li (ed.) *Deng Xiaoping de waijiao sixiang yu shijian*, [*The Ideas and Practice of Deng Xiaoping's Foreign Policy*], Harbin: Heilongjiang chubanshe: 16–26.

Gong, Yang (ed.) (2003) *Sichao: Zhongguo 'xin zuopai' ji qi yingxiang*, [*Thought Wave China's 'New Left' and its Influence*], Beijing: Zhongguo shehui kexue chubanshe.

Gore, A. (1994) 'Remarks Prepared for Delivery to International Telecommunications Union', Buenos Aires, 21 March, online, available: <*http://www.iitf.nist.gov/documents/speeches/032194_gore_giispeech. html*> (accessed 20 February 2002).

Gries, P. H. (2004) *China's New Nationalism: Pride, Politics and Diplomacy*, Berkeley: University of California Press.

Guo Xiangzhi (1990) ' "Yi guo liang zhi" gouxiang de lilun yu shijian', [The Concept of 'One Country, Two Systems' in Theory and Practice], *Taiwan yanjiu* (1): 5–17.

Haacke, J. (2002) 'Seeking Influence: China's Diplomacy Toward ASEAN after the Asian Crisis', *Asian Perspective* 26(4): 13–52.

He, Qinglian (2000) 'China's Listing Social Structure', online, available: <*http://cosa.uchicago.edu/Socialstructure.htm*> (accessed 10 June 2005).

He, Xiquan and Jiang, Li (2000) 'Guoji jiduan shli de xianzhuang ji fazhan xieshi', [The Present Situation Development and Trend of Extremist International Forces], in Zhongguo xiandai guoji guanxi yanjiu suo (China Research Institute of Contemporary International Relations) (ed.) *Quanqiu zhanlue da geju*, [*The Broad Situation of Global Strategy*], Beijing: Shishi chubanshe: 558–65.

Held, D., McGrew, A., Goldblatt, D. and Perraton, J. (1999) *Global Transformations: Politics, Economics and Culture*, Cambridge: Polity Press.

Hideo, Osashi (2004) 'The Impact of China's Rise on Sino-Japanese Economic Relations', in K. Ryosei and J. Wang (eds), *The Rise of China and a Changing East Asian Order*, Tokyo and New York: Japan Centre for International Exchange: 175–94.

House Committee on International Relations (2004) Online, available: <*http://wwwc.house.gov/international_relations/108/kel060204.htm*> (accessed 4 July 2004).

Hsu, Immanuel C. Y. (1983) *China without Mao*, Oxford: Oxford University Press.

Hu, Jintao (1999) 'Zhonggong zhongyang zhengzhiju changwei, guojia fu zhuxi Hu Jintao fabiao dianshi jianghua', [Television Talk by Member of the Standing Committee of the Politburo and Vice State President Hu Jintao], *People's Daily*, 10 May: 1, online, available: <*http://www.people.com.cn/ item/ldhd/hjt.html*> (accessed 14 February 2005).

Hu, Yaobang (1982) 'Quan mian kaizhuang shehuizhuyi xiandaihua jianshe de xin jumian – zai zhongguo gongchangdang di shi er ci quanguo daibiao da hui shang de bao gao', [Completely Open Up the New Situation for Socialist Modernisation – Report to the Twelfth National Congress of the CPC], online, available: <*http://news.xinhuanet.com/ziliao/2003–01/20/ content_696971.htm*> (accessed 3 March 2005).

Huang Jiming (1999) 'Jiji zai aiguo zhuyi de weida qizhi xia', [Come Together under the Great Banner of Patriotism], *People's Daily*, 27 May.

Hughes, C. (1997a) *Taiwan and Chinese Nationalism: National Identity and Status in International Society*, London and New York: Routledge.

—— (1997b) 'Globalisation and Nationalism: Squaring the Circle in Chinese International Relations Theory', *Millennium: Journal of International Studies*, 26 (1): 103–24.

—— (2000) 'Nationalism in Chinese Cyberspace', *Cambridge Review of International Affairs*, Vol XIII, No 2, Spring/Summer: 195–209.

—— (2003) 'Fighting the Smokeless War: ICTs and International Security', in Hughes and Wacker: 139–61.

—— (2005) 'Interpreting Nationalist Texts: A Post-Structuralist Approach', *Journal of Contemporary China*, 14(3), May: 57–77.

—— and Wacker, G. (2003) *China and the Internet: Politics of the Digital Leap Forward*, London and New York: Routledge Curzon.

Human Rights Watch (2003) *A Question of Patriotism: Human Rights and Democratization in Hong Kong*, online, available: <*http://www.hrw.org/backgrounder/asia/china/hk0904/*> (accessed 5 June 2005).

JETRO (Japan External Trade Organization) (2005) *Special Survey of Japanese Business in China – Impact of the April Anti-Japan Demonstrations*, online, available: <*http://www.jetro.go.jp/en/stats/statistics/*> (accessed 15 June 2005).

Jiang, Xiyuan and Xia Liping (2004) *Zhongguo heping jueqi*, [*Peaceful Rise of China*], Beijing: Zhongguo shehui kexue chubanshe.

Jiang, Yiwei (1983) 'Guanyu gongye jingji zeren zhi de yixie lilun wenti', *Renmin Ribao* (*People's Daily*), 19 August, cited in Schram (1984): 455.

Jiang, Yongjing (1985) 'Sun Zhongshan xiansheng de geming sixiang', [The Revolutionary Thought of Mr Sun Yat-sen], in *Zhonghua minguo jian guo shi*, [*The History of the Founding of the ROC*], Taipei.

Jiang, Zemin (1991) 'Jiang Zemin zong shuji zhi xin Li Tieying He Dongchang qiangdiao jinxing zhongguo jindai shi xiandai shi ji guoqing jiaoyu', [General Secretary Jiang Zemin Sends a Letter to Li Tieying and He Dongchang, Stressing the Practice of Chinese Modern History, Contemporary History and National Condition Education], *People's Daily*, 6 June.

—— (1992) 'Jiakuai gaige kaifang he xiandaihua jianshe bufa, duoqu you zhongguo tese shehuizhuyu shiye de geng da shenli', [Speed Up the Steps of Building Reform and Opening and Modernisation, Seize the Great Victory in the Project of Building Socialism with Chinese Characteristics], *Shisida yilai*: 1–2.

—— (1995a) 'Zhengque chuli shehuizhuyi xiandaihua jianshe de ruogan zhongda guanxi', [Correctly Handle Some Major Relationships in the Building of Socialist Modernisation], *Shisida yilai* (2): 1460–77.

—— (1995b), 'Nuli shishe kejiao xingguo de zhanlue', *Shisi da zhongyao wenxian*, (zhong): 1381–96.

—— (1997) 'Gaoju Deng Xiaoping lilun weida qizhi, ba jianshe you Zhongguo tese shehui zhuyi shiye quanmian tuixiang ershiyi shiji', [Hold High the Great Banner of Deng Xiaoping Theory, Take the Project of Building Socialism with Chinese Characteristics Forwards into the Twentieth Century],

Zhonggong shiwu da baogao budai duben, [*Study Guide to the Report to the Fifteenth CPC Congress*], Hong Kong: Mingliu chubanshe: 1–60.

—— (1998a) 'Aiguo zhuyi he woguo zhishifenzi de shiming', [Patriotism and the Mission of Our Country's Intellectuals], Party Documentation Centre: 359–64.

—— (1998b) 'Xinwen gongzuo de jiben fangzhen wenti', Party Documentation Centre: 354–5.

—— (1998c) 'Ren yao you zheng qi he gu qi', [People Need Righteousness and Backbone], Party Documentation Centre: 371–3.

—— (1998d) 'Guanyu shehuizhuyi jinsheng wenming jianshe de wenti', [On Problems in Building Socialist Spiritual Civilization], Party Documentation Centre: 348–9.

—— (1998e) 'Dang de lingdao ganbu yao yi shen zuo ze, lingxian chuifan', [The Party's Leading Cadres Should Set a Leading Example], Party Documentation Centre: 388–9.

—— (1998f) 'Guanyu xuanzhuan sixiang gongzuo de zongzhi he jidian xiwang', [On the Overall Direction and Some Hopes for Propaganda Work], Party Documentation Centre: 392–5.

—— (1998g) 'Fahui wo jun de zhengzhi youshi, da li jiaqiang jundui de jingshen wenming jianshe', [Wield the Superiority of Our Army, Strive to Strengthen the Army's Building of Socialist Spiritual Civilisation], Party Documentation Centre: 41.

—— (1998h) 'Renzhen xuexi Deng Xiaoping tongzhi de geming fengge', [Resolutely Study the Revolutionary Style of Comrade Deng Xiaoping], Party Documentation Centre: 408–9.

—— (1998i) 'Jiaqiang guoqing jiaoyu', Party Documentation Centre: 347.

—— (1999a) 'Zai huanying wo guo zhu nansilafu lianmeng gongheguo gongzuo renyuan dahui shang de jiang hua', [Speech at the Large Meeting to Welcome Workers from Our Country's Embassy in the Yugoslav Republic], online, available: *<http://www.people.com.cn/item/ldhd/hjt.html>* (accessed 14 February 2005).

—— (1999b) 'Zai qingzhu zhonghua renmin gongheguo chengli wushi zhounian da hui shang de jianghua', *Shiwu da yilai*: 1060–2.

—— (2001) 'Full Text of Jiang's Speech at CPC Anniversary Gathering', online, available: *<http://english.peopledaily.com.cn/english/200107/01/archive.html>* (accessed 8 August 2005).

—— (2002) 'Full Text of Jiang Zemin's Report at 16th Party Congress', online, available: *<http://www.china.org.cn/english/features/49007.html>* (accessed 8 August 2005).

Johnston, A. I. (2003) 'Is China a Status-Quo Power?', *International Security*, 27(4) (Spring): 5–56.

Kang, Xiaoguang (1994) 'Zhongguo xiandaihua de mailuo yu chu lu', [The Evolution and the Way Out for China's Modernisation], *ZLGL* (1): 10–12.

Kang, Youwei (1897) 'Shang Qingdi di wu shu', [Fifth Memorial to the Qing Emperor], in Zhongguo Shixuehui (ed.) (2000), *Wushu bianfa*, Vol. II, Shanghai: Shanghai renmin chubanshe: 188–97.

Kelly, D. and He, B. (1992) 'Emergent Civil Society and the Intellectuals in China', in Robert F. Miller (ed.) *The Developments of Civil Societies in Communist Systems*, Sydney: Allen and Unwin.

Kissinger, H. (1973) 'Memcon, Kissinger and Mao, 12 November 1973', in William Burr (ed.), *The Kissinger Transcripts*, New York: New Press: 203–6.

Koizumu, J. (2002) 'Asia in a New Century – Challenge and Opportunity', Speech at the Boao Forum for Asia, online, available: <*http://www.kantei.go.jp/foreign/koizumispeech/2002/04/12boao_e.html*> (accessed 10 June 2005).

Larson, W. (1993) 'Literary Modernism and Nationalism in Post-Mao China', in Larson, W. and Wedell-Wedellsbor, A. (eds) (1993) *Inside Out: Modernism and Postmodernism in Chinese Literary Culture*, Aarhus: Aarhus University Press: 172–92.

Lee, Teng-hui (1988) 'First International Press Conference', in Government Information Office (ed.) *President Lee's Selected Addresses and Messages 1988*, Taipei: GIO.

—— (1990) 'Opening a New Era for the Chinese People', in Lee Teng-hui (ed.) *Creating the Future*, Taipei: GIO: 3–12.

—— (1991) 'Toward the 21st Century Arm in Arm – the Republic of China and the New Asian-Pacific Situation', Lee Teng-hui (ed.) *Creating the Future*, Taipei: GIO: 121–30.

—— (1999) 'Responses to Questions Submitted by Deutsche Welle: Lee Teng Hui President Republic of China', online, available: <*http://www.fas.org/news/taiwan/1999/0709.htm*> (accessed 8 August 2005).

Leung, Julian Y. M. (1992) 'Education in Hong Kong and China: Toward Convergence?', in Postiglione (ed.): 265–72.

Li, Dahong (1994) 'Taiwan zhengtan chongman jiaoju de yi nian', [A Year Full of Political Competition in Taiwan], *Liaowang* (24 January): 36–7.

Li, Fan (1994) 'Shichang jingji fazhan de zhengzhi huangjing ji qi dui Zhongguo xiandaihua de yingxiang', [The Political Environment of the Development of the Market Economy and Its Influence on China's Modernisation], *ZLGL* (1): 20–6.

Li, Keming (1993) 'Jiushi niandai wo guo jiaoyu fazhan he tizhi gaige de jige wenti', [Some Problems in the Development and Structural Reform of Our Country's Education in the 1990s], *Jiaoyu xue* (1): 102–9.

Li, Kemu (1999) *Guangming Ribao*, 14 May: 11.

Li, Kuo-chih (1984) *Zhang Zhidong de Waijiao zhengce*, [Zhang Zhidong's Foreign Policy], Taipei: Academia Sinica.

Li, Peng (1988) *Zhenfen jingshen, shenhua gaige, ba gaodeng jiaoyu gongzuo tuixiang qianjin* (*zai quanguo jiaoyu gongzuo huiyi shang de jianghua*), [Invigorate the Spirit, Deepen the Reforms, Take the Reforms in Higher Education Forward (Speech at the National Conference on Higher Education

Work)], in Ma and Liu, *Guanyu jiaoyu tizhi gaige de wenjian*, [*Documents Related to Reform of the Education System*]: 317–20.

—— (1990) 'Continue to Work for Stable Political, Economic and Social Development in China', *Third Session of the Seventh NPC*: 7–58.

Li, Qing (1987) ' "Yi guo liang zhi" yu aiguo tongyi zhanxian de xin xingshi', ['One Country, Two Systems' and the New Form of the Patriotic United Front], Zhong yang she hui zhu yi xue yuan, Tong yi zhan xian li lun jiao yan shi (ed.) *Yige guojia liang zhong zhidu: lilun yu shixian wenxian ziliao xuanji*, [*One Country, Two Systems: Selected Literature and Materials on Theory and Practice*].

Li, Qingyuan (1993) 'Jingji gaige yu zhengzhi wending', [Economic Reform and Political Stability], *ZLGL* (1): 10–11.

Li, Rui (1984) 'Jin kuai qiyong yi dai xin ren – du *Chen Yun wenxuan* zhong youguan ganbu gongzuo de lunshu', *People's Daily*, 23 March, cited and translated in Schram (1984): 450.

Li, Shenzhi (1994) 'Cong quanqiuhua guandian kan Zhongguo de xiandaihua wenti', [Viewing China's Problems of Modernisation from the Perspective of Globalization], *ZLGL* (1): 5–6.

—— (1999) 'Feng yu cang huang wushi nian: guoqing ye duyu', [Fifty Years of Storms and Disturbances], in Li Shenzhi, *Feng yu cang huang wushi nian: Li Shenzhi wenxuan* (second edition), Hong Kong: Mingbao chubanshe (2003). English version in *China Perspectives*, 32 (November–December): 4–12.

Li, Tieying (1988) *Gaige jiaqiang deyu gongzuo, peiyang zaojiu 'siyou' xinren (zai quanguo zhongxiao deyu gongzuo huiyi shang de jianghua)*, [Reform and Strengthen Ethical Work to Raise New People with the 'Four Haves' (Talk at the National Conference on Middle and Elementary Ethical Education Work)], in Ma and Liu (education volume): 340–4.

—— (1990) 'Gaodeng jiaoyu bixu jianchi shehuizhuyi fangxiang', [Higher Education Must Uphold the Socialist Direction], in Ma and Liu: 375–9.

—— (1991) 'Nuli jianshe you zhongguo tese de shehui zhuyi jiaoyu tixi', [Strive to Build a Socialism with Chinese Characteristics, Education System], in Ma and Liu: 400–7.

—— (1993) 'Shehuizhuyi xiandaihua jianshe de moji gongcheng: renzhen xuexi, xuanzhuan he shishi "zhongguo jiaoyu gaige he fazhan gangyao" ', *Jiaoyu xue* (3): 23–9.

Li, Xiguang, Liu Kang, Xiong Lei, Zhu Weiyi, Han Song, Wu Jianping, Shi Anbin and Wang Minjuan (1996) *Yaomohua Zhongguo de beihou*, [*Behind the Demonization of China*], Beijing: Zhongguo shehui kexue chubanshe.

Li, Xiju (2003) *Zhang Zhidong yu Qing mo xin zheng yanjiu*, [*Research on Zhang Zhidong and the New Politics of the Late Qing*], Shanghai: Shanghai shudian chubanshe.

Li, Zehou (1990) 'Manshuo "xi ti zhong yong" ', [Comments on 'Western Substance Chinese Function'], *Zhongguo xiandai sixiang shi lun*, [*On Chinese Contemporary Thought*], Taipei: Fengyun shidai chuban gongci: 397–434. Originally in *Kongzi yanjiu* (*Confucius Research*), 1987: 1.

—— (1996a) ' "Xi ti zhong yong" jian yi', [Simple Explanation of 'Western Substance Chinese Function'], *Zou wo ziji de lu*, [*Taking My Own Road*], Taipei: sanmin shuju: 195–9. Originally in *Zhongguo wenhua bao*, 9 July 1986.

——(1996b) 'Er, xi ti zhong yong', [Western Substance Chinese Function: 2], *Zou wo ziji de lu*: 213–17. Originally in *Tuanjie bao*, 27 September 1986.

Lieberthal, K. (1995) *Governing China*, New York: W. W. Norton.

Lin Zhijun and Ma Licheng (1999) *Huhan: dangjin zhongguo de wu zhong shengyin*, [*Outcry: Five Voices in Recent China*], Taipei: Tianxia yuanjian chuban gufen youxian gongsi.

Lu, Zhongwei (ed.) (2003) *Fei chuantong anquan lun*, [*On Non-Traditional Security*], Beijing: Shishi chubanshe.

Ma Licheng (2002) 'Zhong Ri guanxi xin siwei – Zhong Ri minjian zhi you', [New Thinking on Sino-Japanese Relations – Concerns between the People of China and Japan], *ZLGL* (6): 41–7.

Ma Licheng and Lin Zhijun (1998) *Jiao feng*, [*Crossed Swords*], Beijing: Jin ri zhongguo chubanshe.

Mao, Zedong (1967) 'On New Democracy', *Selected Works of Mao Tse-tung*, Vol. II, Peking: Foreign Languages Press: 339–84.

—— (1977a) 'On the Ten Major Relationships', *Selected Works of Mao Tse-tung*, Vol. V, Peking: Foreign Languages Press: 284–307.

—— (1977b) 'On the Correct Handling of Contradictions Among the People', *Selected Works of Mao Tse-tung*, Vol. V: 384–421.

—— (1989) [1957] 'On Ideological Work', in R. MacFarquhar, T. Cheek and E. Wu (eds) *The Secret Speeches of Chairman Mao: From the Hundred Flowers to the Great Leap Forward*, Cambridge, Mass. and London: Cambridge University Press: 321–50.

—— (1998) 'On the Question of the Differentiation of the Three Worlds', *Mao Zedong on Diplomacy*, Beijing: Foreign Languages Press: 454–5.

Mearsheimer, J. J. (2001) *The Tragedy of Great Power Politics*, New York and London: W. W. Norton and Co.

Nathan, A. and Link, P. (2001) *The Tiananmen Papers*, London: Little, Brown.

Nolan, P. (2001) *China and the Global Business Revolution*, Basingstoke and New York: Palgrave.

Oksenberg, M., Sullivan, L. R. and Lamberts, M. (eds) (1990) *Beijing Spring, 1989 Confrontation and Conflict: The Basic Documents*, Armonk, NY: M. E. Sharpe.

Peng, Zhen (1983) 'Report on the Draft of the Revised Constitution of the People's Republic of China', *Fifth Session of the Fifth National People's Congress*, Beijing: Foreign Languages Press: 65–108.

Postiglione, G. A. (ed.) (1992) *Education and Society in Hong Kong: Toward One Country and Two Systems*, Hong Kong: Hong Kong University Press.

Qiao, M. (2002) 'Duojiahua qushi bu hui gaibian', [The Trend Towards Multipolarity Cannot Change], *Dangdai Yatai* (*Contemporary Asia Pacific*), (6):10–13.

Raman, B. (2003) 'Understanding China: The View from India', *Asia Times*, 14 June, online, available: <*http://www.atimes.com/atimes/South_Asia/ EF14Df01.html*> (accessed 9 July 2005).

Resolution on CPC History (1949–81) (1981) Beijing: Foreign Languages Press.

Rice, C. (2000) 'Promoting the National Interest', *Foreign Affairs* 79(1): 45–62.

Rong, Jingben (1994) 'Jianli guoji zhengzhi jingji zhixu shi jiejue minzu wenti de genben tujing', [Establishing International Political and Economic Order is the Basic Way to Solve the National Problem], *ZLGL* (3): 2–6.

Samuels, R. (1994) *Rich Nation, Strong Army: National Security and Technological Transformation in Japan*, Ithaca, New York: Cornell University Press.

Sautman, B. (1991) 'Politicization, Hyperpoliticization, and Depoliticization of Chinese Education', *Comparative Education Review* (November): 669–89.

Schram, S. (1984) ' "Economics in Command?" Ideology and Policy since the Third Plenum', *China Quarterly* (September): 417–61.

Segal, A. (2003) *Digital Dragon: High Technology Enterprises in China*, Ithaca, New York and London: Council on Foreign Relations.

Shakya, T. (1999) *The Dragon in the Land of Snows: A History of Modern Tibet since 1947*, London: Pimlico.

Shen, Guofang (2003) 'Dangjin shijie de duojihua xieshi he daguo guanxi', [The Trend of Multipolarity in the Present World and Relations between the Great Powers], *Zhongguo dang zheng ganbu luntan*, [*China Party and Government Cadre Forum*], (1): 39–41.

Shi, Liuzi (1997) *Beijing di xia wan yan xu*, [*Beijing's Underground Ten-Thousand Word Letters*], Hong Kong: Minjing chubanshe.

Shi, Yinhong (2003) 'Zhong ri jiejin yu "waijiao geming" ', [The Closeness of China and Japan and the 'Diplomatic Revolution'], *ZLGL* (2): 71–5.

Song, Huaijiang (2002) *Lianxiang jituan chuanji 18 nian*, [*The 18-Year Saga of the Legend Group*], Taipei: Zhixun yinhang.

Song Qiang, Zhang Zangzang, Qiao Bian, Gu Qingsheng and Tang Zhengyu (1996) *Zhongguo keyi shuo bu: lengzhan hou shidai de zhengzhi yu qinggan jueze*, [*China Can Say No: Political and Emotional Choices in the Post-Cold War Period*], Beijing: Zhonghua gonshang lianhe chubanshe.

Spence, J. D. (1992) 'Film and Politics: Bai Hua's *Bitter Love*', in *Chinese Roundabout: Essays in History and Culture*, New York: W. W. Norton and Co.: 277–92.

Suettinger, R. (2004) 'The Rise and Descent of "Peaceful Rise" ', *China Leadership Monitor*, online, available: <*http://www.chinaleadershipmonitor.org/ 20044/rs.pdf*> (accessed 3 February 2005).

Suganama, U. (2000) *Sovereign Rights and Territorial Space in Sino-Japanese Relations: Irredentism and the Diaoyu/Senkaku Islands*, Honolulu: University of Hawaii Press.

Sum, Ngai-Ling (2003) '(Re-)Imagining "Greater China": Silicon Valley and the Strategy of Siliconization', in Hughes and Wacker: 102–26.

Sun, Liping (1994) 'Xiandaihua jincheng zhong Zhongguo ge zhong shehui guanxi de xin bianhua', [New Transformations in the Various Social Relationships in the Process of China's Modernisation], (1): 17–19.

Sutherland, D. (2001) 'Policies to Build "National Champions": China's National Team of Enterprise Groups', in Nolan: 67–139.

Taiwan Affairs Office (2000) *The One-China Principle and the Taiwan Issue*, Beijing: Taiwan Affairs Office and Information Office, State Council of the PRC.

Tang Zhengyu (1996) 'Ezhi fan er jiang zhongguo daorule geng da de guoji hezuao huanjing', [Containment Will Only Lead China to a Situation of More International Cooperation], in Song, Q. *et al. Zhongguo keyi shuo bu*, [*China Can Say No*].

Tian Xinjian (1993) 'Dongya anquan de fenxi yu zhanwang', [Analysis and Outlook for East Asian Security], *ZLGL* (1): 21–2.

Toffler, A. (1980) *The Third Wave*, New York: Morrow.

United Nations (1993) 'A Report of the Regional Meeting for Asia of the World Conference on Human Rights, Bangkok, 2 April, United Nations General Assembly, A/CONF.157/ASRM/8, 7 April.

Wan, Li (1985) 'Zai quanguo jiaoyu gongzuo huiyi shang de jiang hua', [Speech at the National Education Work Conference], 17 May, in Ma and Liu (eds) *Guanyu jiaoyu tizhi gaige de wenjian*, [*Documents Related to Reform of the Education System*], 1992: 259–66.

Wang, Hui (1994) 'Wenhua pipan lilun yu dangdai Zhongguo minzuzhuyi wenti', [Cultural Criticism and the Problem of China's Contemporary Nationalism], *ZLGL* (4): 17–20.

Wang, Hui (2003) 'Dangdai zhongguo de sixiang zhuangkuang yu xiandai xing wenti', [Problems Concerning Contemporary China's Ideological Situation and the Nature of Modernisation], in Gong, Yang (ed.) (2003).

Wang, Ruoshui (1997) *Hu Yaobang xia tai de Beijing: rendao zhuyi zai zhongguo de mingyun*, [*Behind the Downfall of Hu Yaobang: The Fate of Humanism in China*], Hong Kong: Mirror Books.

Wang, Shan (1994) *Di san zhi yanjing kan Zhongguo*, [*Viewing China through the Third Eye*], Taipei: Zhouzhi wenhua.

Wang, Xiaodong (under the pen name Shi Zhong) (1994) 'Zhongguo xiandaihua mianjian de tiaozhan', [The Challenges Facing China's Modernisation], *ZLGL* (1): 7–9.

—— (2005) 'Chinese Nationalism under the Shadow of Globalization', speech at the London School of Economics, 7 February, online, available: *http://www.lse.ac.uk/collections/asiaResearchCentre/pdf/WANGXiaodong Final Transcript English.pdf* (accessed 6 June 2005).

Wang, Zaixi (1993) 'Taiwan xian shi zhang xuanju qingkuang toushi', [Perspective on the Situation of Taiwan's Elections for County Magistrates and City Mayors], *Liaowang* (13 December): 31–2.

—— (1994) 'Zongguan taiwan "sheng shi zhang" xuanju jieguo', [An Overview of the Results of Taiwan's Elections for Provincial and City Heads], *Liaowang* (26 January): 55.

Waters, M. (1995) *Globalization*, London and New York: Routledge.

Wendt, Alexander (1999) *Social Theory of International Politics*, Cambridge: Cambridge University Press.

Whiting, A. S. (1989) *China Eyes Japan*, Berkeley and Los Angeles: University of California Press.

Wong, J. Y. (2003) 'British Legacy in Hong Kong: Putting the Mass Demonstrations of 1 July 2003 in Historical Perspective, 1895–2003', paper presented to the Department of International Relations, LSE. Original version presented to International Conference on Paradigms and Perspectives I, Hong Kong Studies, Hong Kong University Centre for Asian Studies, December 2003.

World Bank (1997) *China 2020: Development Challenges in the New Century*, Washington, DC: World Bank.

—— (1998) *World Bank Atlas 1998*, Washington, DC: World Bank.

WTO (World Trade Organization) (2003) *International Trade Statistics 2003*, online, available: <*http://www.wto.org/english/res_e/statis_e/its2003_e/its03_byregion_e.pdf*> (accessed 14 July 2005).

Xiao, Cuilin (1992) 'China's Open Door Policy in Education: A Content Analysis of the Chinese Education Newspaper', *Compare*, 18:2, cited in W. O. Lee, in Postiglione (ed.): 239.

Xiao, Gongqin (1994a) 'Ran zhengquan yu fenli jituanhua: Zhongguo xiandaihua de liang zhong xianjin', [Weak Authority and Divided Corporatism: Two Pitfalls of China's Modernisation], *ZLGL* (1): 1–4.

—— (1994b) 'Minzu zhuyi yu Zhongguo zhuan xing shiqi de yishi xingtai', [Nationalism and China's Ideology in the Period of Reformation], *ZLGL* (5): 21–5.

—— (2003) ' "Xin zuopai" yu dangdai Zhonnguo zhishifenzi de sixiang wenhua', [The 'New Left' and the Ideological Culture of China's Contemporary Intellectuals], in Gong, Yang (ed.) *Sichao*: 401–27.

Xiong, Guangkai (2003) 'The Global Challenge of International Terrorism', speech at the Munich Conference on Security Policy, 2 August, online, available: <*http://www.securityconference.de/konferenzen/*> (accessed 4 July 2005).

Xu, J. (1993) *Xu Jiatun Xianggang huiyi lu*, [*Xu Jiatun's Memoirs of Hong Kong*], Vols. I–II, Taipei: Lianhe bao chubanshe.

Xu, L. (1995) 'The "Shekou Storm": Changes in the Mentality of Chinese Youth Prior to Tiananmen', *China Quarterly* (142): 541–72.

Xu Xianqun and Lin Zhengyi (2002) *Jiang Zemin keji sixiang yanjiu* (*Research on Jiang Zemin's Thinking on Technology*), Hangzhou: Zhejiang kexue jishu chubanshe.

Yahuda, M. (1995) *Hong Kong: China's Challenge*, London and New York: Routledge.

Yan, Chuanrong and Yang, Huasheng (1990) 'Taiwan zhengzhi zhuan xing de tedian ji zhuyao maodun', [Special Points and Contradictions of Taiwan's Political Transformation], *Taiwan yanjiu* (1): 18–24.

Yan, Xuetong (1995) 'Zhongguo jueqi de keneng xuanze', *ZLGL* (6), reprinted in Yan Xuetong (2000): 111–20.

—— (1999) 'Guoji huanjing ji waijiao sikao', [Considerations on the International Environment and Foreign Relations], *Xiandai guoji guanxi* (8): 7–11.

—— (2000) *Meiguo baquan yu Zhongguo anquan*, Tianjin: Tianjin renmin chubanshe.

Yin, Baoyun (1994) 'Minzu zhuyi yu xiandai jingji fazhan', [Nationalism and the Development of the Contemporary Economy], *ZLGL* (3): 13–15.

Yu, Yongding and Zheng Bingwen (eds) (2000) *Zhongguo 'ru shi' yanjiu baogao: jinru WTO de Zhongguo chanye*, [*The Research Report on China's Entry into the WTO*], Beijing: Shehui kexue wenxian chubanshe.

Yuan Ming (1992) *Minzhu zhongguo*, August.

Zhang, Chengxian (1993) 'Shichang jingji yu jiaoyu gaige', [Market Economy and Education Reform] (report on a conference held January 1993, Beijing), *Jiaoyu xue*, 2: 44–5.

Zhang, Chunjiang and Ni, Jianmin (2000) *Guojia Xinxi Anquan Baogao*, [*Report on National Information Security*], Beijing: Renmin chubanshe.

Zhao, Suisheng (1997) 'Chinese Intellectuals' Quest for National Greatness and Historical Writing in the 1990s', *China Quarterly*, 152: 725–45.

—— (2004) *A Nation-State by Construction: Dynamics of Modern Chinese Nationalism*, Stanford, Carolina: Stanford University Press.

Zhao, Zhenkai (1985) *Waves*, tr. Bonnie S. McDougall and Susette Ternent Cooke, Hong Kong: Chinese University Press.

Zhao, Ziyang (1987) *Yanzhe you zhongguo tese de shehui zhuyi daolu qian jin*, [*Follow the Road of Socialism with Chinese Characteristics to Advance*], online, available: <http://www.people.com.cn/GB/shizheng> (accessed 14 January 2005).

Zheng, Yongnian (1999) *Discovering Chinese Nationalism in China: Modernization, Identity and International Relations*, Cambridge: Cambridge University Press.

Zhongguo Qingnian bao (1983) 'Wuran xu qingchu, shenghuo yao meihua', [Pollution Needs to be Purged, Life Should be Beautified], *ZQB*, *PD*, 17 November (cited in Schram: 440).

Zhou, Zhiping *et al.* (1993) 'Deng Xiaoping jiaoyu zhanlue sixiang xingcheng yu fazhan de lishi guocheng he beijing tiaojian', [The Historical Process and Background Conditions of the Formation and Development of Deng Xiaoping's Education Strategy], *Jiaoyu xue*, 2: 6–11.

Zhu, Aili (1990) 'Taiwan "zongtong" xuanju hou de zhengci zouxiang', [The Direction of Policy after Taiwan's 'Presidential' Elections], *Taiwan Yenjiu* (1): 1–4.

Zou Jingwen (ed.) (2001) *Li Denghui zhizheng gao bai shilu*, [*Lee Teng-hui's Testament*], Taibei: Yinke.

Zweig, D. (2002) *Internationalizing China: Domestic Interests and Global Linkages*, Ithaca and London: Cornell University Press.

Journals and newspapers

BR   *Beijing Review*
FT   *Financial Times*
JFRB   *Jiefang ribao* (*Liberation Daily*)
LHB   *Lianhe bao* (*United Daily News*) (Taiwan)
            Liaowang (*Outlook*)
MB   *Ming bao* (Hong Kong)
PD   *Renmin ribao* (*People's Daily*)
SCMP   *South China Morning Post*
WHB   *Wenhui bao* (Hong Kong)
Xinhua New China News Agency
Zhengming
ZLGL   *Zhanlue yu guanli* (*Strategy and Management*)
ZQB   *Zhongguo qingnian bao* (*China Youth Daily*)
ZSB   *Zhongguo shibao* (*China Times*) (Taiwan)
ZYS   *Zhongyang shibao* (*Central Daily News*) (Taiwan)

Official documents

National People's Congress (NPC)

1979, 1 January: 'Message to Compatriots in Taiwan', online: *http:// www.china.org.cn/english/taiwan/7943.htm*; Chinese version: 'Zhonghua renmin gongheguo quanguo renmin daibiao da hui changwuweiyuanhui gao Taiwan tongbao shu', online: *http://news.xinhuanet.com/ziliao/2005– 02/05/content_2550226.htm*

1990: *The Third Session of the Seventh National People's Congress of the People's Republic of China (1990)*, Beijing: Foreign Languages Press.

1995: Zhonghua renmin gongheguo jiaoyu fa, *Shisi da yilai zhongyao wenxian xuanbian*, Vol. II: 1293–1309.

Central Committee (CC)

1985, 27 May: *Zhonggong zhongyang guanyu jiaoyu tizhi gaige de jueding* (*Central Committee of the CPC Resolution on Reform of the Education System*), in Ma and Liu (eds), *Guanyu jiaoyu tizhi gaige de wenjian* (*Documents Related to Reform of the Education System*): 11–15.

1987, 29 May: *Zhonggong zhongyang guanyu gaijin he jiaqiang gaodeng xuexiao sixiang zhengzhi zongzuo de jueding* (*Central Committee of the CPC Resolution on Improving and Strengthening Political Thought Work in Higher Education*), in Ma and Liu (eds), *Guanyu jiaoyu tizhi gaige de wenjian* (*Documents Related to Reform of the Education System*): 302–7.

1988, 25 December: *Zhonggong zhongyang guanyu gaige he jiaqiang zhongxiaoxue deyu gongzuo de tongzhi* (*Central Committee of the CCP Circular on Reform and Strengthening Middle and Primary School Ethical Education Work*), in Ma and Liu (eds): 356–60.

1993, February: Zhongguo jiaoyu gaige he fazhan gangyao (Outline of China's Education Reform and Development), *Shisida yi lai zhongyao wenxian*: 59–87.

1994, August: Aiguo zhuyi jiaoju shishi gangyao (Outline for Implementing Patriotic Education), *Shisi da yilai zhongyao wenxian xuanbian*: 920–51.

1995, 6 May: Zhonggong zhongyang, guowuyuan guanyu jiasu kexue jishu jinbu de jueding, *Shisi da zhongyao wenxian*, Vol. II: 1342–62.

2001: Organisation Department, *Zhongguo diaocha baogao: xin xingshi xia renmin neibu maodun yanjiu (China Investigation Report 2000–2001: Studies of Contradictions among the People under New Conditions)*, Beijing: Zhongyang bianyi chubanshe.

Education Commission (EC)

1983, 24 August: 'Guanyu jiaqiang aiguo zhuyi xuanzhuan jiaoyu de yijian', [Views on the Strengthening of the Teaching of Patriotic Ideology], Dalian/education: 16.

1984, 12 September: 'Jiaoyubu guanyu gaodeng xuexiao kaishe gongchangzhuyi sixiang pinde ke de ruogan guiding', [Education Commission Regulations on Establishing Classes on Communist Thought and Ethics in Higher Education], in Ma and Liu (education): 16.

1988, 22 August: *Guojia jiaoyu weiyuanhui guanyu lingfa 'zhongxue deyu dagang' (shixing gao) deng wenjian de tongzhi*, [Circular on the 'Outline for Middle-School Ethics' (draft) and Other Documents], in Ma and Liu (education): 345–52.

1989, 8 November: *Guanyu zai zhong xiao xue yuwen, lishi, dili deng xueke jiaoxue zhong jiaqiang zhengzhi jiaoyu yu guoqing jiaoyu de yijian*, [*Views on Strengthening Political Education and National Condition Education in Middle and Elementary School Language, History, and Geography Course Teaching*].

1990, 13 April: *Guojia jiaoyu weiyuanhui guanyu jin yi bu jiaqiang zhong xiao xue deyu gongzuo de yijian*, [*Views of the Education Commission on Some Progress in Strengthening Ethical Education Work in Middle and Junior Schools*], in Ma and Liu (education): 386–90.

Document collections

Ma Hong and Liu Guoguang (eds) (1992) *Zhongguo Gaige quanshu (1978–1991)*, [*Compendium of China's Reforms 1978–1991*] (5 vols), Dalian chubanshe.

NPC, 1983, *Fifth Session of the Fifth National People's Congress*, Beijing: Foreign Languages Press.

PDC Zhonggong zhongyang wenxian yanjiu shi (Party Documentation Centre) (1998) *Mao Zedong, Deng Xiaoping, Jiang Zemin Talk on World View, Views of Human Live and Views of Values*, Hong Kong: Mingliu chubanshe.

PDC (1999) *Shisi da yilai zhongyao wenxian xuan bian*, [*Selection of Important Documents since the Fourteenth Party Congress*], Beijing: Renmin chubanshe.

PDC (2002) *Jiang Zemin lun you Zhongguo tese shehuizhuyi*, [*Jiang Zemin on Socialism with Chinese Characteristics*], Beijing: Zhonggong zhongyang wenxian chubanshe.

The Thirteenth Party Congress and China's Reforms (1987), Beijing: Beijing Review Publications.

Executive Yuan (Taiwan)

Guidelines for National Unification (14 March 1991) 2223rd meeting of ROC Executive Yuan.

Mainland Affairs Council (Taiwan)

1993: *There is No 'Taiwan Question', Only a 'China Question'*.

Textbooks

Sixiang pinde, [*Thought and Value*], compiled by Renmin jiaoyu chubanshe zhengzhi shi and Beijing jiaoyu ju jiao xue yanjiu suo, Vol. III (1997), Vol. V (1996), Vol. VII (1996), Vol. IX (1997).

Sixiang zhengzhi, [*Thought and Politics*], Vol. I (1997), compiled by Guangdong gaodeng jiaoyu chubanshe and Guangdong jiaoyu chubanshe.

Yuwen (*Language*) (1997), Vols. I–V, compiled by Beijing jiaoyu kexue yanjiu yuan and jichu jiaoyu yanjiu yuan, Beijing: Beijing chubanshe.

Other collections

SWB   *BBC Summary of World Broadcasts*

Index

863 Plan 43, 59
9/11 Incident 1, 3, 124, 136, 138, 142, 155
9 December Movement (1936) 38

Africa 131
Ah Q 27
AIDS 41
Albright, Madeleine 81
Anhui province 36
Anshan steelworks 41
AOL-Time Warner 79
ASEAN Regional Forum (ARF) 136, 155
Asia Pacific Economic Cooperation (APEC) 1, 138
Asian Cup 151
Asian Financial Crisis 81, 139, 140
Asian Tigers (Four Tigers) 62, 65
Asian values 108
Association of Southeast Asian Nations (ASEAN) 137, 138, 140, 141
Australia 81

Bai Hua 22
Balkans 83
Behind the Demonization of China 104, 109, 110, 148, 155
Bei Dao (aka Zhao Zhenkai) 21
Beijing Spring 1978–9 13, 27, 58, 112
Belgrade Embassy Incident 1, 2, 82–6, 111, 112, 133, 139
Bitter Love 22
Bo Yibo 41

Bo'ao Forum 142, 143
Bosnia 96
bourgeois liberalisation 53, 54, 56, 57, 59, 66, 94, 96; 1987 campaign against 39–43
Boxer Rebellion 79
Brezhnev, Leonid 25, 107
Bruno, Giordano 31
Bush, President George W. 1, 131, 153; Taiwan policy 138

Canada 105
Ceaucescu, Nicolai 99
Central Asia 136, 142
Central Military Commission 60, 84, 89
Che Guevara 121
Chechnya 96, 138
Chen Shui-bian 116, 127, 128, 129, 138, 144, 145
Chen Yue 93
Chen Yun 19, 20, 28, 30, 42, 61, 93
Chiang Kaishek 6, 18, 33, 75
China Can Say No 80, 86, 104–6, 109, 110, 111, 116, 133, 148
China Investigation Report 2000–2001 120, 124
China's Road Under the Shadow of Globalization 111, 148
Chinese Communist Party (CCP): 2nd Congress 18; 8th Congress 96; 12th Congress 24, 26, 65; 13th Congress 43–9, 54, 55; 14th Congress 48, 61, 63, 67–9, 70, 98–9, 123, 124, 132; 15th Congress 3, 79, 108, 132, 133,

141; 16th Congress 1, 7, 90–1, 114, 115, 119, 120, 122, 139, 150
Chirac, Jacques 144
'clash of civilisations' 101
Clinton, Bill 1, 81, 84, 139; Taiwan policy 81, 138, 139–40
Cold War 8, 54, 55, 66, 67, 122, 130, 134, 135
Communist Party of the Soviet Union (CPSU) 99
Confucianism 5, 6, 36, 62, 96, 100–101, 145
Constitution of the PRC 22, 26
containment of China 107
Copernicus, Nicolaus 31
corruption 82, 100
Cox Report 83
Crossed Swords 108, 148
Cultural Revolution 11, 13, 15–16, 20, 28, 42, 50, 52, 56, 61, 64, 95, 100, 111, 113
curriculum in schools 72–6

Dalai Lama 132
Darfur 155
democracy and democratisation 58, 62, 64, 69, 73, 82, 100, 101, 103, 105, 108, 111, 112, 113, 114, 116, 134, 156; international 115; Taiwan 6, 9, 126–30; Hong Kong 9, 125–6
Democracy Wall 13, 15, 112; *see also* Beijing Spring
Democratic Progressive Party (DPP) 126, 129
Deng Jiaxuan 35, 74
Deng Liqun 28, 43, 94, 95, 100
Deng Nan 61
Deng Pufang 95
Deng Xiaoping 7, 8, 9, 50, 53, 54, 55, 61, 79, 84, 88, 89, 93, 94, 95, 97, 98, 100, 102, 104, 107 108, 110, 111, 112, 113, 115, 131, 133; bourgeois liberalisation, 40; culture 56; definition of socialism 29, 31, 56, 63–5, 69; Deng Xiaoping Theory 4, 62, 79, 85, 86, 87, 89–90, 114, 122, 131, 133, 138, 141, 142, 143, 144, 147, 149, 156; Hong Kong and Taiwan 26,

125, 126, 127, 145; independence and self reliance 25, 67; patriotism and patriotic education 14–22, 42, 57, 73; primary stage of socialism 44, 45; leadership succession 11–13; last years 60–1; military doctrine 49; normalisation of US relations 16; scientific and technological revolution 30, 36; selected works 63, 65–7, 69, 122–3, 134; socialist spiritual civilisation 22–6; Southern Tour 4, 62–7; spiritual pollution 26–9; three worlds theory 16
Diaoyu archipelago 147, 150, 152
Ding Guan'gen 59, 60
Drifte, Reinhard 137
Du Shu 101

East China Sea 147
East Turkestan Independence Movement (ETIM) 137–8
Eastcom 78
Eddison 31
Education Commission 38, 49, 50–1, 57, 60, 70, 72, 73
education: 1978 conference 12; 1985 conference 32; expansion and reform 24, 32–3, 49, 58, 60, 70–6, 88; Four Haves 42; Education Law (1995) 73; Outline of the Reform and Development of China's Education (1993) 70–3; *see also* patriotic education
Eight Armies 79
Eight Points for Taiwan policy 127
Einstein, Albert 31, 69
'enlightened nationalism' (*mingzhi de minzu zhuyi*) 103
EP3 Reconnaissance Plane Incident 1, 3, 116
espionage 82–3
Europe 83, 115, 117
European Union (EU) 55, 145, 149

Falungong 111
Fan Liqin 95, 96, 98, 107, 110
Fang Lizhi 36–7, 39, 40, 69
Fang Ning 111
fascism 112, 148

Feng Zhaokui 149–50
Fernandez, George 140
Five Hearts Education 101
Five Principles of Peaceful
    Coexistence 17, 26, 88, 90, 130,
    135, 140
Four Cardinal Principles 13–14, 40,
    47, 59, 68, 94, 111, 112, 126
Four Haves 42
Four Modernisations 11, 15, 24, 39,
    45, 60
Four Nos (Chen Shui-bian) 128
Foreign Leap Forward 12
France 83, 105, 134, 145
Frankfurt School 100, 148
Fu Manchu 109
Fudan University 100

G7/G8 55, 66, 135
Galileo 31
Gan Yang 116
Gao Xingjian 20
GATT (General Agreement on Tariffs
    and Trade) 55
Genome project 76
geography 57
Germany 134, 139, 144, 146, 153
'going out' strategy 78
'good neighbour' foreign policy 141,
    148, 149, 154
Great Leap Forward 11, 13, 111
Great Wall 42, 52, 73, 88
Gu Qingsheng 105–6
Gulf War 55, 96

Habermas, Jurgen 100
Hainan Island 47
He Dongchang 38, 60
He Qinglian 118–19, 120
*Heart to Heart Talks with the
    General Secretary* 106–7
Hefei 36, 37, 39
Held, David 3
history 57, 68, 148, 149, 150, 151,
    152
Hitler, Adolf 94, 97, 110
Hollywood 105, 109
homosexuality 41
Hong Kong 9, 17, 18, 26, 28, 29, 40,
    48, 50, 55, 63, 72, 78, 80, 81, 83,
    89, 94, 119, 122, 124, 128, 130,
    131, 141, 147, 149
Hu Angang 100, 107
Hu Jintao 7, 119, 122, 123, 125,
    142, 143, 150, 155, 156; Belgrade
    crisis 85–8
Hu Qiaomu 28
Hu Yaobang 20, 22, 24, 28, 34–5,
    58, 59, 123; downfall 39–40, 43,
    48, 49, 51, 147; and Japan 38, 40
Hua Guofeng 11, 12, 108
Huang Puping 62–3
human rights 58, 66, 82, 83, 86, 88,
    111, 112, 131, 132, 133, 134, 137,
    138
humanism 35
humanitarian intervention 83, 84,
    134, 136, 138, 154, 155
Hundred Flowers Campaign (1986)
    35
Huntington, Samuel 62, 101, 131

IBM 76, 78
'ideological regeneration' 99
Independence and self-reliance 25,
    26, 85, 87, 88, 90
India 17, 94, 132, 140, 141, 154
Indonesia; atrocities 81–2, 106, 109
information security 78
information technology 77–8
International Monetary Fund (IMF)
    82
Internet 9, 55, 62, 78; e-commerce
    55, 78; e-government 78; first
    e-mail 42; political activity 81, 86,
    92, 116, 148, 149, 150, 151
Iraq 55, 83, 98
Islam 131

Jakarta 81, 82
Japan 5, 6, 12, 13, 14, 16, 18, 29, 31,
    36, 38, 63, 65, 74, 77, 83, 84, 89,
    94, 97, 102, 105, 110, 111, 116,
    145, 146–53, 154, 155, 156
Jiang Mianheng 62
Jiang Xiyuan 143, 144–6
Jiang Zemin 1, 2, 7, 8, 37, 44, 59, 60,
    67, 79, 83, 89, 93, 102, 106, 107,
    108, 111, 112, 115, 120, 121, 132,
    133, 136, 139, 140, 141, 142, 142,

147, 148, 150, 154; Belgrade crisis 83, 86, 87, 88; definition of socialism 79; Hong Kong 125; Indonesia crisis 82; patriotic education 56–8; science and technology 76–7; socialism with Chinese characteristics 63; Taiwan 80, 127; *see also* Three Represents
Jiaotong University 59
Johnston, Alastair Iain 134, 153

Kang Xiaoguang 99
Kang Youwei 5
Karimov, Islam 155
Kashmir 136
Kelly, James 140
Kim Jong Il 110
King of Chu 107
Kissinger, Henry 16, 26
KMT (Kuomintang) 6, 13, 33, 73, 126, 127, 128
Koizumi, Junichiro 148
Koo-Wang Talks (Singapore) 80
Korea 65, 94, 96, 102, 139, 144
Korean War 74
Kosovo 86, 133, 134, 135, 136

language teaching 57, 73
Latin America 62, 115, 118
Lee, Bruce 109
Lee Kuan Yew 65
Lee Teng-hui 80, 88, 89, 126, 127, 128, 131, 132, 133, 135
Lee, Wen Ho 82
Legend 78–9
Lenovo (*see Legend*)
Li Dazhao 74
Li Fan 102
Li Hongzhang 26
Li Peng 41, 44, 49, 51, 59, 60, 85, 123, 132
Li Ruihan 44, 59, 60, 100
Li Shenzhi 102–3, 111–12, 113, 114, 121, 143
Li Siguang 64
Li Tieying 44, 51, 60, 72, 119
Li Zehou 35–6, 41
Li Zhaoxing 152
Liang Qichao 5, 108

Lien Chan 129, 130
liberals and liberalism 92, 100, 104, 106–11, 112, 113, 116, 118, 121,
Liberation Daily (*Jiefang ribao*) 62–3, 152
Lin Zhijun 108–10
Liu Binyan 37, 39, 40
Liu Chuanzhi 78–9
Liu Huaqing 93
Liu Shaoqi 74
London School of Economics 113
Long March 74; rocket 86
Lu Xun 27, 108

Ma Licheng 108–10, 148–9, 150, 153
Macao 17, 18, 72, 89, 122
Machimura, Nobutaka 152
Mang Ke 22
Mao Zedong 6, 11, 15, 37, 56, 61, 73, 74, 75, 90, 93, 98, 100, 107, 108, 110, 114, 117, 146; cult 56; foreign policy and three worlds theory 16, 17; Hong Kong and Taiwan 26;
Marcos, Ferdinand 39
Marx 31, 108; Marxism 51, 56, 62, 65, 68, 94, 96, 116, 130, 148; Leninism–Mao Zedong Thought 13–14, 68, 73, 79, 90, 108; Marxism and humanism 35; and feudalism 36; and science 36–7; sinification of 6
May Fourth Movement 13, 52, 53, 58, 101, 111, 146, 152
McDonald's 109
Mearsheimer, John 153
Meiji Restoration 98
Microsoft 76
Middle East 144
military doctrine and policy 49, 60–1, 84, 89
Mongolia (Inner) 18
Most Favoured Nation status 81
Mugabe, Robert 155
Mulan 109
multilateralism 130, 131–5, 136–7, 142, 148, 154
multipolarity 1, 67, 69, 87, 90, 97,

115, 130–32, 134–5, 136, 139, 140, 155

Nakasone, Yasuhiro 38
Nanjing 85; Nanjing Massacre 58
National Condition Study Group 99
national team 59
nationalities policy 123–5
NATO 83, 84, 86, 87, 112, 132
Nauru 129
neo-authoritarianism 62, 92, 100, 114
New Left 92, 100–101, 116, 121
New Life Movement 6
New Security Concept 136–7
Newton, Isaac 31
Nixon, Richard 67
Nolan, Peter 77
Non-Aligned Movement 132
Non-Governmental Organisations (NGOs) 143
non-traditional security 135–6, 138
Northeast Asia 144
Northern Expedition 18
Northwestern University, Xian 151
nuclear weapons 35, 64, 74, 86, 89, 98, 139, 140

Olympic Games 1, 98, 132
'one centre and two basic points' 47
'one China' policy/principle 107, 109, 129, 138, 146
'one country, two systems' 17, 68, 100, 125, 126, 141, 145
Opium War 29, 31, 42, 57, 79, 88, 98, 113
orientalism 101
Osama Bin Laden 136
Outcry: Five Voices of Contemporary China 108–10, 148
overseas Chinese 72, 75, 76, 81, 83, 85, 88, 122, 141–2, 147

Pakistan 140
Pan Yue 93
Park Chung Hee 102
patriotic education 8, 26–7, 42, 51, 56–8, 60, 73, 79, 147, 153
patriotism 7

Patten, Chris 131
peaceful evolution 57, 58, 60, 67, 94, 107
peaceful rise (of China) 130, 139, 142–6, 148, 152, 154, 155, 156
Peking (Beijing) University 39
Peng Zhen 23, 24
People's First Party 129
'personnel great power' (*rencai qiangguo*) 70, 76–7
Peter the Great 98
Philippines 118
pornography 59
post-colonialism 101, 105, 117
post-modernism 2, 36, 96, 117
'pragmatic nationalism' (*wushi minzu zhuyi*) 102
pragmatism 12
primary stage of socialism 44, 67, 93
princelings 62, 93, 95, 118
Protestant ethic 101

Qian Sanqiang 64
Qian Xuesen 64
Qin Shi Huangdi (First Emperor) 75
Qing dynasty 6, 33, 58, 108, 117, 144
Qu Xiao 50

Reagan, Ronald 107, 116
religion 120, 124–5, 133, 136,
renaissance and rejuvenation (Chinese) 59, 60, 152
Resolution on CCP History (1949–81) 14, 16–17, 56
'reverse racism' 112, 113
revolution; definition of 64, 69; *see also* scientific and technological revolution
Rhee, Syngman 102
Rice, Condoleeza 153
River Elegy 52, 105, 112
Russell, Bertrand 108
Russia 83, 94, 97, 98, 103, 132, 134, 136, 139, 141, 144

SARS 129
Sasser, James 85
Sautman, Barry 33

scarred generation 20, 50
science and technology; and
    modernity 24, 95; and patriotism
    12, 70, 76–9, 88, 114; policy 48,
    71
scientific and technological
    revolution 8, 30–4, 47, 54, 55, 60,
    64, 67, 69, 76
secession 136
Senkaku archipelago *see* Diaoyu
    archipelago
Serbia 84
Shanghai 1, 5, 18, 27, 35, 37, 41, 44,
    59, 61, 62, 63, 100, 109, 138, 143,
    151, 152
Shanghai Communique 16
Shanghai Cooperation Organisation
    (SCO) 136, 137, 138
Shanghai Institute of International
    Studies 143
Shekou 29; 'Shekou strom' 49–50
'shelving sovereignty' 141, 147,
    155
Shen Guofang 138
Shenzhen 29, 49–50, 63
Shi Jixing 78
Shi Yinhong 149
Shih, Stan 129
Shougang steel corp. 77
Singapore 65, 75, 80, 119
smokeless war 67, 82
Social Darwinism 94, 108
socialism 51, 58, 59, 66, 79, 87, 90,
    97, 100, 111; 'with Chinese
    characteristics' 6, 52, 55, 60, 63,
    67, 72, 73, 77, 90–1, 108, 114,
    115; and feudalism 37; primary
    stage 44, 67; *see also* Deng
    Xiaoping; definition of socialism
socialist democracy 52
socialist market economy 67–8
Song Ping 61
Soong, James 129
South 97
South Asia 140
South China Sea 140, 141
Southeast Asia (see also ASEAN) 65,
    81, 94, 118, 140, 141, 145
Southern Tour 4, 62–7, 68, 69, 76,
    108, 111, 128

Soviet Union 25, 44, 55, 62, 93, 95,
    96, 99, 107, 112, 134, 141; *see
    also* Russia
Special Economic Zones (SEZs) 28,
    29, 47, 62, 63, 109
spiritual civilisation 6, 8, 22–6, 28,
    40, 68, 70, 77, 80
spiritual pollution 26–9, 40, 42, 59,
    63, 79, 94
Spratly Islands 49
Stalin, Joseph 110
strategic partnership 89, 108, 136
Strategy and Management 99, 101,
    103, 148, 149
Strike Hard campaign 124
student demonstrations (1985–7)
    37–8; *see also* Tiananmen
Su Xiaokang 52
Sudan 155
Suettinger, Robert 142
Sun Liping 99
Sun Yatsen 5, 6, 15, 59, 101, 108, 111

Taiwan: 6, 7, 9, 13, 14, 17, 24–5, 26,
    28, 47, 55, 65, 72, 75, 80, 82, 84,
    88, 89, 94, 96, 107, 110, 119, 122,
    124, 135, 136, 139, 147, 152, 154,
    156; 1995–6 crisis 1, 9, 80, 81, 83,
    103, 104, 105, 108, 109, 111, 124,
    129, 132–3, 139, 141, 142, 152,
    144, 145–46; democratisation
    126–30; and 'peaceful rise' 142–4,
    154; 2000 presidential election
    115, 129; 2004 presidential
    election 138, 145; referendum
    129–30, 138; *see also* United
    Front
Tang Zhengyu 105
teaching materials 72, 73–6, 150,
    151; *see also* history
technology *see* science and
    technology
techno-nationalism 8, 33–9, 40, 61,
    121
Ten Thousand Word Letter(s) 94–5,
    96, 97–8
terrorism 1, 115, 118, 124, 136, 137,
    138, 143, 144
textbooks *see* teaching materials
Thailand 118

Thatcher, Margaret 26, 107, 116, 122
third eye (*Viewing China Through the Third Eye*) 93–4, 95, 96–7, 103
Third World 115
'thought emancipation' 12, 72, 108, 145
Three Benefits 69
Three Faces 29, 47, 143
Three Major Tasks 7, 14, 24, 64, 90
Three Nos policy (US) 81, 83, 108
Three Principles of the People 6
Three Represents 8, 9, 90, 114, 115, 118, 120, 121, 122, 124, 150, 154
ti-yong (essence-function) dichotomy 5, 7, 32, 35–6, 47, 68, 72, 73, 101–2, 106,
Tiananmen Square 73, 96, 110; 1985–6 demonstrations 39; 1989 demonstrations and Massacre 1, 7, 52–3, 58, 64, 73, 108, 111, 122, 125, 147; sanctions 79
Tibet 9, 17, 18, 123, 131, 135, 136
Toffler, Alvin 30
Torch Plan 43, 59, 76
Tung Chee-Hwa 125
Turkestan 124; East Turkestan Independence Movement (ETIM) 137, 138
Twelve Major Relationships 80, 106
'two-states theory' 88, 128, 135

unification 7, 8, 14, 68
unipolarity 83
United Front 6, 17–18, 38, 40, 59, 75, 123, 126, 127–8, 129, 130
United Kingdom (Britain) 26, 83, 105, 144
United Nations 16, 83, 85, 111, 130, 131, 132, 135, 149, 151, 155
United States of America 75, 84, 86, 88, 89, 96, 97, 98, 101, 102, 104, 105, 106, 109, 110, 112, 115, 116, 121, 132, 134, 135, 136, 138, 140, 144, 148, 149, 150, 152, 154; 1995–6 crisis 80, 81, 104, 108; Iraq 83; Quadrennial Defense Review 83; relations with PRC 16, 25

Uygurs 124
Uzbekistan 136, 155

Vatican 31
Vietnam 16, 25, 49, 98

Wan Li 31–2, 33
Wang Hui 101, 116–17,
Wang Jyng Ping 130
Wang Ruoshui 28
Wang Ruowang 37, 39, 40
Wang Shan 93–4, 95, 96–7, 98, 107, 108, 139
Wang Shaoguang 100
Wang Xiaodong 103–4, 105, 111–15, 121, 133, 148, 155
Wang Zhen 41
Weapons of Mass Destruction (WMD) 143
Weber, Max 101
Wen Jiabao 122, 125, 142, 143, 145, 150, 155
Wendt, Alexander 154
Westernisation; 52, 'complete Westernisation' 37, 39–40, 41, 54
World Bank 139
World Health Assembly (WHA) 129
World Health Organization (WHO) 130
World Trade Organization (WTO) 1, 3, 55, 78, 84, 116, 118–20, 121, 132, 135, 140
Wuchang 63

Xia Liping 143, 144–6
Xian 78, 151
Xiao Gongqin 100–1
Xinjiang 9, 18, 124, 130, 131, 135, 142
Xiong Guangkai 138
Xu Wenlong 129

Yan Xuetong 132, 133, 135, 139, 155
Yan'an 12, 22, 23, 56
Yang Baibing 60
Yang Shangkun 60
Yasukuni Shrine 38, 148
Ye Jianying 22

Yellow Emperor 18, 98, 100
Yeltsin, Boris 132
Yuan Ming 61
Yuan Shikai 5
Yugoslavia 83, 99, 107, 112

Zeng Qinhong 120, 121, 142
Zhang Jinfu 86
Zhang Wannian 89
Zhang Zhidong 5, 6, 58, 68
Zhao, Suisheng 4, 52
Zhao Wei 148
Zhao Ziyang 20, 41, 56, 62, 96;
    democracy 46–7; primary stage of
    socialism 44–6

Zhejiang Posts and
    Telecommunications Bureau 78
Zheng Bijian 142, 143
Zheng Chenggong 75
Zheng Zhemin 30
Zhengming 83, 84
Zhou Enlai 11, 17, 18, 74, 75, 102,
    143
Zhu Bangzao 86
Zhou Guanwu 77
Zhu De 74
Zhu Rongji 1, 61, 83–5, 116,
    153
Zhuhai 63; orgy 151, 152
Zimbabwe 155